Some Shapers of Man

Short Stories

Paintings

Sculpture

Poetry

Essays

Fables

THE DRAMA by HONORÉ DAUMIER
Courtesy of Bayerischen Staatsgemäldesammlungen

HOLT, RINEHART AND WINSTON, INC.
NEW YORK   CHICAGO   SAN FRANCISCO   ATLANTA   DALLAS

SOME
SHAPERS
OF
MAN

EXIT FROM THE THEATRE, SCHOOL OF DAUMIER
Nelson Gallery—Atkins Museum (Nelson Fund) Kansas City, Missouri

JOHN H. BENS
MERRITT COLLEGE

To my parents
and to my wife, Allis

PREFACE

Is man aware of what shapes him to think, feel, and act as he does? The question seems worthwhile. If man is not aware, the chances are excellent that the loudest voice, the brightest color, and the strongest wind will shape him. (Sometimes, of course, the loudest, brightest, and strongest forces masquerade as the softest, weakest, and most subdued.)

If man is not aware, the chances are excellent that the forces that sculpted him in his early life will dominate his adult life. That man cannot avoid being shaped and shaping others is a truism. Loud voices, soft voices, voices from the past may be good and/or bad shapers. *Some Shapers of Man* is devised to aid the student in acquiring an awareness of the shapers—to be less slave and more free, to be less puppet and more actor, to be less vegetable and more man.

The shaping forces examined in the text are Home and Family; Religion and Fate; School; Mass Media and the Popular Arts; Peers and Environment; and the Fine Arts. Family, church, and school attempt to shape man directly, particularly to shape the young. Peer group and environment provide the setting and the rules for man's hour upon the stage. The mass media and the popular arts are the voice of the peer group and environment. The fine arts are perhaps the glass, either microscope or magnifying mirror, that enables man—if he knows of the existence of the glass and will look—to see himself and his world most clearly.

In the second paragraph the sentence beginning, "*Some Shapers of Man* is devised to aid the student in acquiring an awareness of the shapers . . ." could have read, "The text attempts to shape the student." It is the premise of this text that *being aware of the shapers in life is important*. Housman's "Yonder See the Morning Blink," Cummings' "mr. youse needn't be so spry," and Saroyan's "The Three Swimmers and the Grocer from Yale" are among the selections included to question the text's premise.

Most of my students in classes at Merritt College for whom *Some Shapers of Man* was designed have told me that man *consciously* acquires less than one fourth of all the thoughts and feelings that determine his actions. According to these students, most of what man thinks and feels and consequently does is a product of *unconscious* acquisition. Whether my students are right or wrong, whether man is or is not aware, is of less interest than the question: *Should* man be conscious of what shapes him to think and feel and act as he does?

J. H. B.

OAKLAND, CALIF.

JANUARY 1968

CONTENTS

Home and Family

(c. 1898) Color aquatint and drypoint, 15⅞ × 11⁵⁄₁₆ in. plate. Collection, The Museum of Modern Art, New York. Gift of Abby Aldrich Rockefeller.

Hide-and-Seek (Cache-cache) by Pavel Tchelitchew

(1940–42) Oil on canvas, 78½ × 84¾ in. Collection, The Museum of Modern Art, New York. Mrs. Simon Guggenheim Fund.

Preliminary Statements for Discussion
and Writing

1. As the twig is bent, so shall the tree grow.

2. How sharper than a serpent's tooth to raise a thankless child.

3. A child is innocent until the world corrupts him.

4. A child is an animal until the world civilizes him.

5. All that I am my mother made me.

6. To see your sweetheart twenty years from now, look at his (her) parents today.

7. We are shaped and fashioned by what we love.

8. Can the acorn fall far from the tree?

9. Man and his home are the microcosm that shapes the macrocosm.

10. Adulthood should be the voyage that children anticipate.

There Will Come Soft Rains*

Ray Bradbury

The house was a good house and had been planned and built by the people who were to live in it, in the year 1980. The house was like many another house in that year; it fed and slept and entertained its inhabitants, and made a good life for them. The man and wife and their two children lived at ease there, and lived happily, even while the world trembled. All of the fine things of living, the warm things, music and poetry, books that talked, beds that warmed and made themselves, fires that built themselves in the fireplaces of evenings, were in this house, and living there was a contentment.

And then one day the world shook and there was an explosion followed by ten thousand explosions and red fire in the sky and a rain of ashes and radio-activity, and the happy time was over.

In the living room the voice-clock sang, *Tick-tock, seven A.M. o'clock, time to get up!* as if it were afraid nobody would. The house lay empty. The clock talked on into the empty morning.

The kitchen stove sighed and ejected from its warm interior eight eggs, sunny side up, twelve bacon slices, two coffees, and two cups of hot cocoa. *Seven nine, breakfast time, seven nine.*

"Today is April 28th, 1985," said a phonograph voice in the kitchen ceiling. "Today, remember, is Mr. Featherstone's birthday. Insurance, gas, light and water bills are due."

Somewhere in the walls, relays clicked, memory tapes glided under electric eyes. Recorded voices moved beneath steel needles:

Eight one, run, run, off to school, off to work, run, run, ticktock, eight one o'clock!

But no doors slammed, no carpets took the quick tread of rubber heels. Outside, it was raining. The voice of the weather box on the front door sang quietly: "Rain, rain, go away, rubbers, raincoats for today." And the rain tapped on the roof.

At eight thirty the eggs were shriveled. An aluminum wedge scraped them into the sink, where hot water whirled them down a metal throat which digested and flushed them away to the distant sea.

Nine fifteen, sang the clock, *time to clean.*

Out of warrens in the wall, tiny mechanical mice darted. The rooms were acrawl with the small cleaning animals, all rubber and metal. They sucked up the hidden dust, and popped back in their burrows.

Ten o'clock. The sun came out from behind the rain. The house stood

---

alone on a street where all the other houses were rubble and ashes. At night, the ruined town gave off a radioactive glow which could be seen for miles.

Ten fifteen. The garden sprinkler filled the soft morning air with golden fountains. The water tinkled over the charred west side of the house where it had been scorched evenly free of its white paint. The entire face of the house was black, save for five places. Here, the silhouette, in paint, of a man mowing a lawn. Here, a woman bent to pick flowers. Still farther over, their images burned on wood in one titanic instant, a small boy, hands flung in the air—higher up, the image of a thrown ball—and opposite him a girl, her hands raised to catch a ball which never came down.

The five spots of paint—the man, the woman, the boy, the girl, the ball—remained. The rest was a thin layer of charcoal.

The gentle rain of the sprinkler filled the garden with falling light.

Until this day, how well the house had kept its peace. How carefully it had asked, "Who goes there?" and getting no reply from rains and lonely foxes and whining cats, it had shut up its windows and drawn the shades. If a sparrow brushed a window, the shade snapped up. The bird, startled, flew off! No, not even an evil bird must touch the house.

And inside, the house was like an altar with nine thousand robot attendants, big and small, servicing, attending, singing in choirs, even though the gods had gone away and the ritual was meaningless.

A dog whined, shivering, on the front porch.

The front door recognized the dog voice and opened. The dog padded in wearily, thinned to the bone, covered with sores. It tracked mud on the carpet. Behind it whirred the angry robot mice, angry at having to pick up mud and maple leaves, which, carried to the burrows, were dropped down cellar tubes into an incinerator which sat like an evil Baal in a dark corner.

The dog ran upstairs, hysterically yelping at each door. It pawed the kitchen door wildly.

Behind the door, the stove was making pancakes which filled the whole house with their odor.

The dog frothed, ran insanely, spun in a circle, biting its tail, and died. It lay in the living room for an hour.

One o'clock.

Delicately sensing decay, the regiments of mice hummed out of the walls, soft as blown leaves, their electric eyes blowing.

One fifteen.

The dog was gone.

The cellar incinerator glowed suddenly and a whirl of sparks leaped up the flue.

Two thirty-five.

Bridge tables sprouted from the patio walls. Playing cards fluttered onto pads in a shower of pips. Martinis appeared on an oaken bench.

But the tables were silent, the cards untouched.

At four thirty the tables folded back into the walls.

Five o'clock. The bathtubs filled with clear hot water. A safety razor dropped into a wall-mold, ready.

Six, seven, eight, nine o'clock.

Dinner made, ignored, and flushed away; dishes washed; and in the study, the tobacco stand produced a cigar, half an inch of gray ash on it, smoking, waiting. The hearth fire bloomed up all by itself, out of nothing.

Nine o'clock. The beds began to warm their hidden circuits, for the night was cool.

A gentle click in the study wall. A voice spoke from above the crackling fireplace:

"Mrs. McClellan, what poem would you like to hear this evening?"

The house was silent.

The voice said, "Since you express no preference, I'll pick a poem at random." Quiet music rose behind the voice. "Sara Teasdale. A favorite of yours, as I recall."

> *"There will come soft rains and the smell of the ground,*
> *And swallows circling with their shimmering sound;*
>
> *And frogs in the pools singing at night,*
> *And wild plum-trees in tremulous white.*
>
> *Robins will wear their feathery fire*
> *Whistling their whims on a low fence-wire;*
>
> *And not one will know of the war, not one*
> *Will care at last when it is done.*
>
> *Not one would mind, neither bird nor tree!*
> *If mankind perished utterly:*
>
> *And Spring herself, when she woke at dawn,*
> *Would scarcely know that we were gone."**

The voice finished the poem. The empty chairs faced each other between the silent walls, and the music played.

At ten o'clock, the house began to die.

The wind blew. The bough of a falling tree smashed the kitchen window. Cleaning solvent, bottled, crashed on the stove.

"Fire!" screamed voices. "Fire!" Water pumps shot down water from the

---

*Reprinted with permission of The Macmillan Company from *Collected Poems* by Sara Teasdale. Copyright 1920 by The Macmillan Company, renewed 1948 by Mamie T. Wheless.

ceilings. But the solvent spread under the doors, making fire as it went, while other voices took up the alarm in chorus.

The windows broke with heat and the wind blew in to help the fire. Scurrying water rats, their copper wheels spinning, squeaked from the walls, squirted their water, ran for more.

Too late! Somewhere, a pump stopped. The ceiling sprays stopped raining. The reserve water supply, which had filled baths and washed dishes for many silent days, was gone.

The fire crackled upstairs, ate paintings, lay hungrily in the beds! It devoured every room.

The house was shuddering, oak bone on bone, the bared skeleton cringing from the heat, all the wires revealed as if a surgeon had torn the skin off to let the red veins quiver in scalded air. Voices screamed, *"Help, help, fire, run!"* Windows snapped open and shut, like mouths, undecided. *Fire, run!* the voices wailed a tragic nursery rhyme, and the silly Greek chorus faded as the sound-wires popped their sheathings. Ten dozen high, shrieking voices died, as emergency batteries melted.

In other parts of the house, in the last instant under the fire avalanche, other choruses could be heard announcing the time, the weather, appointments, diets; playing music, reading poetry in the fiery study, while doors opened and slammed and umbrellas appeared at the doors and put themselves away—a thousand things happening, like the interior of a clock shop at midnight, all clocks striking, a merry-go-round of squeaking, whispering, rushing, until all the film spools were burned and fell, and all the wires withered and the circuits cracked.

In the kitchen, an instant before the final collapse, the stove, hysterically hissing, could be seen making breakfasts at a psychopathic rate, ten dozen pancakes, six dozen loaves of toast.

The crash! The attic smashing kitchen down into cellar and subcellar. Deep freeze, armchairs, filmtapes, beds, were thrown in a cluttered mound deep under.

Smoke and silence.

Dawn shone faintly in the east. In the ruins, one wall stood alone. Within the wall, a voice said, over and over again and again, even as the sun rose to shine upon the heaped rubble and steam:

"Today is April 29th, 1985. Today is April 29th, 1985. Today is..."

Questions

1. Do any of the devices in the house seem impossible, even for the future?

2. The author, Ray Bradbury, is very imaginative. Which of the devices most appeals to you?

3. Can you think of a device to add to those in the house to make living in the house more comfortable or easier?

4. The only living creature in the story is the dog. What has happened and what does happen to him?

5. Bradbury's story seems to ask the question if man had the knowledge to construct such a house, why hadn't he the knowledge to . . . ?

6. Why is it ironic that Mrs. McClellan's favorite poem was "There Will Come Soft Rains"?

7. What kind of a family wouldn't you expect to live in this house?

8. If this home is the microcosm of the world, what would the world be? How would you describe the life of the people in such a world?

9. How important apparently is the physical world in the shaping of man?

10. If the catastrophe that struck in "There Will Come Soft Rains" is to be averted, how is man to be shaped?

The Knife*

BRENDAN GILL

Michael threw himself down, locked his hands over one of his father's knees, and began, in a loud whisper, "'Our Father, who art in heaven, hallowed be thy name, kingdom come, will be done, earth as it is in heaven, give us this day—'"

Carroll folded his newspaper. Michael should have been in bed an hour ago. "Take it easy, kid," he said. "Let's try it again, slow."

Michael repeated distinctly. "'Our Father, who art in heaven, hallowed . . .'" The boy's pajamas, Carroll saw, were dirty at the cuffs; probably he had not brushed his teeth. "'. . . as we forgive them, who trespass against us'—what does 'trespass' mean, Dad?"

"Why, hurting anybody."

"Do I trespass anybody?"

"Not much, I guess. Finish it up."

Michael drew a breath. "'And lead us not into temptation, but deliver us from evil. Amen.'"

"Now," his father said, brushing back Michael's tangled hair, "what about a good 'Hail, Mary'?"

"All right," Michael said. "'Hail, Mary, full of grace, the Lord is with thee, blessed art thou among women, and blessed is the fruit of thy womb, Jesus.'" Michael lifted his head to ask if a womb got fruit like a tree, but thought better of it. His father never answered questions seriously, the way his mother used to. Michael decided to wait and ask Mrs. Nolan. "Is Mrs. Nolan coming tomorrow?" he asked.

"She'll be here, all right," Carroll said. "I give you ten seconds to finish the prayer."

Michael grinned at the ultimatum. "I thought you wanted me to go slow. 'Holy Mary, Mother of God, pray for us sinners, now and at the hour of our death. Amen.'" He unlocked his fingers. "Will she?"

"Will she what?"

"Will she now and at the hour of our death, A-men?"

The words of Michael's prayer caught in Carroll's mind and stayed there, a long way beyond his smiling face. "Yes," he said, and set his pipe in the broken dish on the table beside him. He had not emptied the dish of ashes in two days. Mrs. Nolan would give him a piece of her mind tomorrow morning, as she did each week when she came in to give the apartment a general cleaning and to do the laundry.

"What good can she do?" Michael asked.

"Climb into bed, young ragamuffin," Carroll said sternly. "It's past nine."

"What *good* can she do?"

"She'll help you get anything you want. I suppose she'll help you climb up into heaven when the time comes. You know all about heaven, don't you?"

Michael felt himself on the defensive. "Of course."

"Well, then, get along with you."

But Michael had something difficult to say. "You mean she'll ask God for anything I want and He'll give it to her for me?"

"She's His mother."

Michael stood up and kissed his father carefully on the cheek. Then he walked from the room, and Carroll could hear his bare feet crossing the hall. The bed creaked as Michael lay down on it. Carroll opened the newspaper, read a paragraph, then dropped it in a white heap on the rug. He felt tired; perhaps tonight he might be able to get some sleep. He got up, slipped his suspenders from his shoulders, unknotted his tie, kicked off his shoes. He had learned to undress quickly in the last six months, since his wife had died.

His pajamas were hanging inside out in the bathroom, where he had left them that morning. When he had undressed he felt Michael's toothbrush with his thumb; it was dry. He should have explained to the child what happened to a person's teeth when he forgot to clean them every night and morning.

Carroll stared at his face in the mirror above the basin. He tried smiling. No one could honestly tell what a man was thinking by the way he smiled. Even Michael, who was like a puppy about sensing moods, could not tell. He entered the bedroom on tiptoe. Feeling the sheets bunched at the foot of the mattress, he remembered that he had made the beds in a hurry. The sheets felt fresh and cool only on Saturdays, when Mrs. Nolan changed them.

Michael was not asleep. "Dad?" he whispered.

"Go to sleep."

"I been asking Hail Mary for something."

"Tomorrow."

"No, I been asking her right now."

Carroll lay on his back with his hands over his eyes. "What've you been asking her for, Mickey?"

Michael hesitated. "I thought I'd better make it something easy first. To see what happened." He sat up in bed. "A jackknife."

A few blocks away the clock in the Metropolitan Life tower was striking ten. Michael was deep in the noisy middle of a dream. Carroll listened to his breathing. He tried matching his own breath to Michael's, to make sleep come, but it was no use. Every night Carroll pretended to himself he was just at the brink of falling off to sleep, but his eyes always widened with wakefulness in the dark. Now, as the clock stopped striking, Carroll got up and walked into the bathroom and dressed. Then he went into the living room, unlocked the outside door of the apartment, and then locked it again before he walked down the two flights of stairs to the sidewalk. Shops reached out of sight down both sides of Lexington Avenue. Carroll walked uptown as he always did. He stopped in front of each bright shop window, studying its contents for the fifth or sixth time. He knew by now the day on which each window was changed and by whom. Certain plaster models, certain fringed crêpe papers were old friends.

At the top of a long slope Carroll waited for the lights to change. On his left was a bar; on his right, across the street, a drugstore. Carroll waited a moment outside the bar. Between the slats of its cheap orange Venetian blinds he could see the gleaming mahogany counter, the stacked glasses, the barman slicing foam from a mug of beer. A man and a girl were sitting at a table by the window, a foot under Carroll's eyes. They did not seem to be speaking. The man's hands lay halfway across the table and the girl's black dress made her throat look soft and white. Carroll turned away and crossed the street to the drugstore. The owner, Sam Ramatsky, stood sniffing the night air under the painted sign bearing his name.

"Well, Mr. Carroll, nice night for March."

"Yes." Carroll wanted only to hear a voice. "How's business?" he asked.

"Can't complain." Sam grinned, shaking his head. "I take that back. It's *lousy*. I got to break myself of this old 'Can't complain.' I got to remember how serious it is. Business is lousy."

Carroll leaned back against Sam's window, which was crammed with hot-water bottles, perfumes, toys, and two cardboard girls in shorts and sandals. The girls had been there for two months. There was dust on their teeth and on their smooth brown legs. "You ought to brush their teeth, Sam," Carroll said, "and run your hand down their legs now and then."

"You walk a lot," Sam said. "I figure on you, ten or eleven, every night."

"I guess I do," Carroll said.

Sam patted his hard belly. "Nothing like exercise keep a man in shape."

Carroll nodded impatiently. It was not Sam's voice he wanted to hear, after all. "Give me a milk shake, Sam."

They walked into the store. Carroll sat down on one of the round stools at the fountain and watched Sam pouring milk into the shaker. "Nothing like milk," Sam said, "keep a man's system clean." Carroll watched the hands of the electric clock above the door. Ten-forty-five. He could not go to bed before twelve. He glanced at the packed counters behind him. "Sell any jackknives, Sam?"

"Sure. I sell everything. That's what keeps me broke. Nothing like keeping a thing in stock to kill demand." Sam lifted a tray of jackknives from a counter, brought it over, and set it down on the fountain. "Beauties," Sam said. "Fifty cents up."

Carroll looked at several of them and finally picked up the biggest and shiniest one. "I'll take this one," he said.

"Such expensive taste! One buck."

Carroll paid for the milk shake and the knife, said "Good night, Sam," and walked out into the street. In another hour and a half he should have walked six miles. By that time his body would be tired enough so that he could sleep. By that time, he hoped, no voice could rouse him.

It was morning when Carroll awoke. He lay with his face on his hands, listening to the sound of the March rain against the windows. He remembered suddenly the absurd song that everyone used to sing: "Though April showers may come your way, they bring the flowers that bloom in May." March rains brought you nothing. March rains only shut you in your room without any hope of escape.

Michael and Mrs. Nolan were talking together in the kitchen. Michael's voice was high with excitement. "Look at it, Mrs. Nolan, look at it! Isn't it beautiful?"

"It is that," Mrs. Nolan said in her deep voice. Carroll sat up in bed. It was too late to give Mrs. Nolan warning.

"Do you ask for things when you say your prayers, Mrs. Nolan?" Michael demanded.

"I do." A pan clattered to the floor. "I've seen many a nice clean sty I'd swap for this dirty kitchen," Mrs. Nolan said. "You live like a couple of savages from week to week. God love you."

"Do you always get what you ask for?" Michael said.

"It all depends. I sort of try to guess what the good Lord wants to give me, and I ask for that."

"That's how I got this knife," Michael said. "It's got a big blade and a little blade and a screwdriver and a thing to punch holes in leather with and a file."

"You must have said yourself a fine prayer," Mrs. Nolan said. There was no hint of surprise in her voice.

"It was only a 'Hail, Mary,'" Michael said, "but I did it very slow, the way Dad told me to." Michael was silent for a moment. "But I'm asking for the real thing tonight. The knife was just to see. Someone's going to be here when you come next week."

Mrs. Nolan made a clucking sound in her mouth. "Someone instead of me?"

"She was here with Dad and me before you came," Michael said, his voice thin with its burden, "and she's coming back."

"Michael!" Carroll shouted.

Michael ran to the doorway. The knife gleamed in his fist. "Look what I got," he said. "I was showing Mrs. Nolan."

"Come here," Carroll said. When Michael reached the edge of the bed Carroll bent over and fastened his arms behind the child's back. There was only one thing to say, and one way to say it, and that was fast. "I'm glad you like it," he said. "I bought it for you at Ramatsky's last night. The biggest and shiniest one he had."

Questions

1. What was the boy going to ask for next?
2. What lesson does the father feel the youngster has to learn? Do you agree with the father?
3. Is the loss of the mother harder on the boy or on his father? In what ways is the loss apparent?
4. If you were making a movie of "The Knife," what directions would you give the actress playing the housekeeper?
5. Why does the author make the family Catholic rather than Unitarian?

Catherine and the Winter Wheat*

P. B. HUGHES

This is the winter wheat that is being hauled along the concession roads in late July or early August in southern Ontario, the winter wheat, the fall wheat—have it how you will.

It is sown in September, about the time of the equinox, when the wind blows northwesterly and the heavy rain has not come. It stands through the winter, withering under the snow like common grass, blazing emerald in spring. By early June it is breast high, fading in color and heading up—as the farmers say, looking to their binders against July when the field will be golden and heavy with grain.

This is the "corn" of the Old Testament, rich stuff revered by men through history, substance "honored above all other things on earth"—as I read in a cookbook a while ago.

Yet it is not for bread that winter wheat is milled, but for cake and pastry flours principally, and macaroni, and no doubt other things. The reason I do not know. My mother used to say the dough had not the elasticity of that made with flour from the hard spring-sown wheat of the West.

Wheat is not generally a principal means of livelihood in Ontario. But with us, long ago, it was our sole cash crop and a crop of one year in the rotation of a field.

Wheat one year was our way; then the field was planted with spring grains, seeded down with grasses for hay and pasture, and allowed to stand for several years. The spring grain was oats for the most part, or oats and barley mixed; it was used to feed the cattle.

Thus the wheat had a particular importance; the miller bought it for money. It was the only crop we sold, and the brief season when we hauled wheat to the mill was always associated with new clothes and toys and coins in our pockets when my sisters and I were young.

One year before the war we carried our wheat, as we always did, to the mill at Streetsville on the Credit River. I was a boy in my first teens before the war—the 1914 war, long ago now. I rode on the sacks, sitting beside my sister Catherine, who was sixteen—or nearly. My father drove the team; and Emily, the oldest of us Laughlin children—seventeen—sat beside him and spelled him with the reins.

The trip in the wagon took hours, though you'd cover it in a few minutes today in a car. But the sun was bright and the day fresh and beautiful after all the rain and humid heat of the summer; and I talked away to

Catherine and thought of the delights to come—of lying under the trees at the miller's while we waited our turn to unload and my father chatted with the men and smoked his pipe, and of the greatest delight of all: when the wagon was empty and my father would give us money and tell us to get about our shopping.

Catherine paid no attention to what I said. Dark and stormy she sat on the jolting wagon, despite the glory of this most glorious day. She had the letter shoved into her blouse, the letter she'd written the night before when everyone was in bed—a secret, portentous letter.

Oh, I heard the lamp being lit and saw the shadowy figure scratching away; and I knew all about her and Tom Skaife and what would be in the letter. So I went to sleep again. Skaife's house was only a mile out of Streetsville. For certain I'd be dispatched to deliver it personally and privately to Tom before we all set out home again; and Tom would be along one night to get her and the two of them off to be married at Hamilton, where Tom worked at the iron works except in the harvest season.

That's the way it was, and that was the reason Catherine's singing was muted that summer and she so fiery and quick to take the corn broom to a boy that got in her way about the place. There wasn't anything against Tom. It was just a matter of their both being so young, and the two years of waiting demanded of them so intolerably too much. Catherine and I were close to one another, and I think I could tell what she was thinking. That is how I knew what was in the letter. I never saw it.

So Catherine brooded on the top of the rumbling wagonload. And I grieved beside her that I was to lose her; but I was a lad brought up on the land and aware already that all life was ordered in awful cycles of growth and generation and decay, and go she must, soon or late. But today there would be the long ride in the sun (which was far-travel to me), the stream of grain as the sacks were emptied, and money rattling in my pocket; and I could not keep on with grieving and regretting when I contemplated these things.

This summer, this trip to the Credit River, this harvest are special in my memory. There was Catherine and Tom Skaife. Then there was the wetness of the past July and the heat. The two factors got strangely mixed up during the course of the day, which is a trick nature is playing all the time while she is weaving away at the destinies of men. My father, unaware of Catherine's letter writing, was unusually preoccupied, worrying about the wheat he carried, for grain is sensitive to the weather in which it has matured and been harvested.

We knew that a good deal of wheat had been turned away at the mill in the last week because of toughness, which is a matter of moisture content and difficult to deal with, though they do have drying equipment at mills today that takes care of a lot of doubtful grain. Millers daren't bin it tough because heating and spoilage are an ever present risk.

At that time before the war, you hauled your rejected grain home again. Then you could dry it out with untold labor by spreading it out on the floor of your barn and keep it or sell it, degraded, for feed. But, at that time of the year, your barn was stuffed with hay and with straw from the threshing; so you really hadn't any floor to spread it on.

My father pondered the matter as he drove; and Emily, sensitive to the moods of others, was quiet. Catherine was wrapped in her own thoughts. Only I was possessed with the high spirits proper to the occasion.

There wasn't much waiting around at the mill. Some years, all the farmers seemed to arrive together and you might be four or five hours in line. Other times, the season was strung out so you could get a load in when you brought it. We all went into the miller's office together. Mr. Jonathan remembered all our names, inquired for my mother, and complained—of his rheumatism, the hard times, the cost of labor, the sad wheat he'd been getting, and how much he'd had to refuse. It was the same each year. But this year it was the toughness of the wheat, caused by the unseasonably damp summer, he grumbled about most.

"Well, William," he said to my father at last, "dump her off. No need to sample Laughlin's wheat, anyway."

The girls and I looked at each other with relief. I felt like jumping up and down, for there was no doubt the worry about selling the wheat had been urgent in the last hour. My father and his father—the old Laughlin who bought our home, Star-of-the-Sea, from the O'Rourkes who built it in '69—were staunch men, and men of substance. But the substance was seldom cash.

My father stood there quite still; and the rest of us, starting for the door of the office, halted when he did not turn to go.·

"No, Jonathan," he said, after a pause. "I guess we'd better sample this. It's not been a good summer."

The miller got up, a little surprised. "H'm. All right. Thought it mightn't have been so bad out your way."

They went on together, and we followed without speaking to each other. My father and the miller opened a lot of the sacks and talked as they pushed their hands into the wheat. Then they carried a couple of sample tins into the office and remained there for what seemed hours to us.

At last my father came out. When we saw his face, our hearts sank. He didn't say anything but climbed back onto the wagon. We got up, too. He worked the wagon around, and we started back toward the road.

At the road, he swung the team down toward the town and halted under the trees in front of the post office. Then he pulled a dollar out of his pocket and told Emily to get something for her mother and some ice cream for us while the horses were fed and watered.

But we didn't move at once. The blow had been heavy. I thought, Catherine is going to give me that letter now to take to Tom while Father is seeing to the horses. Then suddenly there were tears in Emily's eyes; and she turned on my father, hurt and passionate.

"Oh, why couldn't you have unloaded the wheat when he told you to? Why haven't you got the money for it? Why did you say it had to be tested?"

My father looked at her and at us. Three pairs of eyes were upon him, puzzled, accusing, in that moment or two before he spoke. Actually he said very little by way of answer.

Only, "Children, you'd better remember this all your lives."

I think we must have stared at him a long time before we turned away, ashamed, realizing the enormity of what had been in our minds, of what Emily had expressed. We got down slowly off the wheat, leaving Father, and went into the shop and ate ice-cream cones, not talking and not looking at each other.

Suddenly Catherine pulled out the letter and tore it across and across, again and again, until it was only small wads of paper too thick to tear. She pushed the bits into her pocket and ran out without a word, her face wet with tears, to where my father was tending the horses.

Emily and I went and got some bit of something for Mother. Eventually we all got back on the wagon and went home with the sun setting in front of us; and that is all there was to that day—but I have remembered.

Questions

1. How has the man who is telling the story been shaped?

2. What was the family's fear about the wheat?

3. What was Catherine more concerned with than the wheat?

4. What had the children wanted their father to do?

5. What was the apparent, immediate effect on Catherine of her father's action?

6. Would you attempt to instill the morality of the father in a child of yours? Why or why not?

All the Years of Her Life*

MORLEY CALLAGHAN

They were closing the drugstore, and Alfred Higgins, who had just taken off his white jacket, was putting on his coat and getting ready to go home. The little gray-haired man, Sam Carr, who owned the drugstore, was bending down behind the cash register, and when Alfred Higgins passed him, he looked up and said softly, "Just a moment, Alfred. One moment before you go."

The soft, confident, quiet way in which Sam Carr spoke made Alfred start to button his coat nervously. He felt sure his face was white. Sam Carr usually said, "Good night," brusquely, without looking up. In the six months he had been working in the drugstore Alfred had never heard his employer speak softly like that. His heart began to beat so loud it was hard for him to get his breath. "What is it, Mr. Carr?" he asked.

"Maybe you'd be good enough to take a few things out of your pocket and leave them here before you go," Sam Carr said.

"What things? What are you talking about?"

"You've got a compact and a lipstick and at least two tubes of toothpaste in your pockets, Alfred."

"What do you mean? Do you think I'm crazy?" Alfred blustered. His face got red and he knew he looked fierce with indignation. But Sam Carr, standing by the door with his blue eyes shining bright behind his glasses and his lips moving underneath his gray mustache, only nodded his head a few times, and then Alfred grew very frightened and he didn't know what to say. Slowly he raised his hand and dipped it into his pocket, and with his eyes never meeting Sam Carr's eyes, took out a blue compact and two tubes of toothpaste and a lipstick, and he laid them one by one on the counter.

"Petty thieving, eh, Alfred?" Sam Carr said. "And maybe you'd be good enough to tell me how long this has been going on."

"This is the first time I ever took anything."

"So now you think you'll tell me a lie, eh? What kind of a sap do I look like, huh? I don't know what goes on in my own store, eh? I tell you you've been doing this pretty steady," Sam Carr said as he went over and stood behind the cash register.

Ever since Alfred had left school he had been getting into trouble wherever he worked. He lived at home with his mother and his father, who was a printer. His two older brothers were married and his sister had got married

last year, and it would have been all right for his parents now if Alfred had
only been able to keep a job.

While Sam Carr smiled and stroked the side of his face very delicately
with the tips of his fingers, Alfred began to feel that familiar terror growing
in him that had been in him every time he had got into such trouble.

"I liked you," Sam Carr was saying. "I liked you and would have trusted
you, and now look what I got to do." While Alfred watched with his alert,
frightened blue eyes, Sam Carr drummed with his fingers on the counter.
"I don't like to call a cop in point-blank," he was saying as he looked very
worried. "You're a fool, and maybe I should call your father and tell him
you're a fool. Maybe I should let them know I'm going to have you locked
up."

"My father's not at home. He's a printer. He works nights," Alfred said.

"Who's at home?"

"My mother, I guess."

"Then we'll see what she says." Sam Carr went to the phone and dialled
the number. Alfred was not so much ashamed, but there was that deep fright
growing in him, and he blurted out arrogantly, like a strong, full-grown man,
"Just a minute. You don't need to draw anybody else in. You don't need
to tell her." He wanted to sound like a swaggering, big guy who could look
after himself, yet the old, childish hope was in him, the longing that someone at home would come and help him. "Yeah, that's right, he's in trouble,"
Mr. Carr was saying. "Yeah, your boy works for me. You'd better come down
in a hurry." And when he was finished Mr. Carr went over to the door and
looked out at the street and watched the people passing in the late summer
night. "I'll keep my eye out for a cop" was all he said.

Alfred knew how his mother would come rushing in; she would rush
in with her eyes blazing, or maybe she would be crying, and she would
push him away when he tried to talk to her, and make him feel her dreadful
contempt; yet he longed that she might come before Mr. Carr saw the cop
on the beat passing the door.

While they waited—and it seemed a long time—they did not speak,
and when at last they heard someone tapping on the closed door, Mr. Carr,
turning the latch, said crisply, "Come in, Mrs. Higgins." He looked hard-
faced and stern.

Mrs. Higgins must have been going to bed when he telephoned, for her
hair was tucked in loosely under her hat, and her hand at her throat held
her light coat tight across her chest so her dress would not show. She came
in, large and plump, with a little smile on her friendly face. Most of the
store lights had been turned out and at first she did not see Alfred, who
was standing in the shadow at the end of the counter. Yet as soon as she
saw him she did not look as Alfred thought she would look: she smiled,
her blue eyes never wavered, and with a calmness and dignity that made
them forget that her clothes seemed to have been thrown on her, she put

out her hand to Mr. Carr and said politely, "I'm Mrs. Higgins. I'm Alfred's mother."

Mr. Carr was a bit embarrassed by her lack of terror and her simplicity, and he hardly knew what to say to her, so she asked, "Is Alfred in trouble?"

"He is. He's been taking things from the store. I caught him red-handed. Little things like compacts and toothpaste and lipsticks. Stuff he can sell easily," the proprietor said.

As she listened Mrs. Higgins looked at Alfred sometimes and nodded her head sadly, and when Sam Carr had finished she said gravely, "Is it so, Alfred?"

"Yes."

"Why have you been doing it?"

"I been spending money, I guess."

"On what?"

"Going around with the guys, I guess," Alfred said.

Mrs. Higgins put out her hand and touched Sam Carr's arm with an understanding gentleness, and speaking as though afraid of disturbing him, she said, "If you would only listen to me before doing anything." Her simple earnestness made her shy; her humility made her falter and look away, but in a moment she was smiling gravely again, and she said with a kind of patient dignity, "What did you intend to do, Mr. Carr?"

"I was going to get a cop. That's what I ought to do."

"Yes, I suppose so. It's not for me to say, because he's my son. Yet I sometimes think a little good advice is the best thing for a boy when he's at a certain period in his life," she said.

Alfred couldn't understand his mother's quiet composure, for if they had been at home and someone had suggested that he was going to be arrested, he knew she would be in a rage and would cry out against him. Yet now she was standing there with that gentle, pleading smile on her face, saying, "I wonder if you don't think it would be better just to let him come home with me. He looks a big fellow, doesn't he? It takes some of them a long time to get any sense," and they both stared at Alfred, who shifted away with a bit of light shining for a moment on his thin face and the tiny pimples over his cheekbone.

But even while he was turning away uneasily Alfred was realizing that Mr. Carr had become aware that his mother was really a fine woman; he knew that Sam Carr was puzzled by his mother, as if he had expected her to come in and plead with him tearfully, and instead he was being made to feel a bit ashamed by her vast tolerance. While there was only the sound of the mother's soft, assured voice in the store, Mr. Carr began to nod his head encouragingly at her. Without being alarmed, while being just large and still and simple and hopeful, she was becoming dominant there in the dimly lit store. "Of course, I don't want to be harsh," Mr. Carr was saying. "I'll tell you what I'll do. I'll just fire him and let it go at that. How's that?"

and he got up and shook hands with Mrs. Higgins, bowing low to her in deep respect.

There was such warmth and gratitude in the way she said, "I'll never forget your kindness," that Mr. Carr began to feel warm and genial himself.

"Sorry we had to meet this way," he said. "But I'm glad I got in touch with you. Just wanted to do the right thing, that's all," he said.

"It's better to meet like this than never, isn't it?" she said. Suddenly they clasped hands as if they liked each other, as if they had known each other a long time. "Good night, sir," she said.

"Good night, Mrs. Higgins. I'm truly sorry," he said.

The mother and son walked along the street together, and the mother was taking a long, firm stride as she looked ahead with her stern face full of worry. Alfred was afraid to speak to her, he was afraid of the silence that was between them, so he only looked ahead too, for the excitement and relief were still pretty strong in him; but in a little while, going along like that in silence made him terribly aware of the strength and the sternness in her; he began to wonder what she was thinking of as she stared ahead so grimly; she seemed to have forgotten that he walked beside her; so when they were passing under the Sixth Avenue elevated and the rumble of the train seemed to break the silence, he said in his old, blustering way, "Thank God it turned out like that. I certainly won't get in a jam like that again."

"Be quiet. Don't speak to me. You've disgraced me again and again," she said bitterly.

"That's the last time. That's all I'm saying."

"Have the decency to be quiet," she snapped. They kept on their way, looking straight ahead.

When they were at home and his mother took off her coat, Alfred saw that she was really only half-dressed, and she made him feel afraid again when she said, without even looking at him, "You're a bad lot. God forgive you. It's one thing after another and always has been. Why do you stand there stupidly? Go to bed, why don't you?" When he was going, she said, "I'm going to make myself a cup of tea. Mind, now, not a word about tonight to your father."

While Alfred was undressing in his bedroom, he heard his mother moving around the kitchen. She filled the kettle and put it on the stove. She moved a chair. And as he listened there was no shame in him, just wonder and a kind of admiration of her strength and repose. He could still see Sam Carr nodding his head encouragingly to her; he could hear her talking simply and earnestly, and as he sat on his bed he felt a pride in her strength. "She certainly was smooth," he thought. "Gee, I'd like to tell her she sounded swell."

And at last he got up and went along to the kitchen, and when he was at the door he saw his mother pouring herself a cup of tea. He watched and he didn't move. Her face, as she sat there, was a frightened, broken face utterly unlike the face of the woman who had been so assured a little while ago in the drugstore. When she reached out and lifted the kettle to pour hot water in her cup, her hand trembled and the water splashed on the stove. Leaning back in the chair, she sighed and lifted the cup to her lips, and her lips were groping loosely as if they would never reach the cup. She swallowed the hot tea eagerly, and then she straightened up in relief, though her hand holding the cup still trembled. She looked very old.

It seemed to Alfred that this was the way it had been every time he had been in trouble before, that this trembling had really been in her as she hurried out half-dressed to the drugstore. He understood why she had sat alone in the kitchen the night his young sister had kept repeating doggedly that she was getting married. Now he felt all that his mother had been thinking of as they walked along the street together a little while ago. He watched his mother, and he never spoke, but at that moment his youth seemed to be over; he knew all the years of her life by the way her hand trembled as she raised the cup to her lips. It seemed to him that this was the first time he had ever looked upon his mother.

Questions

1. Is there a hero or heroine of the story?

2. Was the mother playing a role in the store?

3. Three views of the mother were given. What has been the true or major view all the years of her life?

4. Has the experience at the drugstore and in "seeing his mother" changed the boy? If he was immature before, is he mature now?

5. Is the view of life presented in the story positive or negative?

6. How do you imagine the boy's family would react to "individuals"? The father is a printer. What does the family read?

7. Are the father in "Catherine and the Winter Wheat" and the mother in this story alike or different?

8. Which of the pictures of youngsters ("Hide-and-Seek" by Tchelitchew, page 3 or "The Four Seasons" by Rockwell, page 106) does the Morley Callaghan story more nearly parallel?

9. Do you imagine the boy's life when he marries will parallel his present family life?

You've Got To Be Taught*

OSCAR HAMMERSTEIN, 2nd

You've got to be taught to hate and fear,
You've got to be taught from year to year,
It's got to be drummed in your dear little ear—
You've got to be carefully taught!

You've got to be taught to be afraid
Of people whose eyes are oddly made,
And people whose skin is a different shade—
You've got to be carefully taught.

You've got to be taught before it's too late,
Before you are six or seven or eight,
To hate all the people your relatives hate—
You've got to be carefully taught!

Questions

1. Prejudice against whom is specifically mentioned?

2. According to the song, who teaches you prejudice and when?

3. Racial and religious prejudice involves hate and fear. What else are we taught to hate and fear in childhood that we continue to hate and fear as adults?

4. Is prejudice more often taught directly rather than indirectly? What do the terms *direct* and *indirect* mean?

5. In the play *South Pacific* from which these lyrics are taken, a Caucasian Marine lieutenant is in love with one of the native girls. In what ways might the playwrights have resolved the difficulty of love between races? How do you imagine the playwrights solved the difficulty?

Don'ts*

D. H. Lawrence

Fight your little fight, my boy
fight and be a man.
Don't be a good little, good little boy
being as good as you can

and agreeing with all the mealy-mouthed, mealy-mouthed
truths that the sly trot out
to protect themselves and their greedy-mouthed, greedy-mouthed
cowardice, every old lout.

Don't live up to the dear little girl who costs
you your manhood, and makes you pay.
Nor the dear old mater who so proudly boasts
that you'll make your way.

Don't earn golden opinions, opinions golden,
or at least worth Treasury notes,
from all sorts of men; don't be beholden
to the herd inside the pen.

Don't long to have dear little, dear little boys
whom you'll have to educate
to earn their living; nor yet girls, sweet joys
who will find it so hard to mate.

Nor a dear little home, with its cost, its cost
that you have to pay,
earning your living while your life is lost
and dull death comes in a day.

Don't be sucked in by the su-superior,
don't swallow the culture bait,
don't drink, don't drink and get beerier and beerier,
do learn to discriminate.

---

*From *The Complete Poems of D. H. Lawrence,* Vol. I. Edited by Vivian de Sola Pinto and F. Warren Roberts. Copyright 1929 by Frieda Lawrence Ravagli. All Rights Reserved. Reprinted by permission of The Viking Press, Inc.

Do hold yourself together, and fight
with a hit-hit here and a hit-hit there,
and a comfortable feeling at night
that you've let in a little air.

A little fresh air in the money sty,
knocked a little hole in the holy prison,
done your own little bit, made your own little try
that the risen Christ should *be* risen.

Questions

1. What does a good boy do according to Lawrence?
2. A good boy according to Lawrence gets what for his goodness?
3. What is the holy prison into which a little air must be let?
4. What would Lawrence probably say about the father in "Catherine and the Winter Wheat" and the mother in "All the Years of Her Life"?
5. Lawrence says, "learn to discriminate." Who will teach you?

Mending Wall*

ROBERT FROST

Something there is that doesn't love a wall,
That sends the frozen-ground-swell under it,
And spills the upper boulders in the sun;
And makes gaps even two can pass abreast.
The work of hunters is another thing:
I have come after them and made repair
Where they have left not one stone on a stone,
But they would have the rabbit out of hiding,
To please the yelping dogs. The gaps I mean,
No one has seen them made or heard them made,
But at spring mending-time we find them there.
I let my neighbor know beyond the hill;
And on a day we meet to walk the line
And set the wall between us once again.
We keep the wall between us as we go.

To each the boulders that have fallen to each.
And some are loaves and some so nearly balls
We have to use a spell to make them balance:
'Stay where you are until our backs are turned!'
We wear our fingers rough with handling them.
Oh, just another kind of out-door game,
One on a side. It comes to little more:
There where it is we do not need the wall:
He is all pine and I am apple orchard.
My apple trees will never get across
And eat the cones under his pines, I tell him.
He only says, 'Good fences make good neighbors.'
Spring is the mischief in me, and I wonder
If I could put a notion in his head:
'*Why* do they make good neighbors? Isn't it
Where there are cows? But here there are no cows.
Before I built a wall I'd ask to know
What I was walling in or walling out,
And to whom I was like to give offence.
Something there is that doesn't love a wall,
That wants it down.' I could say 'Elves' to him,
But it's not elves exactly, and I'd rather
He said it for himself. I see him there
Bringing a stone grasped firmly by the top
In each hand, like an old-stone savage armed.
He moves in darkness as it seems to me,
Not of woods only and the shade of trees.
He will not go behind his father's saying,
And he likes having thought of it so well
He says again, 'Good fences make good neighbors.'

Questions

1. Why do the two farmers meet once a year to walk the wall on either side?

2. What does the damage to the piled stone walls if hunters and their dogs do not do it?

3. Because it is spring, and the young farmer feels mischievous, what does he want to make the old farmer say caused the damage?

4. "He is pine and I am apple orchard" proves what to the young farmer?

5. The old farmer "moves in darkness . . . not of woods only and the shade of trees." What is this darkness he moves in?

6. What apparently shaped the old man to think and say what he does? What predictions will you make concerning the sons of the young farmer?

Sonnet to Gath*

EDNA ST. VINCENT MILLAY

Country of hunchbacks!—where the strong, straight spine,
Jeered at by crooked children, makes his way
Through by-streets at the kindest hour of day,
Till he deplore his stature, and incline
To measure manhood with a gibbous line;
Till out of loneliness, being flawed with clay,
He stoop into his neighbour's house and say,
"Your roof is low for me—the fault is mine."
Dust in an urn long since, dispersed and dead
Is great Apollo; and the happier he;
Since who amongst you all would lift a head
At a god's radiance on the mean door-tree,
Saving to run and hide your dates and bread,
And cluck your children in about your knee?

Questions

1. What does the expression "country of hunchbacks" mean?

2. Why does the person with a strong straight spine walk down by-streets in Gath?

3. When the roof is too low in Gath, what does the person with the straight spine do and say?

4. Would the people of Gath welcome the god Apollo as he walked in their midst, and would they tell their children to emulate the god?

5. What makes a country a country of hunchbacks?

6. Would the mother in "All the Years of Her Life" and the father in "Catherine and the Winter Wheat" hide the food and call in the children if a god appeared in their midst?

Children

ANONYMOUS

Little children
Are so sweet
They always wait
To cross the street.
They help their mother
And their father
And never want
To be a bother.

Eletelephony*

LAURA E. RICHARDS

Once there was an elephant,
Who tried to use the telephant—
No! no! I mean an elephone
Who tried to use the telephone—
(Dear me! I am not certain quite
That even now I've got it right.)

Howe'er it was, he got his trunk
Entangled in the telephunk;
The more he tried to get it free,
The louder buzzed the telephee—
(I fear I'd better drop the song
Of elephop and telephong!)

Questions

1. Is what most college students feel about poetry today an outcome of childhood home experiences? What beliefs besides religious and political beliefs do you share with your parents?

2. What are the two poems' differences and similarities?

---

3. Of the two children's poems given, which would you choose for your child? Why? Would a child choose the same one?

4. As adults we often look on childhood through "rose-colored glasses." Is one of the two poems more "rose-colored" than the other?

5. You might want to write a sentimental poem about a little girl, a little boy, a puppy, your mother, the flag, a teacher, or spring. Or perhaps you would prefer to write the opposite of such a poem.

6. If in answer to question 2 you said "Eletelephony" is not obviously preaching, what will a child probably learn indirectly from the poem?

The Wind and the Sun*

ÆSOP

A dispute once arose between the Wind and the Sun as to which was the stronger of the two. They agreed, therefore, to try their strength upon a traveler to see which should be able to take his cloak off first. The Wind began and blew with all his might and main, a cold and fierce blast; but the stronger he blew the closer the traveler wrapped his cloak about him and the tighter he grasped it with his hands. Then broke out the Sun and with his welcome beams he dispersed the vapor and the cold. The traveler felt the genial warmth and as the Sun shone brighter and brighter, he sat down, overcome with the heat, and cast his cloak on the ground. Thus the Sun was declared the conqueror.

Questions

1. Who is proven the more powerful in the contest?

2. What is the moral or lesson of the fable?

3. Is this lesson one that most parents teach their children? Should they?

4. In the play *The Skin of Our Teeth* by Thornton Wilder, a John Q. Public character says, "God help me but I liked the war. People are at their best during wartime." How do you interpret "at their best"? Do you agree with the character?

Under the Horse-Chestnut Tree

(*painting—see p. 2*)

MARY CASSATT

Hide-and-Seek

(*painting—see p. 3*)

PAVEL TCHELITCHEW

Questions

1. Mother and child figures usually evoke what sentiments in viewers?
2. In your opinion how does Cassatt want the viewer to feel as a result of the picture?
3. What do the two pictures have in common? What is the primary difference?
4. Norman Rockwell (p. 106) pictures the four seasons. Compare and contrast the seasons as Tchelitchew presents them.
5. When a person says regarding a painting, "But I wouldn't want it hanging in my living room," what is he telling you about himself?

Religion and Fate

The Hand of God by Carl Milles

Courtesy of Ateljé Sundahl, Stockholm

And God Created
Man in His Own Image
by Ivan Albright

(1930–31) Oil on canvas, 48 × 26 in.
Courtesy of The Art Institute of Chicago

Preliminary Statements for Discussion
and Writing

1. The meek shall inherit the earth.

2. Nice guys finish last.

3. Man is fate.

4. If there were no God, it would be necessary to invent him.

5. Therefore all things whatsoever ye would that man should do to you, do ye even so unto them. You are your brother's keeper.

6. Morality is the offspring of hypocrisy out of economics.

7. We will live as if we were God's spies.

8. One man's religion is another's superstition.

9. Adam remarked to Eve as they left the Garden of Eden, "Well, everything is in a state of transition."

10. Whatever will be, will be.

The Monkey's Paw*

W. W. Jacobs

Without, the night was cold and wet, but in the small parlor of Lakesnam Villa the blinds were drawn and the fire burned brightly. Father and son were at chess, the former, who possessed ideas about the game involving radical changes, putting his king into such sharp and unnecessary perils that it even provoked comment from the white-haired old lady knitting placidly by the fire.

"Hark at the wind," said Mr. White, who, having seen a fatal mistake after it was too late, was amiably desirous of preventing his son from seeing it.

"I'm listening," said the latter, grimly surveying the board as he stretched out his hand. "Check."

"I should hardly think that he'd come tonight," said his father, with his hand poised over the board.

"Mate," replied the son.

"That's the worst of living so far out," bawled Mr. White, with sudden and unlooked-for violence; "of all the beastly, slushy, out-of-the-way places to live in, this is the worst. Pathway's a bog, and the road's a torrent. I don't know what people are thinking about. I suppose because only two houses on the road are let, they think it doesn't matter."

"Never mind, dear," said his wife soothingly; "perhaps you'll win the next one."

Mr. White looked up sharply, just in time to intercept a knowing glance between mother and son. The words died away on his lips, and he hid a guilty grin in his thin gray beard.

"There he is," said Herbert White, as the gate banged to loudly and heavy footsteps came toward the door.

The old man rose with hospitable haste, and opening the door, was heard condoling with the new arrival. The new arrival also condoled with himself, so that Mrs. White said, "Tut, tut!" and coughed gently as her husband entered the room, followed by a tall burly man, beady of eye and rubicund of visage.

"Sergeant-Major Morris," he said, introducing him.

The sergeant-major shook hands, and taking the proffered seat by the fire, watched contentedly while his host got out whisky and tumblers and stood a small copper kettle on the fire.

At the third glass his eyes got brighter, and he began to talk, the little family circle regarding with eager interest this visitor from distant parts, as

---

*Reprinted by permission of Dodd, Mead & Company, Inc. from *The Lady of the Barge* by W. W. Jacobs.

he squared his broad shoulders in the chair and spoke of strange scenes and doughty deeds, of wars and plagues and strange peoples.

"Twenty-one years of it," said Mr. White, nodding at his wife and son. "When he went away he was a slip of a youth in the warehouse. Now look at him."

"He don't look to have taken much harm," said Mrs. White politely.

"I'd like to go to India myself," said the old man, "just to look round a bit, you know."

"Better where you are," said the sergeant-major, shaking his head. He put down the empty glass and, sighing softly, shook it again.

"I should like to see those old temples and fakirs and jugglers," said the old man. "What was that you started telling me the other day about a monkey's paw or something, Morris?"

"Nothing," said the soldier hastily. "Leastways, nothing worth hearing."

"Monkey's paw?" said Mrs. White curiously.

"Well, it's just a bit of what you might call magic, perhaps," said the sergeant-major off-handedly.

His three listeners leaned forward eagerly. The visitor absent-mindedly put his empty glass to his lips and then set it down again. His host filled it for him.

"To look at," said the sergeant-major, fumbling in his pocket, "it's just an ordinary little paw, dried to a mummy."

He took something out of his pocket and proffered it. Mrs. White drew back with a grimace, but her son, taking it, examined it curiously.

"And what is there special about it?" inquired Mr. White, as he took it from his son and, having examined it, placed it upon the table.

"It had a spell put on it by an old fakir," said the sergeant-major, "a very holy man. He wanted to show that fate ruled people's lives, and that those who interfered with it did so to their sorrow. He put a spell on it so that three separate men could each have three wishes from it."

His manner was so impressive that his hearers were conscious that their light laughter jarred somewhat.

"Well, why don't you have three, sir?" said Herbert White cleverly.

The soldier regarded him in the way that middle age is wont to regard presumptuous youth. "I have," he said quietly, and his blotchy face whitened.

"And did you really have the three wishes granted?" asked Mrs. White.

"I did," said the sergeant-major, and his glass tapped against his strong teeth.

"And has anybody else wished?" inquired the old lady.

"The first man had his three wishes, yes," was the reply. "I don't know what the first two were, but the third was for death. That's how I got the paw."

His tones were so grave that a hush fell upon the group. "If you've had your three wishes, it's no good to you now, then, Morris," said the old man at last. "What do you keep it for?"

The soldier shook his head. "Fancy, I suppose," he said slowly. "I did have some idea of selling it, but I don't think I will. It has caused enough mischief already. Besides, people won't buy. They think it's a fairy tale, some of them, and those who do think anything of it want to try it first and pay me afterward."

"If you could have another three wishes," said the old man, eyeing him keenly, "would you have them?"

"I don't know," said the other. "I don't know."

He took the paw, and dangling it between his front finger and thumb, suddenly threw it upon the fire. White, with a slight cry, stooped down and snatched it off.

"Better let it burn," said the soldier solemnly.

"If you don't want it, Morris," said the old man, "give it to me."

"I won't," said his friend doggedly. "I threw it on the fire. If you keep it, don't blame me for what happens. Pitch it on the fire again, like a sensible man."

The other shook his head and examined his new possession closely. "How do you do it?" he inquired.

"Hold it up in your right hand and wish aloud," said the sergeant-major, "but I warn you of the consequences."

"Sounds like the *Arabian Nights,*" said Mrs. White, as she rose and began to set the supper. "Don't you think you might wish for four pairs of hands for me?"

Her husband drew the talisman from his pocket and then all three burst into laughter as the sergeant-major, with a look of alarm on his face, caught him by the arm. "If you must wish," he said gruffly, "wish for something sensible."

Mr. White dropped it back into his pocket, and placing chairs, motioned his friend to the table. In the business of supper the talisman was partly forgotten, and afterward the three sat listening in an enthralled fashion to a second installment of the soldier's adventures in India.

"If the tale about the monkey paw is not more truthful than those he has been telling us," said Herbert, as the door closed behind their guest, just in time for him to catch the last train, "we shan't make much out of it."

"Did you give him anything for it, father?" inquired Mrs. White, regarding her husband closely.

"A trifle," said he, coloring slightly. "He didn't want it, but I made him take it. And he pressed me again to throw it away."

"Likely," said Herbert, with pretended horror. "Why, we're going to be rich, and famous, and happy. Wish to be an emperor, father, to begin with; then you can't be henpecked."

He darted round the table, pursued by the maligned Mrs. White armed with an antimacassar.

Mr. White took the paw from his pocket and eyed it dubiously. "I don't know what to wish for, and that's a fact," he said slowly. "It seems to me I've got all I want."

"If you only cleared the house, you'd be quite happy, wouldn't you?" said Herbert, with his hand on his shoulder. "Well, wish for two hundred pounds, then; that'll just do it."

His father, smiling shamefacedly at his own credulity, held up the talisman, as his son, with a solemn face somewhat marred by a wink at his mother, sat down at the piano and struck a few impressive chords.

"I wish for two hundred pounds," said the old man distinctly.

A fine crash from the piano greeted the words, interrupted by a shuddering cry from the old man. His wife and son ran toward him.

"It moved," he cried, with a glance of disgust at the object as it lay on the floor. "As I wished it twisted in my hands like a snake."

"Well, I don't see the money," said his son, as he picked it up and placed it on the table, "and I bet I never shall."

"It must have been your fancy, father," said his wife, regarding him anxiously.

He shook his head. "Never mind, though; there's no harm done, but it gave me a shock all the same."

They sat down by the fire again while the two men finished their pipes. Outside, the wind was higher than ever, and the old man started nervously at the sound of a door banging upstairs. A silence unusual and depressing settled upon all three, which lasted until the old couple rose to retire for the night.

"I expect you'll find the cash tied up in a big bag in the middle of your bed," said Herbert, as he bade them good night, "and something horrible squatting up on top of the wardrobe watching you as you pocket your ill-gotten gains."

II

In the brightness of the wintry sun next morning as it streamed over the breakfast table Herbert laughed at his fears. There was an air of prosaic wholesomeness about the room which it had lacked on the previous night, and the dirty, shriveled little paw was pitched on the sideboard with a carelessness which betokened no great belief in its virtues.

"I suppose all old soldiers are the same," said Mrs. White. "The idea of our listening to such nonsense! How could wishes be granted in these days? And if they could, how could two hundred pounds hurt you, father?"

"Might drop on his head from the sky," said the frivolous Herbert.

"Morris said the things happened so naturally," said his father, "that you might if you so wished attribute it to coincidence."

"Well, don't break into the money before I come back," said Herbert, as he rose from the table. "I'm afraid it'll turn you into a mean, avaricious man, and we shall have to disown you."

His mother laughed, and followed him to the door, watched him down the road, and returning to the breakfast table, was very happy at the expense of her husband's credulity. All of which did not prevent her from scurrying to the door at the postman's knock, nor prevent her from referring somewhat shortly to retired sergeant-majors of bibulous habits when she found that the post brought a tailor's bill.

"Herbert will have some more of his funny remarks, I expect, when he comes home," she said, as they sat at dinner.

"I dare say," said Mr. White, pouring himself out some beer; "but for all that, the thing moved in my hand; that I'll swear to."

"You thought it did," said the old lady soothingly.

"I say it did," replied the other. "There was no thought about it. I had just—What's the matter?"

His wife made no reply. She was watching the mysterious movements of a man outside, who, peering in an undecided fashion at the house, appeared to be trying to make up his mind to enter. In mental connection with the two hundred pounds, she noticed that the stranger was well dressed and wore a silk hat of glossy newness. Three times he paused at the gate, and then walked on again. The fourth time he stood with his hand upon it, and then with sudden resolution flung it open and walked up the path. Mrs. White at the same moment placed her hands behind her, and hurriedly unfastening the strings of her apron, put that useful article of apparel beneath the cushion of her chair.

She brought the stranger, who seemed ill at ease, into the room. He gazed furtively at Mrs. White, and listened in a preoccupied fashion as the old lady apologized for the appearance of the room, and her husband's coat, a garment which he usually reserved for the garden. She then waited as patiently as her sex would permit for him to broach his business, but he was at first strangely silent.

"I—was asked to call," he said at last, and stooped and picked a piece of cotton from his trousers. "I came from Maw and Meggins."

The old lady started. "Is anything the matter?" she asked breathlessly. "Has anything happened to Herbert? What is it? What is it?"

Her husband interposed. "There, there, mother," he said hastily. "Sit down, and don't jump to conclusions. You've not brought bad news, I'm sure, sir," and he eyed the other wistfully.

"I'm sorry—" began the visitor.

"Is he hurt?" demanded the mother.

The visitor bowed in assent. "Badly hurt," he said quietly, "but he is not in any pain."

"Oh, thank God!" said the old woman, clasping her hands. "Thank God for that! Thank—"

She broke off suddenly as the sinister meaning of the assurance dawned upon her and she saw the awful confirmation of her fears in the other's averted face. She caught her breath, and turning to her slower-witted husband, laid her trembling old hand upon his. There was a long silence.

"He was caught in the machinery," said the visitor at length, in a low . voice.

"Caught in the machinery," repeated Mr. White, in a dazed fashion, "yes."

He sat staring blackly out at the window, and taking his wife's hand between his own, pressed it as he had been wont to do in their old courting days nearly forty years before.

"He was the only one left to us," he said, turning gently to the visitor. "It is hard."

The other coughed, and rising, walked slowly to the window. "The firm wished me to convey their sincere sympathy with you in your great loss," he said, without looking around. "I beg that you will understand I am only their servant and merely obeying orders."

There was no reply; the old woman's face was white, her eyes staring, and her breath inaudible; on the husband's face was a look such as his friend the sergeant might have carried into his first action.

"I was to say that Maw and Meggins disclaim all responsibility," continued the other. "They admit no liability at all, but in consideration of your son's services they wish to present you with a certain sum as compensation."

Mr. White dropped his wife's hand, and rising to his feet, gazed with a look of horror at his visitor. His dry lips shaped the words, "How much?"

"Two hundred pounds," was the answer.

Unconscious of his wife's shriek, the old man smiled faintly, put out his hands like a sightless man, and dropped, a senseless heap to the floor.

III

In the huge new cemetery, some two miles distant, the old people buried their dead, and came back to a house steeped in shadow and silence. It was all over so quickly that at first they could hardly realize it, and remained in a state of expectation as though of something else to happen—something else which was to lighten this load, too heavy for old hearts to bear. But the days passed, and expectation gave place to resignation—the hopeless resignation of the old, sometimes miscalled apathy. Sometimes they hardly exchanged a word, for now they had nothing to talk about, and their days were long to weariness.

It was about a week after that the old man, waking suddenly in the night, stretched out his hand and found himself alone. The room was in darkness, and the sound of subdued weeping came from the window. He raised himself in bed and listened.

"Come back," he said tenderly. "You will be cold."

"It is colder for my son," said the old woman, and wept afresh.

The sound of her sobs died away on his ears. The bed was warm, and his eyes heavy with sleep. He dozed fitfully, and then slept until a sudden wild cry from his wife awoke him with a start.

"The monkey's paw!" she cried wildly. "The monkey's paw!"

He started up in alarm. "Where? Where is it? What's the matter?"

She came stumbling across the room toward him. "I want it," she said quietly. "You've not destroyed it?"

"It's in the parlor, on the bracket," he replied, marvelling. "Why?"

She cried and laughed together, and bending over, kissed his cheek.

"I only just thought of it," she said hysterically. "Why didn't I think of it before? Why didn't you think of it?"

"Think of what?" he questioned.

"The other two wishes," she replied rapidly. "We've only had one."

"Was not that enough?" he demanded fiercely.

"No," she cried triumphantly; "we'll have one more. Go down and get it quickly, and wish our boy alive again."

The man sat up in bed and flung the bedclothes from his quaking limbs. "Good God, you are mad!" he cried, aghast.

"Get it," she panted; "get it quickly, and wish— Oh, my boy, my boy!"

Her husband struck a match and lit the candle. "Get back to bed," he said unsteadily. "You don't know what you are saying."

"We had the first wish granted," said the old woman feverishly; "why not the second?"

"A coincidence," stammered the old man.

"Go. and get it and wish," cried the old woman, and dragged him toward the door.

He went down in the darkness, and felt his way to the parlor, and then to the mantelpiece. The talisman was in its place, and a horrible fear that the unspoken wish might bring his mutilated son before him ere he could escape from the room seized upon him, and he caught his breath as he found that he had lost the direction of the door. His brow cold with sweat, he felt his way round the table, and groped along the wall until he found himself in the small passage with the unwholesome thing in his hand.

Even his wife's face seemed changed as he entered the room. It was white and expectant, and to his fears seemed to have an unnatural look upon it. He was afraid of her.

"Wish!" she cried, in a strong voice.

"It is foolish and wicked," he faltered.

"Wish!" repeated his wife.

He raised his hand. "I wish my son alive again."

The talisman fell to the floor, and he regarded it shudderingly. Then he sank trembling into a chair as the old woman, with burning eyes, walked to the window and raised the blind.

He sat until he was chilled with the cold, glancing occasionally at the

figure of the old woman peering through the window. The candle end, which
had burnt below the rim of the china candlestick, was throwing pulsating
shadows on the ceiling and walls, until, with a flicker larger than the rest,
it expired. The old man, with an unspeakable sense of relief at the failure
of the talisman, crept back to his bed, and a minute or two afterward the
old woman came silently and apathetically beside him.

Neither spoke, but both lay silently listening to the ticking of the clock.
A stair creaked, and a squeaky mouse scurried noisily through the wall. The
darkness was oppressive, and after lying for some time screwing up his courage, the husband took the box of matches, and striking one, went down
stairs for a candle.

At the foot of the stairs the match went out, and he paused to strike
another, and at the same moment a knock, so quiet and stealthy as to be
scarcely audible, sounded on the front door.

The matches fell from his hand. He stood motionless, his breath suspended until the knock was repeated. Then he turned and fled swiftly back
to his room, and closed the door behind him. A third knock sounded
through the house.

"*What's that?*" cried the old woman, starting up.

"A rat," said the old man, in shaking tones—"a rat. It passed me on the
stairs."

His wife sat up in bed listening. A loud knock resounded through the
house.

"It's Herbert!" she screamed. "It's Herbert!"

She ran to the door, but her husband was before her, and catching her
by the arm, held her tightly.

"What are you going to do?" he whispered hoarsely.

"It's my boy; it's Herbert!" she cried, struggling mechanically. "I forgot
it was two miles away. What are you holding me for? Let go. I must open
the door."

"For God's sake don't let it in," cried the old man, trembling.

"You're afraid of your own son," she cried, struggling. "Let me go. I'm
coming, Herbert; I'm coming."

There was another knock, and another. The old woman with a sudden
wrench broke free and ran from the room. Her husband followed to the
landing, and called after her appealingly as she hurried downstairs. He heard
the chain rattle back and the bottom bolt drawn slowly and stiffly from the
socket. Then the old woman's voice, strained and panting.

"The bolt," she cried loudly. "Come down. I can't reach it."

But her husband was on his hands and knees groping wildly on the
floor in search of the paw. If he could only find it before the thing outside
got in. A perfect fusillade of knocks reverberated through the house, and he
heard the scraping of a chair as his wife put it down in the passage against
the door. He heard the creaking of the bolt as it came slowly back, and at

the same moment he found the monkey's paw, and frantically breathed his third and last wish.

The knocking ceased suddenly, although the echoes of it were still in the house. He heard the chair drawn back and the door opened. A cold wind rushed up the staircase, and a long loud wail of disappointment and misery from his wife gave him courage to run down to her side, and then to the gate beyond. The street lamp flickering opposite shone on a quiet and deserted road.

Questions

1. The author uses the real and unreal, the practical and the exotic in his story. Make lists of the two.

2. What was the purpose of the spell put on the monkey's paw?

3. Why does Jacobs, the author, make the old man the last of the three who could use the paw? What happened to the first two who used it?

4. What were the old man's first, second, and third wishes?

5. A person says, "If fate governs all, then I cannot be held responsible for what I do." React.

6. How can the fact that the old man's three wishes came true be explained logically (the wisdom of the eye)?

7. The storm, the bright sunny day, the street light swaying in the wind, and the deserted street do what for the author?

8. Students delight in "The Monkey's Paw" and get angry at "God Sees the Truth, but Waits." Can you explain why one is liked and the other is not?

9. If students are not going to like a story, should it be omitted from the book?

God Sees the Truth, but Waits*

LEO N. TOLSTOY

In the town of Vladimir lived a young merchant named Ivan Dmitrich Aksionov. He had two shops and a house of his own.

Aksionov was a handsome, fair-haired, curly-headed fellow, full of fun, and very fond of singing. When quite a young man he had been given to drink, and was riotous when he had had too much; but after he married he gave up drinking, except now and then.

One summer Aksionov was going to the Nizhny Fair, and as he bade good-bye to his family, his wife said to him, "Ivan Dmitrich, do not start to-day; I have had a bad dream about you."

Aksionov laughed, and said, "You are afraid that when I get to the fair I shall go on a spree."

His wife replied: "I do not know what I am afraid of; all I know is that I had a bad dream. I dreamt you returned from the town, and when you took off your cap I saw that your hair was quite grey."

Aksionov laughed. "That's a lucky sign," said he. "See if I don't sell out all my goods, and bring you some presents from the fair."

So he said good-bye to his family, and drove away.

When he had travelled half-way, he met a merchant whom he knew, and they put up at the same inn for the night. They had some tea together, and then went to bed in adjoining rooms.

It was not Aksionov's habit to sleep late, and, wishing to travel while it was still cool, he aroused his driver before dawn, and told him to put in the horses.

Then he made his way across to the landlord of the inn (who lived in a cottage at the back), paid his bill, and continued his journey.

When he had gone about twenty-five miles, he stopped for the horses to be fed. Aksionov rested awhile in the passage of the inn, then he stepped out into the porch, and, ordering a samovar to be heated, got out his guitar and began to play.

Suddenly a troika drove up with tinkling bells and an official alighted, followed by two soldiers. He came to Aksionov and began to question him, asking him who he was and whence he came. Aksionov answered him fully, and said, "Won't you have some tea with me?" But the official went on cross-questioning him and asking him, "Where did you spend last night? Were you alone, or with a fellow-merchant? Did you see the other merchant this morning? Why did you leave the inn before dawn?"

Aksionov wondered why he was asked all these questions, but he described

*From *Twenty-Three Tales* by Leo Tolstoy, translated by Louise and Aylmer Maude. Reprinted by permission of Oxford University Press.

all that had happened, and then added, "Why do you cross-question me as if I were a thief or a robber? I am travelling on business of my own, and there is no need to question me."

Then the official, calling the soldiers, said, "I am the police-officer of this district, and I question you because the merchant with whom you spent last night has been found with his throat cut. We must search your things."

They entered the house. The soldiers and the police-officer unstrapped Aksionov's luggage and searched it. Suddenly the officer drew a knife out of a bag, crying, "Whose knife is this?"

Aksionov looked, and seeing a blood-stained knife taken from his bag, he was frightened.

"How is it there is blood on this knife?"

Aksionov tried to answer, but could hardly utter a word, and only stammered: "I—don't know—not mine."

Then the police-officer said: "This morning the merchant was found in bed with his throat cut. You are the only person who could have done it. The house was locked from inside, and no one else was there. Here is this blood-stained knife in your bag, and your face and manner betray you! Tell me how you killed him, and how much money you stole?"

Aksionov swore he had not done it; that he had not seen the merchant after they had had tea together; that he had no money except eight thousand rubles of his own, and that the knife was not his. But his voice was broken, his face pale, and he trembled with fear as though he were guilty.

The police-officer ordered the soldiers to bind Aksionov and to put him in the cart. As they tied his feet together and flung him into the cart, Aksionov crossed himself and wept. His money and goods were taken from him, and he was sent to the nearest town and imprisoned there. Enquiries as to his character were made in Vladimir. The merchants and other inhabitants of that town said that in former days he used to drink and waste his time, but that he was a good man. Then the trial came on: he was charged with murdering a merchant from Ryazan, and robbing him of twenty thousand rubles.

His wife was in despair, and did not know what to believe. Her children were all quite small; one was a baby at her breast. Taking them all with her, she went to the town where her husband was in jail. At first she was not allowed to see him; but after much begging, she obtained permission from the officials, and was taken to him. When she saw her husband in prison-dress and in chains, shut up with thieves and criminals, she fell down, and did not come to her senses for a long time. Then she drew her children to her, and sat down near him. She told him of things at home, and asked about what had happened to him. He told her all, and she asked, "What can we do now?"

"We must petition the Czar not to let an innocent man perish."

His wife told him that she had sent a petition to the Czar, but it had not been accepted.

Aksionov did not reply, but only looked downcast.

Then his wife said, "It was not for nothing I dreamt your hair had turned grey. You remember? You should not have started that day." And passing her fingers through his hair, she said: "Vanya dearest, tell your wife the truth; was it not you who did it?"

"So you, too, suspect me!" said Aksionov, and, hiding his face in his hands, he began to weep. Then a soldier came to say that the wife and children must go away; and Aksionov said good-bye to his family for the last time.

When they were gone, Aksionov recalled what had been said, and when he remembered that his wife also had suspected him, he said to himself, "It seems that only God can know the truth; it is to Him alone we must appeal, and from Him alone expect mercy."

And Aksionov wrote no more petitions; gave up all hope, and only prayed to God.

Aksionov was condemned to be flogged and sent to the mines. So he was flogged with a knot, and when the wounds made by the knot were healed, he was driven to Siberia with other convicts.

For twenty-six years Aksionov lived as a convict in Siberia. His hair turned white as snow, and his beard grew long, thin, and grey. All his mirth went; he stooped; he walked slowly, spoke little, and never laughed, but he often prayed.

In prison Aksionov learnt to make boots, and earned a little money, with which he bought *The Lives of the Saints*. He read this book when there was light enough in the prison; and on Sundays in the prison-church he read the lessons and sang in the choir; for his voice was still good.

The prison authorities liked Aksionov for his meekness, and his fellow-prisoners respected him: they called him "Grandfather," and "The Saint." When they wanted to petition the prison authorities about anything, they always made Aksionov their spokesman, and when there were quarrels among the prisoners they came to him to put things right, and to judge the matter.

No news reached Aksionov from his home, and he did not even know if his wife and children were still alive.

One day a fresh gang of convicts came to the prison. In the evening the old prisoners collected round the new ones and asked them what towns or villages they came from, and what they were sentenced for. Among the rest Aksionov sat down near the newcomers, and listened with downcast air to what was said.

One of the new convicts, a tall, strong man of sixty, with a closely-cropped grey beard, was telling the others what he had been arrested for.

"Well, friends," he said, "I only took a horse that was tied to a sledge, and I was arrested and accused of stealing. I said I had only taken it to get home quicker, and had then let it go; besides, the driver was a personal friend of mine. So I said, 'It's all right.' 'No,' said they, 'you stole it.' But how or where I stole it they could not say. I once really did something wrong, and ought by rights to have come here long ago, but that time I was not found out. Now I have been sent here for nothing at all. . . . Eh, but it's lies I'm telling you; I've been to Siberia before, but I did not stay long."

"Where are you from?" asked some one.

"From Vladimir. My family are of that town. My name is Makar, and they also call me Semyonich."

Aksionov raised his head and said: "Tell me, Semyonich, do you know anything of the merchants Aksionov of Vladimir? Are they still alive?"

"Know them? Of course I do. The Aksionovs are rich, though their father is in Siberia: a sinner like ourselves, it seems! As for you, Gran'dad, how did you come here?"

Aksionov did not like to speak of his misfortune. He only sighed, and said, "For my sins I have been in prison these twenty-six years."

"What sins?" asked Makar Semyonich.

But Aksionov only said, "Well, well—I must have deserved it!" He would have said no more, but his companions told the newcomers how Aksionov came to be in Siberia; how some one had killed a merchant, and had put the knife among Aksionov's things, and Aksionov had been unjustly condemned.

When Makar Semyonich heard this, he looked at Aksionov, slapped his own knee, and exclaimed, "Well, this is wonderful! Really wonderful! But how old you've grown, Gran'dad!"

The others asked him why he was so surprised, and where he had seen Aksionov before; but Makar Semyonich did not reply. He only said: "It's wonderful that we should meet here, lads!"

These words made Aksionov wonder whether this man knew who had killed the merchant; so he said, "Perhaps, Semyonich, you have heard of that affair, or maybe you've seen me before?"

"How could I help hearing? The world's full of rumours. But it's a long time ago, and I've forgotten what I heard."

"Perhaps you heard who killed the merchant?" asked Aksionov.

Makar Semyonich laughed and replied: "It must have been him in whose bag the knife was found! If some one else hid the knife there, 'He's not a thief till he's caught,' as the saying is. How could any one put a knife into your bag while it was under your head? It would surely have woke you up."

When Aksionov heard these words, he felt sure this was the man who had killed the merchant. He rose and went away. All that night Aksionov lay awake. He felt terribly unhappy, and all sorts of images rose in his mind. There was the image of his wife as she was when he parted from her to go to the fair. He saw her as if she were present; her face and her eyes rose before him; he heard her speak and laugh. Then he saw his children, quite little, as they were at that time: one with a little cloak on, another at his mother's breast. And then he remembered himself as he used to be—young and merry. He remembered how he sat playing the guitar in the porch of the inn where he was arrested, and how free from care he had been. He saw, in his mind, the place where he was flogged, the executioner, and the people standing around; the chains, the convicts, all the twenty-six years of his prison life, and his premature old age. The thought of it all made him so wretched that he was ready to kill himself.

"And it's all that villain's doing!" thought Aksionov. And his anger was so great against Makar Semyonich that he longed for vengeance, even if he himself should perish for it. He kept repeating prayers all night, but could get no peace. During the day he did not go near Makar Semyonich, nor even look at him.

A fortnight passed in this way. Aksionov could not sleep at night, and was so miserable that he did not know what to do.

One night as he was walking about the prison he noticed some earth that came rolling out from under one of the shelves on which the prisoners slept. He stopped to see what it was. Suddenly Makar Semyonich crept out from under the shelf, and looked up at Aksionov with frightened face. Aksionov tried to pass without looking at him, but Makar seized his hand and told him that he had dug a hole under the wall, getting rid of the earth by putting it into his highboots, and emptying it out every day on the road when the prisoners were driven to their work.

"Just you keep quiet, old man, and you shall get out too. If you blab, they'll flog the life out of me, but I will kill you first."

Aksionov trembled with anger as he looked at his enemy. He drew his hand away, saying, "I have no wish to escape, and you have no need to kill me; you killed me long ago! As to telling of you—I may do so or not, as God shall direct."

Next day, when the convicts were led out to work, the convoy soldiers noticed that one or other of the prisoners emptied some earth out of his boots. The prison was searched and the tunnel found. The Governor came and questioned all the prisoners to find out who had dug the hole. They all denied any knowledge of it. Those who knew would not betray Makar Semyonich, knowing he would be flogged almost to death. At last the Governor turned to Aksionov whom he knew to be a just man, and said: "You are a truthful old man; tell me, before God, who dug the hole?"

Makar Semyonich stood as if he were quite unconcerned, looking at the Governor and not so much as glancing at Aksionov. Aksionov's lips and hands trembled, and for a long time he could not utter a word. He thought, "Why should I screen him who ruined my life? Let him pay for what I have suffered. But if I tell, they will probably flog the life out of him, and maybe I suspect him wrongly. And, after all, what good would it be to me?"

"Well, old man," repeated the Governor, "tell me the truth: who has been digging under the wall?"

Aksionov glanced at Makar Semyonich, and said, "I cannot say, your honour. It is not God's will that I should tell! Do what you like with me; I am in your hands."

However much the Governor tried, Aksionov would say no more, and so the matter had to be left.

That night, when Aksionov was lying on his bed and just beginning to doze, some one came quietly and sat down on his bed. He peered through the darkness and recognized Makar.

"What more do you want of me?" asked Aksionov. "Why have you come here?"

Makar Semyonich was silent. So Aksionov sat up and said, "What do you want? Go away, or I will call the guard!"

Makar Semyonich bent close over Aksionov, and whispered, "Ivan Dmitrich, forgive me!"

"What for?" asked Aksionov.

"It was I who killed the merchant and hid the knife among your things. I meant to kill you too, but I heard a noise outside, so I hid the knife in your bag and escaped out of the window."

Aksionov was silent, and did not know what to say. Makar Semyonich slid off the bed-shelf and knelt upon the ground. "Ivan Dmitrich," said he, "forgive me! For the love of God, forgive me! I will confess that it was I who killed the merchant, and you will be released and can go to your home."

"It is easy for you to talk," said Aksionov, "but I have suffered for you these twenty-six years. Where could I go to now? ... My wife is dead, and my children have forgotten me. I have nowhere to go. ..."

Makar Semyonich did not rise, but beat his head on the floor. "Ivan Dmitrich, forgive me!" he cried. "When they flogged me with the knot it was not so hard to bear as it is to see you now ... yet you had pity on me, and did not tell. For Christ's sake forgive me, wretch that I am!" And he began to sob.

When Aksionov heard him sobbing he, too, began to weep. "God will forgive you!" said he. "Maybe I am a hundred times worse than you." And at these words his heart grew light, and the longing for home left him. He no longer had any desire to leave the prison, but only hoped for his last hour to come.

In spite of what Aksionov had said, Makar Semyonich confessed his guilt. But when the order for his release came Aksionov was already dead.

Questions

1. God sees the truth, but waits for what?

2. Tolstoy's story was written in Russia in the 1800s. Why might this story be particularly appealing to a reader who lived under a religious despot?

3. What is the evidence against Aksionov?

4. When his wife, too, suspects him, to whom does he turn?

5. Defend the argument that what happened to Aksionov was for the good.

6. Why does Tolstoy introduce the fact of Aksionov's drinking in his youth?

7. Everything in a story should contribute to it and should aid the author in what he is trying to accomplish. What does the dream do for Tolstoy?

8. What leads Aksionov to suspect that Makar Semyonich committed the murder?

9. When Aksionov says, "Maybe I am a hundred times worse than you," is he being a hypocrite, attempting to make Makar feel less bad, or is he perhaps telling a truth? Make a case for the fact that he is telling the truth.

10. Might the story "Black Is My Favorite Color" (page 159) be entitled "God Sees the Truth, but Waits"?

11. How are the stories "God Sees the Truth, but Waits" and "The Monkey's Paw" alike and different?

The History of Susanna*

There dwelt a man in Babylon, called Joacim: and he took a wife, whose name was Susanna, the daughter of Chelcias, a very fair woman, and one that feared the Lord. Her parents also were righteous, and taught their daughter according to the law of Moses. Now Joacim was a great rich man, and had a fair garden joining unto his house: and to him resorted the Jews; because he was more honourable than all others. The same year were appointed two of the ancients of the people to be judges, such as the Lord spake of, that wickedness came from Babylon from ancient judges, who seemed to govern the people. These kept much at Joacim's house: and all that had any suits in law came unto them.

Now when the people departed away at noon, Susanna went into her husband's garden to walk. And the two elders saw her going in every day, and walking; so that their lust was inflamed toward her. And they perverted their own mind, and turned away their eyes, that they might not look unto heaven, nor remember just judgments. And albeit they both were wounded with her love, yet durst not one shew another his grief. For they were ashamed to declare their lust, that they desired to have to do with her. Yet they watched diligently from day to day to see her. And the one said to the other, Let us now go home: for it is dinner time. So when they were gone out, they parted the one from the other, and turning back again they came to the same place; and after that they had asked one another the cause, they acknowledged their lust: then appointed they a time both together, when they might find her alone.

And it fell out, as they watched a fit time, she went in as before with two maids only, and she was desirous to wash herself in the garden: for it was hot. And there was no body there save the two elders, that had hid themselves, and watched her. Then she said to her maids, Bring me oil and washing balls, and shut the garden doors, that I may wash me. And they did as she bade them, and shut the garden doors, and went out themselves at privy doors to fetch the things that she had commanded them: but they saw not the elders, because they were hid.

Now when the maids were gone forth, the two elders rose up, and ran unto her, saying, Behold, the garden doors are shut, that no man can see us, and we are in love with thee; therefore consent unto us, and lie with us. If thou wilt not, we will bear witness against thee, that a young man was with thee: and therefore thou didst send away thy maids from thee. Then Susanna sighed, and said, I am straitened on every side: for if I do this thing, it is

*From the Apocrypha: Daniel: 13. The Apocrypha contains certain writings of doubtful authority or authorship that are excluded or considered secondary in the Bible (Douay and King James versions).

death unto me: and if I do it not, I cannot escape your hands. It is better for me to fall into your hands, and not do it, than to sin in the sight of the Lord. With that Susanna cried with a loud voice: and the two elders cried out against her. Then ran the one, and opened the garden door. So when the servants of the house heard the cry in the garden, they rushed in at a privy door, to see what was done unto her. But when the elders had declared their matter, the servants were greatly ashamed: for there was never such a report made of Susanna.

And it came to pass the next day, when the people were assembled to her husband Joacim, the two elders came also full of mischievous imagination against Susanna to put her to death; and said before the people, Send for Susanna, the daughter of Chelcias, Joacim's wife. And so they sent. So she came with her father and mother, her children, and all her kindred. Now Susanna was a very delicate woman, and beauteous to behold. And these wicked men commanded to uncover her face, (for she was covered) that they might be filled with her beauty. Therefore her friends and all that saw her wept.

Then the two elders stood up in the midst of the people, and laid their hands upon her head. And she weeping looked up toward heaven: for her heart trusted in the Lord. And the elders said, As we walked in the garden alone, this woman came in with two maids, and shut the garden doors, and sent the maids away. Then a young man, who there was hid, came unto her, and lay with her. Then we that stood in a corner of the garden, seeing this wickedness, ran unto them. And when we saw them together, the man we could not hold: for he was stronger than we, and opened the door, and leaped out. But having taken this woman, we asked who the young man was, but she would not tell us: these things do we testify. Then the assembly believed them, as those that were the elders and judges of the people: so they condemned her to death.

Then Susanna cried out with a loud voice, and said, O everlasting God, that knowest the secrets, and knowest all things before they be: thou knowest that they have borne false witness against me, and, behold, I must die; whereas I never did such things as these men have maliciously invented against me. And the Lord heard her voice. Therefore when she was led to be put to death, the Lord raised up the holy spirit of a young youth, whose name was Daniel: who cried with a loud voice, I am clear from the blood of this woman. Then all the people turned them toward him, and said, What mean these words that thou hast spoken? So he standing in the midst of them, said, Are ye such fools, ye sons of Israel, that without examination or knowledge of the truth ye have condemned a daughter of Israel? Return again to the place of judgment: for they have borne false witness against her.

Wherefore all the people turned again in haste, and the elders said unto him, Come, sit down among us, and shew it us, seeing God hath given thee the honour of an elder. Then said Daniel unto them, Put these two aside one far from another, and I will examine them. So when they were put asunder one from another, he called one of them, and said unto him, O thou that art waxen old in wickedness, now thy sins which thou hast committed aforetime are come to light: for thou hast pronounced false judgment, and hast condemned the innocent, and hast let the guilty go free; albeit the Lord saith, The innocent and righteous shalt thou not slay. Now then, if thou hast seen her, tell me, Under what tree sawest thou them companying together? Who answered, Under a mastick tree. And Daniel said, Very well; thou hast lied against thine own head; for even now the angel of God hath received the sentence of God to cut thee in two.

So he put him aside, and commanded to bring the other, and said unto him, O thou seed of Chanaan, and not of Juda, beauty hath deceived thee, and lust hath perverted thine heart. Thus have ye dealt with the daughters of Israel, and they for fear companied with you: but the daughter of Juda would not abide your wickedness. Now therefore tell me, Under what tree didst thou take them companying together? Who answered, Under a holm tree. Then said Daniel unto him, Well; thou hast also lied against thine own head: for the angel of God waiteth with the sword to cut thee in two, that he may destroy you. With that all the assembly cried out with a loud voice, and praised God, who saveth them that trust in him. And they arose against the two elders, (for Daniel had convicted them of false witness by their own mouth;) and according to the law of Moses they did unto them in such sort as they maliciously intended to do to their neighbour: and they put them to death.

Thus the innocent blood was saved the same day. Therefore Chelcias and his wife praised God for their daughter Susanna, with Joacim her husband, and all the kindred, because there was no dishonesty found in her. From that day forth was Daniel had in great reputation in the sight of the people.

Questions

1. If the Elders had at one time been good men, what led them astray?

2. How did Daniel prove the Elders were bearing false witness? Was Daniel simply a clever lawyer?

3. How would you differentiate between love and lust?

4. What had shaped the people that they would agree to Susanna's execution?

5. If you were listing seven wrongs or sins in the order of their badness, where would you place "bearing false witness"? Lust? Willful stupidity?

6. Dancers, painters, dramatists—many different artists have presented "The History of Susanna." What questions should occur to these artists as they plan their presentation?

7. In your estimation is the Bible's authority strengthened or weakened because of the existence of the Apocrypha?

Where the Mind Is Without Fear*

RABINDRANATH TAGORE

Where the mind is without fear and the head is held high;
Where knowledge is free;
Where the world has not been broken up into fragments of narrow
    domestic walls;
Where words come out from the depths of truth;
Where tireless striving stretches its arms towards perfection;
Where the clear stream of reason has not lost its way into the dreary
    desert sand of dead habit;
Where the mind is led forward by Thee into ever-widening thought
    and action—
Into that heaven of freedom, my Father, let my country awake.

Questions

1. Every line beginning with *where* leads us to anticipate what?

2. In your estimation what is the American dream? What is everyman's dream?
    To what would we like to awake?

3. The poet wants his country to awake to what kind of riches?

4. The life we are leading is a dream, according to the poet. He describes what
    he wants us to awaken to. How would he describe what he wants us to awaken
    from?

5. Where do we learn what is real, what is important? Are the real and the
    important the same?

6. The poet asks God to awaken his country to that heaven of freedom. What
    stands in the way of man's awakening himself?

Abou Ben Adhem

LEIGH HUNT

Abou Ben Adhem (may his tribe increase!)
Awoke one night from a deep dream of peace,
And saw, within the moonlight in the room,
Making it rich, and like a lily in bloom,

---

*Reprinted with permission of The Macmillan Company from *Gitanjali* by Rabindranath
Tagore.

An angel writing in a book of gold.
Exceeding peace had made Ben Adhem bold,
And to the Presence in the room he said,
"What writest thou?"—The vision raised its head,
And with a look made of all sweet accord,
Answered, "The names of those who love the Lord."
"And is mine one?" said Abou. "Nay, not so,"
Replied the angel. Abou spoke more low,
But cheerily still; and said, "I pray thee, then,
Write me as one who loves his fellow-men."

The angel wrote, and vanished. The next night
It came again, with a great wakening light,
And showed the names whom love of God had blessed,
And lo! Ben Adhem's name led all the rest!

Questions

1. The name and the words "may his tribe increase" lead you to believe Abou Ben Adhem lives where?

2. What was the angel writing in the book of gold?

3. Loving one's fellowmen is equal to what, according to the poet?

4. "Abou Ben Adhem" and "Old Timers" have to do with a man. Are the men different? Which poet is the more direct teacher?

5. Apparently Abou Ben Adhem spoke truthfully when he told the angel what to write describing him. How does one go about being an Abou Ben Adhem?

6. After the first visit and the angel's answer, the angel returns to Heaven. Who might the angel have spoken to who changed his thinking? Reconstruct their conversation.

Incident*

(*For Eric Walrond*)

COUNTEE CULLEN

Once riding in old Baltimore,
    Heart-filled, head-filled with glee,
I saw a Baltimorean
    Keep looking straight at me.

Now I was eight and very small,
    And he was no whit bigger,
And so I smiled, but he poked out
    His tongue, and called me, "Nigger."

I saw the whole of Baltimore
    From May until December;
Of all the things that happened there
    That's all that I remember.

Questions

1. How old was the "I" and the boy from Baltimore?
2. What would we expect a youngster normally to remember from a seven- or eight-month visit to a large city?
3. Do we tend to remember the good or bad of our past experiences?
4. The poet, if he was the "I," has perhaps never felt good about Baltimore since the incident. If there is a place, or an object, or a person that is distasteful to you, are you conscious of the reason for your distaste?

God's Grandeur*

GERARD MANLEY HOPKINS

The world is charged with the grandeur of God.
    It will flame out, like shining from shook foil;
    It gathers to a greatness, like the ooze of oil
Crushed. Why do men then now not reck his rod?
    And all is seared with trade; bleared, smeared with toil;
    And wears man's smudge and shares man's smell: the soil
Is bare now, nor can foot feel, being shod.

And for all this, nature is never spent;
    There lives the dearest freshness deep down things;
And though the last lights off the black West went
    Oh, morning, at the brown brink eastward, springs—
Because the Holy Ghost over the bent
    World broods with warm breast and with ah! bright wings.

---

*From *Poems of Gerard Manley Hopkins* by Gerard Manley Hopkins. Reprinted by permission of Oxford University Press.

Questions

1. We speak of a charged battery. Does Hopkins use the word *charged* in a similar way?

2. The ooze of crushed oil and the leap of light from shook foil remind the poet of what?

3. To reck God's rod is an unusual expression. Can you define it?

4. In lines four through seven, is Hopkins pleased or displeased with man?

5. What evidence does Hopkins offer in the last stanza that nature is not spent, that the world is still charged with the grandeur of God?

6. Hopkins might shape a reader to his belief, leave him untouched, or turn him against the poem and belief. What will determine the effect of "God's Grandeur" on the reader?

The Road Not Taken*

ROBERT FROST

Two roads diverged in a yellow wood,
And sorry I could not travel both
And be one traveler, long I stood
And looked down one as far as I could
To where it bent in the undergrowth;

Then took the other, as just as fair,
And having perhaps the better claim,
Because it was grassy and wanted wear;
Though as for that the passing there
Had worn them really about the same,

And both that morning equally lay
In leaves no step had trodden black.
Oh, I kept the first for another day!
Yet knowing how way leads on to way,
I doubted if I should ever come back.

I shall be telling this with a sigh
Somewhere ages and ages hence:
Two roads diverged in a wood, and I—
I took the one less traveled by,
And that has made all the difference.

Questions

1. In the first stanza what is the problem facing the traveler (the poet)?

2. In the second stanza the poet explains how the paths were different. What was the difference?

3. He takes one, saving the other path for another day, but what does he know?

4. Which path did he take? The poet remembers the incident and the path. You have had to choose between paths a number of times. Do you recall some of your conscious choices? What were some of your choices that you realize now were unconscious?

5. Of the two paths Frost had to choose between, which is the path of the poet, and which is the path of most of the rest of us?

6. John Q. Public is walking in the woods and the path becomes two paths. Later in the day, or week, or year, how do the poet and John Q. react to the incident?

Old Timers*

CARL SANDBURG

I am an ancient reluctant conscript.
On the soup wagons of Xerxes I was a cleaner of pans.
On the march of Miltiades' phalanx I had a haft and head;
I had a bristling gleaming spear-handle.

Red-headed Cæsar picked me for a teamster.
He said, "Go to work, you Tuscan bastard!
Rome calls for a man who can drive horses."

The units of conquest led by Charles the Twelfth,
The whirling whimsical Napoleonic columns:
They saw me one of the horseshoers.

I trimmed the feet of a white horse Bonaparte swept the night stars with.

---

*From *Cornhuskers* by Carl Sandburg. Copyright 1918 by Holt, Rinehart and Winston, Inc. Copyright 1946 by Carl Sandburg. Reprinted by permission of Holt, Rinehart and Winston, Inc.

Lincoln said, "Get into the game; your nation takes you."
And I drove a wagon and team, and I had my arm shot off
At Spottsylvania Court House.

I am an ancient reluctant conscript.

Questions

1. Why doesn't Sandburg use the word *soldier* rather than *conscript?* *Ancient* and *reluctant* will not make sense, perhaps, until you have read the entire poem.
2. How does Sandburg tell you his conscript has existed through all time?
3. What role does the conscript play in the wars?
4. How does Sandburg want you to feel about the conscript?
5. Would the ancient, reluctant conscript ever be a conscientious objector? Explain.
6. A contemporary newspaper columnist calls John Q. Public a sucker because John Q. fights our wars for us. Discuss the journalist's statement.

nobody loses all the time*

E. E. CUMMINGS

nobody loses all the time

i had an uncle named
Sol who was a born failure and
nearly everybody said he should have gone
into vaudeville perhaps because my Uncle Sol could
sing McCann He Was a Diver on Xmas Eve like Hell Itself which
may or may not account for the fact that my Uncle

Sol indulged in that possibly most inexcusable
of all to use a highfalootin phrase
luxuries that is or to
wit farming and be
it needlessly
added

my Uncle Sol's farm
failed because the chickens
ate the vegetables so
my Uncle Sol had a
chicken farm till the
skunks ate the chickens when

my Uncle Sol
had a skunk farm but
the skunks caught cold and
died and so
my Uncle Sol imitated the
skunks in a subtle manner

or by drowning himself in the watertank
but somebody who'd given my Uncle Sol a Victor
Victrola and records while he lived presented to
him upon the auspicious occasion of his decease a
scrumptious not to mention splendiferous funeral with
tall boys in black gloves and flowers and everything and

i remember we all cried like the Missouri
when my Uncle Sol's coffin lurched because
somebody pressed a button
(and down went
my Uncle
Sol

and started a worm farm)

Questions

1. The first line of the poem possibly makes the reader think he is going to read about a winner. Who was the born failure?

2. Why might a stamp collection, hula lessons, and a swimming pool be called luxuries? Why is farming a luxury in the poem?

3. What happened on the farm of the man who was the born failure?

4. What kind of a funeral is a scrumptious, splendiferous funeral? Does the poet want to make you unhappy?

5. How do we know Sol's body was lowered mechanically into the grave?

6. What happens to a corpse in the grave? How did Uncle Sol finally achieve success?

7. Are both Cummings and Sandburg ("Old Timers") telling us of losers? If so, who are the winners?

The Parable of the Sower

ST. MATTHEW, FROM CHAPTER 13

The same day went Jesus out of the house, and sat by the sea side.

And great multitudes were gathered together unto him, so that he went into a ship, and sat; and the whole multitude stood on the shore.

And he spake many things unto them in parables, saying, Behold, a sower went forth to sow;

And when he sowed, some seeds fell by the way side, and the fowls came and devoured them up:

Some fell upon stony places, where they had not much earth: and forthwith they sprung up, because they had no deepness of earth:

And when the sun was up, they were scorched; and because they had no root, they withered away.

And some fell among thorns; and the thorns sprung up, and choked them:

But others fell into good ground, and brought forth fruit, some an hundredfold, some sixtyfold, some thirtyfold.

Who hath ears to hear, let him hear.

And the disciples came, and said unto him Why speakest thou unto them in parables?

He answered and said unto them, Because it is given unto you to know the mysteries of the kingdom of heaven, but to them it is not given.

Therefore speak I to them in parables: because they seeing see not; and hearing they hear not, neither do they understand.

Questions

1. What is the parable or story Christ told? What does it mean in your estimation?

2. What question do his disciples put to him? What is Christ's reply?

3. Christ's explanation of the parable is to be found in Matthew 13:18–23. What is the explanation?

4. What is the most effective way in your estimation to teach (does *teach* mean *shape?*) others? How many different ways can you list?

Appointment in Samarra*

W. SOMERSET MAUGHAM

DEATH SPEAKS: There was a merchant in Bagdad who sent his servant to market to buy provisions and in a little while the servant came back, white and trembling, and said, Master, just now when I was in the market-place I was jostled by a woman in the crowd and when I turned I saw it was Death that jostled me. She looked at me and made a threatening gesture; now, lend me your horse, and I will ride away from this city and avoid my fate. I will go to Samarra and there Death will not find me. The merchant lent him his horse, and the servant mounted it, and he dug his spurs in its flanks and as fast as the horse could gallop he went. Then the merchant went down to the market-place and he saw me standing in the crowd and he came to me and said, Why did you make a threatening gesture to my servant when you saw him this morning? That was not a threatening gesture, I said, it was only a start of surprise. I was astonished to see him in Bagdad, for I had an appointment with him tonight in Samarra.

Questions

1. The servant claimed he was looked at angrily. How was the look explained when the master went to the market place?

2. If our death is fated, can one logically claim our lives are fated?

3. This fable is used at the opening of the novel *Appointment in Samarra* by John O'Hara. What might you predict about the leading character in the novel?

4. Were you the master would you or wouldn't you explain what had happened to your children?

5. What does it mean to live one's life as if one were God's spy? Did the servant so live his life?

The Hand of God

(*sculpture—see p. 34*)

CARL MILLES

---

*Reprinted from *Sheppey*. By permission of the Literary Executor of W. Somerset Maugham and William Heinemann Ltd.

And God Made Man in His Own Image

(painting—see p. 35)

IVAN ALBRIGHT

Questions

1. Does the sculptor Carl Milles want you to react positively or negatively to God and man?

2. Had the sculptor wanted you to feel the opposite (of your answer to question 1), what might he have done to the hand of God and the figure of man?

3. In your estimation, how does the painter Ivan Albright want you to feel about man and God?

4. How do both Milles and Albright want the viewer to feel about them as artists?

5. The Bible says God created man in his own image. What words do we usually use to describe the man who has the appearance of God?

School

Or Does the Pupil Know More? by Francisco de Goya y Lucientes

¿Si sabrà mas el discipulo?

Education Strengthens the Nation

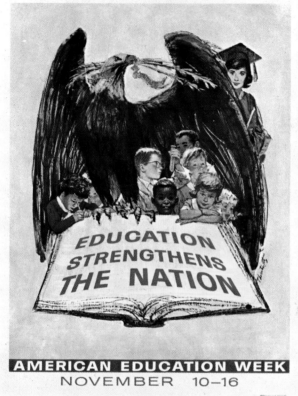

Courtesy of the National Education Association

Preliminary Statements for Discussion
and Writing

1.   Devising the question is more difficult than answering it.

2.   The job of the school is to preserve the status quo.

3.   Wisdom is to the soul what health is to the body.

4.   The school gets the child too late.

5.   What we *like* determines what we *are* and is the sign of what we are; to teach taste is inevitably to form character.

6.   Those who can, do. Those who can't, teach.

7.   History will tell lies as usual.

8.   The best teacher is he whose students say, "We did it ourselves."

9.   The school is society's laboratory.

10. If it isn't boring, it isn't education.

11. Students are more influenced by fellow students than by teachers or books.

The Last Lesson*

ALPHONSE DAUDET

I started for school very late that morning and was in great dread of a scolding, especially because M. Hamel had said that he would question us on participles, and I did not know the first word about them. For a moment I thought of running away and spending the day out of doors. It was so warm, so bright! The birds were chirping at the edge of the woods; and in the open field back of the saw-mill the Prussian soldiers were drilling. It was all much more tempting than the rule for participles, but I had the strength to resist, and hurried off to school.

When I passed the town hall there was a crowd in front of the bulletin-board. For the last two years all our bad news had come from there—the lost battles, the draft, the orders of the commanding officer—and I thought to myself, without stopping:

"What can be the matter now?"

Then, as I hurried by as fast as I could go, the blacksmith, Wachter, who was there, with his apprentice, reading the bulletin, called after me:

"Don't go so fast, bub; you'll get to your school in plenty of time!"

I thought he was making fun of me, and reached M. Hamel's little garden all out of breath.

Usually, when school began, there was a great bustle, which could be heard out in the street, the opening and closing of desks, lessons repeated in unison, very loud, with our hands over our ears to understand better, and the teacher's great ruler rapping on the table. But now it was all so still! I had counted on the commotion to get to my desk without being seen; but, of course, that day everything had to be as quiet as Sunday morning. Through the window I saw my classmates, already in their places, and M. Hamel walking up and down with his terrible iron ruler under his arm. I had to open the door and go in before everybody. You can imagine how I blushed and how frightened I was.

But nothing happened. M. Hamel saw me and said very kindly:

"Go to your place quickly, little Franz. We were beginning without you."

I jumped over the bench and sat down at my desk. Not till then, when I had got a little over my fright, did I see that our teacher had on his beautiful green coat, his frilled shirt, and the little black silk cap, all embroidered, that he never wore except on inspection and prize days. Besides, the whole school seemed so strange and solemn. But the thing that surprised me most was to see, on the back benches that were always empty, the village people sitting quietly like ourselves; old Hauser, with his three-cornered hat,

---

*From *Monday Tales* by Alphonse Daudet. Courtesy of Little, Brown and Company.

the former mayor, the former postmaster, and several others besides. Everybody looked sad; and Hauser had brought an old primer, thumbed at the edges, and he held it open on his knees with his great spectacles lying across the pages.

While I was wondering about it all, M. Hamel mounted his chair, and, in the same grave and gentle tone which he had used to me, said:

"My children, this is the last lesson I shall give you. The order has come from Berlin to teach only German in the schools of Alsace and Lorraine. The new master comes to-morrow. This is your last French lesson. I want you to be very attentive."

What a thunder-clap these words were to me!

Oh, the wretches; that was what they had put up at the town-hall!

My last French lesson! Why, I hardly knew how to write! I should never learn any more! I must stop there, then! Oh, how sorry I was for not learning my lessons, for seeking birds' eggs, or going sliding on the Saar! My books, that had seemed such a nuisance a while ago, so heavy to carry, my grammar, and my history of the saints, were old friends now that I couldn't give up. And M. Hamel, too; the idea that he was going away, that I should never see him again, made me forget all about his ruler and how cranky he was.

Poor man! It was in honor of this last lesson that he had put on his fine Sunday-clothes, and now I understood why the old men of the village were sitting there in the back of the room. It was because they were sorry, too, that they had not gone to school more. It was their way of thanking our master for his forty years of faithful service and of showing their respect for the country that was theirs no more.

While I was thinking of all this, I heard my name called. It was my turn to recite. What would I not have given to be able to say that dreadful rule for the participle all through, very loud and clear, and without one mistake? But I got mixed up on the first words and stood there holding on to my desk, my heart beating, and not daring to look up. I heard M. Hamel say to me:

"I won't scold you, little Franz; you must feel bad enough. See how it is! Every day we have said to ourselves: 'Bah! I've plenty of time. I'll learn it to-morrow.' And now you see where we've come out. Ah, that's the great trouble with Alsace; she puts off learning till to-morrow. Now those fellows out there will have the right to say to you: 'How is it; you pretend to be Frenchmen, and yet you can neither speak nor write your own language?' But you are not the worst, poor little Franz. We've all a great deal to reproach ourselves with.

"Your parents were not anxious enough to have you learn. They preferred to put you to work on a farm or at the mills, so as to have a little more money. And I? I've been to blame also. Have I not often sent you to water my flowers instead of learning your lessons? And when I wanted to go fishing, did I not just give you a holiday?"

Then, from one thing to another, M. Hamel went on to talk of the French language, saying that it was the most beautiful language in the world —the clearest, the most logical; that we must guard it among us and never forget it, because when a people are enslaved, as long as they hold fast to their language it is as if they had the key to their prison. Then he opened a grammar and read us our lesson. I was amazed to see how well I understood it. All he said seemed so easy, so easy! I think, too, that I had never listened so carefully, and that he had never explained everything with so much patience. It seemed almost as if the poor man wanted to give us all he knew before going away, and to put it all into our heads at one stroke.

After the grammar, we had a lesson in writing. That day M. Hamel had new copies for us, written in a beautiful round hand: France, Alsace, France, Alsace. They looked like little flags floating everywhere in the school-room, hung from the rod at the top of our desks. You ought to have seen how every one set to work, and how quiet it was! The only sound was the scratching of the pens over the paper. Once some beetles flew in; but nobody paid any attention to them, not even the littlest ones, who worked right on tracing their fish-hooks, as if that was French, too. On the roof the pigeons cooed very low, and I thought to myself:

"Will they make them sing in German, even the pigeons?"

Whenever I looked up from my writing I saw M. Hamel sitting motionless in his chair and gazing first at one thing, then at another, as if he wanted to fix in his mind just how everything looked in that little school-room. Fancy! For forty years he had been there in the same place, with his garden outside the window and his class in front of him, just like that. Only the desks and benches had been worn smooth; the walnut-trees in the garden were taller, and the hop-vine that he had planted himself twined about the windows to the roof. How it must have broken his heart to leave it all, poor man; to hear his sister moving about in the room above, packing their trunks! For they must leave the country next day.

But he had the courage to hear every lesson to the very last. After the writing, we had a lesson in history, and then the babies chanted their ba, be, bi, bo, bu. Down there at the back of the room old Hauser had put on his spectacles and, holding his primer in both hands, spelled the letters with them. You could see that he, too, was crying; his voice trembled with emotion, and it was so funny to hear him that we all wanted to laugh and cry. Ah, how well I remember it, that last lesson!

All at once the church-clock struck twelve. Then the Angelus. At the same moment the trumpets of the Prussians, returning from drill, sounded under our windows. M. Hamel stood up, very pale, in his chair. I never saw him look so tall.

"My friends," said he, "I—I—" But something choked him. He could not go on.

Then he turned to the blackboard, took a piece of chalk, and, bearing on with all his might, he wrote as large as he could:

"Vive La France!"

Then he stopped and leaned his head against the wall, and, without a word, he made a gesture to us with his hand:

"School is dismissed—you may go."

Questions

1. How did Franz know the day was to be an unusual one?

2. How is Franz similar to the young boy in the story "Catherine and the Winter Wheat"?

3. After conquering a country, what would you immediately seek to control to shape the people to your way of thinking?

4. Why did the teacher have to leave the country immediately?

5. If The Tribe in "The Way It Spozed To Be" (p. 75) faced what Franz did, would school become important? Would the quality of the education change?

The Way It Spozed To Be*

JAMES HERNDON

We had come out of the library from our first meeting with the principal, just the new teachers. I walked down the hall with a man named Skates whom I'd just met. It was mid-afternoon; the hall was dark. Suddenly, a trio of girls burst upon us as if they had been lying in ambush. One jumped ahead, pointing a finger at me.

You a new teacher?

Uh-huh. Yes.

What grade?

All of them, it looks like.

You teach the eighth?

Yes. Eighth too.

What you teach to the eighth grade?

English. Social studies. No, only English to the eighth grade.

The other two girls were hanging back, giggling. This girl crowded me, standing right next to me, looking straight up. I kept my head absurdly raised, feeling that if I bent down I'd graze the top of her head with my chin. I kept stepping back in order to get a look at her, and also to get away from her. She kept moving forward. She talked very loudly, smiling and grinning all the time but still almost shouting every word, having a fine time. It was okay with me.

What your name?

Herndon. Mr. Herndon.

Okay, Mr. Hern-don, saying Hern-dawn, accent last syllable as I was to hear it spoken from then on by all students. Okay, Mr. Hern-don, you all right. I'm gonna be in your class. You better believe it! I'm in your class!

Well, fine, I said. Good. The two girls giggled in the background. Skates stood around, waiting. The girl ignored all of them; her business was with me.

It seemed to be over. I waved my hand at her and started to move off. She grabbed me by the arm.

I ain't done! Listen you Mr. Hern-don, my name Ruth. Ruth! You'll hear about me, don't worry about it! And what I say, Mr. Hern-don, you don't cause me no trouble and I don't cause you none! You hear?

That suits me, I said. Well, see you later, Ruth, girls. Skates and I started off.

You don't cause me none, and I don't cause you none! she yelled once more, and then the three of them took off, sprinting down the hall away from us, laughing like hell and yelling at the top of their lungs.

The first day, sure enough, there was Ruth in my eighth grade B class. She was absolutely the craziest-looking girl I've ever seen. Her hair was a mass of grease, matted down flat in some places, sticking straight out in several others. Her face was faintly Arabic, and she was rather handsome, and very black. Across her forehead a tremendous scar ran in a zigzag pattern from somewhere above the hairline on her left side across to her right eye, cutting into the eyebrow. The scar was dead white. Her entire figure seemed full of energy and power; she was, every time I saw her, completely alert and ready. She could have been any age from fifteen to twenty-five. I once tried to look up her age, but on every sheet, the space after *Age* was simply left blank. No one knew, and apparently no one knew why it was that no one knew.

True to her word, she didn't cause me any trouble that first day. She sat in the second desk in her row and all she did was grab all the pencils I handed out for that row and refuse to pass them back. The row burst into an uproar, demanding their pencils. The other rows, not having thought of this themselves, yelled derisively, That row ain't gittin' any!

Please pass the pencils back, Ruth, I said, reasonably but loudly, since I wanted to be heard. In the back of my mind I was still wondering how she got in my class, or at least how she knew she was going to be in my class.

Ruth jumped up immediately. Don't go to hollering at me! she yelled. You got *plenty* of pencils! You *spozed* to give 'em all out! They ain't your pencils! You *spozed* to give 'em out! I *need* these pencils!

The class yelled out, Whooooo-eee! Whooo-eee! They all made the same sound. Everyone stood up, laughing and yelling whoo-eee except for the kids in Ruth's row who all screamed, We ain't got no pyenculs!

I advanced on the row. Sit down! I shouted at everybody. I did have plenty of pencils, and I was going to give one to each kid in the row and forget about it. Let her keep the goddam pencils! But as I came toward the row, Ruth suddenly flung the handful of pencils out into the room, screeched No! and launched herself backwards into space. She actually flew through the air and landed on her back on the floor after crashing—some part of her body or head, I couldn't tell—against a desk and a kid or two. Later—as other girls from other classes landed on their heads with a bang—I came to call this the Plop Reflex but all I could think of at the time was getting this damn girl off the floor. As I moved, she jumped up, full of life, and fled for the door.

I'm trying to tell about my year teaching—learning to teach—in a junior high school near San Francisco. It was a Negro school, about 98 per cent Negro they told me downtown in the district office, as if to say not entirely Negro. Its principal, Mr. Grisson, announced candidly that he was new at his job, that he expected to make some mistakes himself and certainly would not be surprised if we made some too. The vice principal, Miss Bentley, likened us to the Army. The Army, she submitted, was an organization of people given certain tasks to perform. So was a school. The school's overall mission was the education of children. "So that learning may take place," Miss Bentley explained, "there must first be order."

Skates had another comparison to suggest. He called our students "The Tribe." Watch out today, he'd yell to me, coming down the hall for lunch, The Tribe's getting edgy! Or, Come into my room; The Tribe's holding a talent show, tap-dancing, strippers, the whole bit. It's a little gift from me, in appreciation of the fact that they didn't eat me up last week.

Still, that was later. On this first day all I knew about my students was that they were divided up into four different groups—a seventh-grade B class which I had twice, an eighth-grade B class, a ninth-grade D class, and a seventh-grade H class. Inquiring around the coffee tables in the teachers' rooms, I learned that the kids were all rated A (high) to H (low) and placed in classrooms together accordingly.

The first day, third period, I pretended to ignore 9D—making out cards and alphabetizing lists while trying to figure out what they might have in mind. They ignored me in turn, steadfastly and actually, roaming the room to try out new seats, applying cosmetics, and listening to transistors. So on the second day, I determined to pass out English books and spellers, to make everything official, and get down to work. The main work, I'd decided, was going to be composition, freely done and at length. The kids were bound to be interested in things they'd written themselves and we could later make some corrections, show up some common faults, use the books to find practical standards for usage and punctuation. The spellers I'd use for regularity; they weren't much good, being just lists of words and a number of rather silly things to do with those words.

Nine D scrambled around for the books and spellers, but then quickly withdrew as soon as it became clear there were enough to go around, which was only when every single person had one of each. Cosmetics came out, kids got up and began searching for new places to sit, a boy took out a transistor radio. I passed out paper; I began to talk about what we were going to do. Cosmetics and conversation continued—not loudly or aggressively, but just as if I weren't addressing them. I began to insist on everyone's attention. Finally a voice said, Teacher, why don't you let us alone?

That stopped it. Oooooh? they all went. The speaker was Verna, a tall, lanky girl, brown, lithe and strong-looking, plain-faced, kinky-haired, without make-up. The tone of the class implied apprehension and excitement; I was now going to throw Verna out. Actually I didn't give a damn. We had everyone's attention; they had momentarily lost. Verna had to say something. I expected an outburst, but instead she said, You should have made us get to work yesterday. All the other teachers made us get to work. If you want us to do work, why didn't you make us yesterday?

She stopped talking and immediately turned around, her back toward me. The class rallied to her support by taking up their conversations where they had left off. Now I was losing. I got ready to start insisting again, wondering what I was going to say if and when they started listening.

Then the door swung open, and a kid walked in, came over and handed me a slip, and found a seat near the back of the room. The class turned around and conversed in a different key. The subject was the newcomer, Maurice, particularly the fact that he had just gotten out of Juvenile Hall in time to make the second day of school. Teacher, Maurice just back from Juvi! shouted somebody, so I wouldn't have any trouble finding out. Maurice himself was subdued, having been warned, I suppose, to be nice or find himself right back in Juvi. But I was winning again; they were so curious about what I was going to say to Maurice that they had to recognize me. I passed a book and speller down the row to him. You spozed to report to the parole officer about Maurice, Teacher! How he do, if he do his work! Do he get in trouble or fighting! . . .

Well now, I said, actually this is not a class about Juvi, but about English. Whoooo-eee! That broke them up. But when they stopped laughing they were attentive enough. I began to talk about how English meant using the language; I was well into my speech about figuring out together what was relatively interesting to do and then figuring out how to do it—which was, naturally, crap since I already had the business of composition in mind —and they were just beginning to get bored (they knew it was crap too) seeing as how I wasn't going either to lecture Maurice about Crime Not Paying or to say anything humorous again, when Bang! Maurice and another boy, locked in each other's arms, fell over their desks and across the desks of the next row and lay there stretched out, struggling. Books, papers, and kids scattered. Whoooo-eee!

Hell! I got over there. Silence. Let go! I shouted, but nothing happened. Maurice was on top, the other kid across a desk, and as I got there Maurice loosed an arm and belted the other kid in the face. Cut it out! I grabbed Maurice. The kid on the bottom let go, but Maurice didn't. I tugged him rather gently. He belted the kid again. I got mad, grabbed Maurice under the arms, and heaved as hard as I could. He flew backwards over the row of desks and landed with a crash on the next row. He landed plenty hard; I imagine it hurt and, also, he must have thought it was all up with him, back to Juvi. He was frantic and mad. He jumped up and started for me. I stood there; he stopped and stood there. He glared. Everybody was frightened. No one in the class looked forward, suddenly, to what was going to happen, which was that Maurice was going to come for me and hit me or I him; the end would be the speedy return of Maurice to Juvenile Hall beaten up by me previously or not. It was inevitable.

We stood there quite a few seconds and then I nodded, turned, and walked swiftly back to my desk and sat down. I hoped I was implying a mutual cease-fire among equals. When I turned around toward the class, Maurice had likewise retreated and was sitting at his desk. We carefully didn't look right at each other, but still in the same general direction, so as not to be accused of avoiding anything either. Maurice had seen the issue—I'd say we saw it exactly alike. We both had something at stake, and we cooperated perfectly.

The class was dumbfounded. They waited, disappointed, but certainly somewhat relieved. The Tribe courted disaster; that doesn't mean they liked it. But they didn't believe the action was over, so they were all attention when I got ready to say something. All right, I said, I guess we can start classwork. The first English assignment is to write a story about what just happened. You can begin writing now, finish it tonight, and have it ready for tomorrow's class.

Whatever they'd expected, that wasn't it. It suddenly seemed like a lousy idea to me, and I decided to admit it and do something else, but before I could Verna said Sh—! loudly and turned around in her seat so her back was to me. The class woke up at that signal and began to yell demands and questions at me. What to write! How we spozed to write without no paper! That ain't no schoolwork, Teacher! You can't make us write about that! I ain't got no pencil! You trying to get us into trouble! No pen! No paper! What to write! What to do!

Shhh—loudly again. This time not from Verna, but from Leon LaTour in the back. None of The Tribe said Shit, only Sh! or, to express extreme disgust, Sheee . . . ! Sh! said Leon LaTour, nobody going to write that. He was addressing the class, not me. He just want to pin it on somebody. He want to find out about it. He want to pull you in on it!

Protestations of innocence and as many accusations and counter-accusations followed that. Finally people's Mamas began to be mentioned, and I had to yell Quiet! again. Well, what if I do want to know? I yelled. Do you know? Something started it didn't it? Here's Maurice pounding on somebody, on Fletcher there, all of a sudden. Do you think he wanted to? So who did start it then?

Accusations, etc. Leon LaTour grinned in the back. Finally Verna jumped up and yelled, Hush up you-all! Sit down big-leg! came an unidentified voice. Forget you! said Verna coldly and everybody hushed. You don't have to get all shook up, said Verna. She was talking to me. Everybody know who start it. Earl he took hold of Maurice's notebook while Maurice writing on them cards you give him for the books, and slip it over onto Fletcher's desk and Maurice look up and find it gone and then he see it on Fletcher's desk and grab it, but Fletcher don't know it Maurice's because he didn't see that Earl put it there so he grab it back and there they go.

No one denied it. Earl was out of his seat and backed up in the corner of the room like John Dillinger facing the FBI. Sit down, Earl, I said. Oooooh? went the class softly. Sh! said Leon LaTour. Verna wasn't convinced. Ain't you sendin' Earl to the office, Teacher? she said flatly.

I was tired of the whole thing. Property. Your Mama. It seemed likely that at the moment Earl was slipping Maurice's notebook over, every other kid in the class was grabbing, poking, pushing, or pulling at some piece of someone else's stuff. I told them so, and looked at the clock; there were only about five minutes left. Okay, I said, now go on and write the assignment, now we all know all about it.

Actually no one wrote the assignment; no one, that is, except for Maurice, who perhaps figured he'd better. The next day all denied any knowledge of its being assigned. I read Maurice's Compostion, as it was entitled. A boy took another boy ['s notebook] in the class and so the boy jump [ed] him to beat [him] the teacher broke it up But the teacher didn't send the boys to the office. (*Corrections mine.*)

Teachers are always willing to give advice to new (or old) teachers, and I talked to them all during those first six or seven weeks. The advice was of two kinds. The first kind, useful enough, was about methods and equipment —sets of flash cards, controlled readers, recorders, easy-correcting tests, good films—but after a short time I was already using most of these. My problem was not what to use but how to get the kids to respond in such a way that they learned something. That brought up the other kind of advice, which was also the most common and which was useless to me. It was about a conglomeration of dodges, tricks, gimmicks to get the kids to do what they were spozed to do, that is, whatever the teacher had in mind for them to do. The purpose of all these tricks was to get and keep an aspect of order, which was reasonable enough I suppose. But the purpose of this order was to enable "learning to take place" (so everyone said—not wanting to be guilty of the authoritarian predilection for order for its own sake) and we all knew that most of the kids weren't learning anything. Everyone agreed that our students were on the average a couple of years below grade level, everyone agreed that was because they were "deprived" kids, but no one agreed that simply because their methods weren't working they ought to try something else.

It's not my purpose or even desire to criticize these teachers—they were as good as or better than most and they had a difficult job—but frankly I could never come to terms with their attitude. They knew certain ways to get control of the class, although even these didn't work consistently because the kids were not easily threatened, having little to lose. The material which was so important, which had to be "covered" once order was established, was supposed to lead toward specific understanding and broader knowledge. But actually what was happening was that teachers were presenting the students, every day, with something for them either to do or not-do, while keeping them through "order" from any other alternative. If a kid couldn't or wouldn't copy a paragraph from the board, he had only the choice of not-doing it, of doing nothing. Almost every teacher admitted that this last was the choice of half the class on any given day. Since their teaching methods were right in other schools, they argued, it must be the fact of "deprivation" which was at fault here. If deprivation was the problem, then something should be done about that deprivation. After that, the school program, being essentially right, would work, since the only reason it didn't work now was that the students were of the wrong kind, *i.e.,* they were deprived.

But I began to think something else was the trouble. Long before we met, my wife had worked for Dr. Thomas French at the Institute for Psychoanalysis in Chicago, and during this time I was reading the first volume of his book *The Integration of Behavior,* which he had sent her. In it he noted that the disintegration of reactions in abnormal behavior seemed to show up goals and processes in a kind of relief, and motivational patterns which might be overlooked in normal behavior were clearly shown in the abnormal. It occurred to me that The Tribe's reactions to this teaching were not different, only more overt, violent, and easily seen than those of normal (or nondeprived) children. Where the middle-class kids were learning enough outside of the classroom or accepting conventional patterns of behavior more readily, so as to make it seem that they were actually learning in school, The Tribe was exposing the system as ineffective for everyone.

During Christmas vacation I came across something that did seem effective: Paul Roberts' book *Patterns of English,* the first high-school English text based on modern linguistics or structural grammar. What impressed me about it was that the exercises seemed both practical and extremely interesting. I immediately tried them out on 7B and they were a great success.

Very briefly, the idea was to teach kids the various different kinds of words (the "parts of speech") by the way in which they occurred in sentences, instead of according to the meaning of the word. That is, a word wasn't to be called a noun because it was a person, place, or thing necessarily, but because it occurred in normal sentences in a certain way. If you took a sentence, "The ———— is new," you could see that only certain words would fit that blank, and those words we could call nouns or anything else; whatever we called them, they still were the only kinds of words which would fit there.

This seemed simple and interesting, and 7B was enthusiastic. They learned the various "patterns" easily, and by the time the year was over had gone through about half the book, which was meant for upper-grade high-school kids. I began now to try it out with 9D and 7H and the results were, relatively, quite as good. We did these patterns once a week and almost all the kids enjoyed making up huge lists of words which would fit certain patterns, and became fairly sure of themselves when it came to naming the patterns. The opposite exercise, that of taking a nonsense sentence like *"The groobs fleegled the grinty wilpentops"* and trying to figure out which words were nouns, adjectives, etc., was a great favorite; it had all the virtues, being new, fun, and not difficult. At the same time, Roberts assured the reader, they were learning the signaling devices for the parts of speech in English. This was the only thing I was able to point to to prove I was teaching something, in the ordinary classroom sense, and I was happy about it.

February and March are dull times in the morning sports page—nothing but the interminable scoring of pro-basketball teams and a vague sense of something about minor-league hockey. The season made itself felt at school. It was the beginning of the second semester and although it was impossible to see just why, it was clear that we were pretty stable. We had our schedule of events—reading, library, spellers—so that everyone would know just what they were not-doing, and the interminable and intellectual discussions of the radicals, led by Verna, about what was wrong with everything. Yet even the sports page began to tell us that some baseball team was contemplating a trade, a new manager; and we had a few changes too about this time.

In 9D Leon LaTour stopped coming to my class. In fact, he didn't come to any classes for the rest of the year. He didn't stop coming to school. He came on time, and spent the day roaming the halls or the yard, joining his class at passing periods to talk, going with them, stopping short at the door of whatever classroom they went into, and going on. Kids began to speak of students beaten up by him, of teachers threatened in the halls, of his talk about setting the fires in the big cans in the halls, which now became almost daily events. In the teachers' room it was branded a scandal—something had better be done, was the consensus. Skates told me that a number of his ninth-graders were coming in after lunch half-drunk and the kids all said they were buying wine from Leon LaTour at a nickel a drink. Skates was in favor of the whole thing, both on account of its being a revolutionary act and also because the student-drunks were too sleepy in class to cause any trouble or make any noise.

I began to stop regularly at the Plantation Club after school for a beer or two myself. The Plantation had South Seas decor, a good jukebox, and was dark and warm. There were always several businessmen from the Negro hotel next door, a traveling man's hotel as the bartender said. He often treated me in an extravagant Uncle Tom manner; he would hurry to serve me, wipe the bar over and over, ask me if the beer was cold enough, if I was comfortable, if the music was too loud or not loud enough. At other times he ignored me completely when I came in, until I began to think about getting up to leave, at which instant he would hurry over and become Uncle Tom again. I couldn't see any resemblance between the salesmen here and The Tribe, and indeed whenever I tried to imagine The Tribe grown up I found I couldn't do it. I could only imagine them now. I counted on something happening in my classes and soon, hoping I could hold out long enough for it. I counted on it. It did occur to me now that perhaps it wouldn't; there were too many things against it, the school structure, other teachers, America itself.

But something did. I still have an ordinary yellow-covered notebook which used to belong to Cerise. Open the cover, and there is a page decorated in ink with curlicues and flourishes which enclose a paragraph: "This is the Slambook belonging to Cerise, who says that nobody can read it without her permission and also anyone who steals it is guilty of a crime." It was all spelled correctly and signed with an elegant and unreadable script.

On the next page there is a list, numbered, of the students of 9D, and this is the key to what follows. For on each page afterwards, there is the name of a kid, and on that page other kids have been invited to comment on his or her character, appearance, courage, brains, or wealth, signing themselves only with a number corresponding to the key in the front. The beauty of this system is that the owner of the Slambook may then show the comments to the kid whose name is at the top of the page and have the pleasure of listening to him beg and plead with her to see the first page so that he may identify the commentators, the girl who said he was good-looking or the boy who said he was chicken. The authors of the remarks can also plead for her not to show it, and the owner thus becomes the center of frantic social activity.

I picked this Slambook up from the floor after the class left one period; when I gave it back to Cerise the next day, saying I didn't want to be guilty of a crime, she said it was already out of date and she had another, so I could have it.

Slambooks suddenly took precedence over everything. Charlene, Connie, and Cerise—the Three Cs, we called them—had them one day; everyone else was making them the next. The Three Cs were the prettiest and whitest girls in the class and their lead was bound to be followed. Since making up slambooks involved doing more work than many kids had done the entire year, I was delighted. Everyone was avidly writing in them, not perhaps in "complete sentences" or the rest of the paraphernalia expected for classwork, but the books were carefully made, the names spelled right, the style of the opening paragraph elegant and complicated and formal. From the appearance and behavior of the class, they might have been involved in some kind of engrossing class project or group work (as of course they were) discussing their progress with each other and writing entries into notebooks to be reported later with the results of their research, discussion, and inquiry.

The whole talk now in the teachers' room was about Slambook season and voices rose in excited competition about how many had been confiscated or destroyed. Methods for ridding the school of Slambooks forever were discussed and, I guess, tried out. All I could see, though, was that The Tribe had finally come across something which *needed to be written down* to be successful or interesting to them, which couldn't even exist without writing, and they were as enthusiastic about it as possible.

The next change in 9D began around the same time. It was, I think, the day I started reading Cerise's book that Geneva came into the room and, instead of going over to sit down, went to the board and began to write a list of the Top Forty songs on it. Geneva was a tall, big girl, middle in the hierarchy of skin-color, hair, features, etc., and middle in other ways too. This morning, as far as I could tell, she simply felt like writing tune titles on the board and did it.

The Top Forty, of course, were those forty rock 'n' roll songs played over and over, all day long, by the disc-jockeys of the local rock 'n' roll station. Geneva planned to write down only the first twenty—at least that's all she did write down and later on twenty became established as the proper number although we all still called it the Top Forty. As kids noticed Geneva chalking up titles, they began to question spellings, order, simple correctness; she made a couple of changes. Top Forty soon became a program, like the pledge of allegiance (or a paragraph on the board for everyone to copy). Something everyone could expect to start the class with from now on, except that almost everyone thought it was something important in itself, which made the difference.

During library periods I kept looking in the back storeroom for anything I could use with my classes and eventually I came across a series of playbooks. I kept them stacked in a corner of the room, since the librarian said that no one else ever used them. Occasionally kids from 9D or 7H would take a look at them.

One day, near the beginning of the period in 9D, with the kids hard at work or not-work, the Slambooks going through their courses, the Top Forty being laboriously written on the board under the watchful eye of Verna and a few critics, I was astonished to see the Three Cs approaching my desk in a body. They were clutching playbooks and they asked me why couldn't we read these plays out loud in class, everyone taking the parts? Why not? I'd already tried to get 9D interested in play-reading some time before. So I said it was a fine idea, but who was going to do the reading? It was an idiotic question. With the Three Cs planning to do something, everyone in the class was suddenly eager to take part. The Cs' own big table was quickly moved up to the front of the room—ten boys shoving each other for the honor of grabbing hold of it—desks shoved out of the way, folding chairs set around it. Trouble began as twenty kids dived for space around the table. I yelled. Everyone finally fell back and, taking the easy way out, I announced that the Three Cs, having introduced the idea, could pick out the players. There followed plenty of threats and counterthreats, some refusals-in-advance-of-expected-rejection, an incipient Plop Reflex or two; the Cs finally extorted enough promises and, with perhaps fifteen minutes left in the period, they began to read the play. That was the first time I realized that the play the Cs were so excited about was *Cinderella*.

It was a terrible reading. Unprepared, the kids stumbled and read too fast, giggled among themselves or argued, forgot their turn in haste to correct someone else, and the audience, prepared at first to listen, soon lost interest and drifted back to their spellers, Slambooks, and cosmetics.

The source of the trouble was the Three Cs. In their haste they had picked *Cinderella* because they saw there was a Prince and a fancy-dress ball and two sisters and a mother who were going to that ball; they saw themselves in starring roles, dancing, dining, diamonds shining and all. They weren't prepared to find Cinderella the heroine and had given that part to a girl named Grace, not concealing the fact that Grace looked, in their opinion, like someone who stayed home and cleaned up all the time. As the play went on and Grace steadily read all the most interesting parts with the fairy godmother and the Prince, the Cs became more and more upset and began to interpose remarks. How could the Prince dance with that ugly old thing? they wanted to know.

By the end of the play they had really become the three jealous women, so much so that they were almost speechless as the Prince began to go around with the glass slipper. When he got to their house and tried the slipper on the first of the mean sisters, he was supposed to read the line, "Oh no! Your foot is much too big for this slipper. You cannot be the lady I seek!" But by the time he got as far as "big," Charlene jumped up in a fury and yelled, Don't you say my feets too big you black monkey! and slammed her book down.

That broke up the play. Everyone began to laugh and yell Whoooo-eee! The other two Cs, having looked ahead now and seen the same fate reserved for them, quit the play too. We ain't playing no part where they get to say our feet too big, Mr. Hern-don! The bell rang about then, and the class rushed out still yelling Whooo-eee! They left *Cinderella* scattered about the room, the chairs knocked over, the table still up in front.

I left the table there. The next day the Cs tried to recruit someone to move it back for them, but the class objected. A number of them had play-books out and were planning to read another play. But first, they called out to me, we got to finish that one about Cinderella. They wanted to know how it came out.

Springtime was the rioting season. The Tribe had given up and was becoming violent. By April the story of the year was over—some details, some dramatics left to tell, but the score was already in. All the promises had lost their appeal and The Tribe was busting out. Fights. Fires. Windows. Food thrown all over. Neighborhood complaints about vandalism. And we lost Ruth. She'd remained in the elite 8B all year, getting along well enough, but in the spring she became determined to carry out minor disturbances to the bitter end, insisting on her rights, why she didn't have to give back the other kid's pen or book, what I was spozed to do. One afternoon after school she imprisoned the school nurse, a secretary, and a woman teacher in a room for forty-five minutes, threatening them with an upraised chair if they moved, thereby giving us an idea of what she meant by trouble. Teachers who had kept things in check all year began to have their problems. Oddly enough, the faculty took it in stride. It happens every year, they seemed to say. We try. We hold 'em for as long as we can. . . .

I viewed the daily slaughter with detachment and no little vanity. If they were beginning to lose, I was just starting to win. If their programs were falling apart, we were just starting to move. 9D not only read almost every day, but they were discussing—all right, they were arguing, squabbling, making a lot of noise, using a lot of bad language—certain questions about play-reading. They were discussing who read well and why, they were telling each other what the play was about, they argued about where certain characters should sit at the table. The most important question to them was what relationship the reader should have to the character he was reading. Two solid factions arose, the first arguing that if the character was a giant, a big kid had to read the part. The second disagreed; they thought that, if the character was a beautiful girl, any girl who *read* beautifully, who *sounded* beautiful, should read it. The kids were making it. Rolling. I was enthusiastic, pleased, proud of them.

In this mood I met with Mr. Grisson in April for his official evaluation of my year's work. He opened the interview by stating that it was always painful to him to have to make judgments, but that it was best to be frank. In short, he found my work unsatisfactory on every count, he could not recommend me for rehire in the district. Furthermore he must say that he considered me unfit for the position of junior-high-school teacher in any school, anywhere, now or in the future, and would so state on my evaluation paper.

On the last day of school, Ramona and Hazel told me I was the nicest and best teacher they ever had. I told them I bet they said that to all their teachers; the class agreed loudly that they did.

Grisson had scheduled an assembly for the afternoon. I sat with Skates in the balcony of the auditorium, surrounded by excited students. On the stage Grisson was giving out awards for the year—for good citizenship, class officers and athletes, and finally for the district-wide spelling contest. He called off the names, waited for the kids to climb up onto the stage, shook their hands, led applause, and frowned into the audience as The Tribe expressed occasional disbelief in the spelling ability of such-and-such a watermelon-head. After it seemed that all the awards had been distributed, Grisson paused significantly. Everyone waited. Then he said, there is one more spelling award which may come as a little surprise. It is my great pleasure now to call up the last winner in the spelling contest—Leon LaTour!

The Tribe went wild, roaring out in what seemed to me equal parts of disbelief, astonishment, glee, and disgust, keeping it up long after Leon LaTour shook Grisson's hand and left the stage. Around us I could see other teachers nodding and smiling; it was another victory—the rebel brought back into the fold, a threat to the system conquered by the carrot. Grisson was leading the way, and everything was okay.

Unfortunately, I was aware that Leon LaTour hadn't ever taken the spelling tests. They were given only in English classes, and Leon LaTour only had one English class—mine; he hadn't been there when I gave it. He hadn't been in any classes then: I suppose Grisson could have called him in and given him the test privately, but it didn't seem likely, nor did it seem likely that Leon LaTour would have come in and taken that test.

In any case Leon LaTour couldn't spell.

So why the award? What the hell? Either Leon LaTour threatened some good-spelling kid to sign his—Leon's—name to his own spelling paper, or else the whole thing was rigged. Like many another event that year there wasn't an answer available, but it was the last day and I didn't have to worry about it. Forget you! I said, talking to myself out loud. Two kids in front of me started to giggle. You hear Mr. Hern-don? one of them said to the other. He say, Forget you!

The movie came on then, something about a Bullfighter and a Kid. The Tribe was restless during it, standing up, talking, scuffling. I was brooding about the position I found myself in. I couldn't remember when I'd worked so hard or concentrated what intelligence and energy I possessed so seriously on a single effort. It seemed unlikely that any kind of work besides teaching was going to satisfy me now, but it seemed even more unlikely that I was going to get another teaching job very soon. It was a kind of bind I wasn't used to.

Around Skates and me the kids stopped scuffling and began to cheer and yell. I looked at the screen. In the movie, the bull had just gored a matador. Two men came out to distract it, and the bull began to chase them around the ring, crashing into the wooden barriers as the men dodged behind them. Time and time again, the bull chased and crashed. The kids yelled and laughed and stood up and fell down again helpless with laughter. Hey Jim! Skates yelled to me, look, The Tribe likes it! They like it! He was laughing now too, raising his fist and waving it in the air.

Suddenly the lights went on in the auditorium, the film stopped, and Grisson appeared on the stage. He warned them that any further demonstrations of that sort wouldn't be tolerated; if it happened again the film would be stopped and they could return to their classrooms. Sh! said The Tribe.

Let 'em alone! Skates called out loudly from the balcony. Hell, he said to me, it's the first time all year they like something. So let 'em alone . . .

Well, the lights went back out, the bull chased everyone around the ring, the kids yelled. In time the movie was over, the lights came on, the kids dismissed, the season over too, and we all went home.

Questions

1. Mr. Skates called the students "The Tribe." Was the title justified?

2. What was the "plop reflex"?

3. According to the assistant principal there had to be order before there could be what? Do you agree? Did Mr. Herndon agree with her? Explain.

4. Why didn't the fight with Maurice, the slambooks, the initial play reading, the transistors, and the wandering around particularly bother Mr. Herndon?

5. How successful were most of the teachers at the school in teaching? According to the author, who in addition to the tribe learned nothing?

6. "... it was another victory—the rebel brought back into the fold, a threat to the system conquered by the carrot." This quoted idea refers to what incident?

7. If the job of the school is to help shape the student, was the junior high in this story doing a good job in your estimation?

The Three Swimmers
and the Grocer from Yale*

WILLIAM SAROYAN

The ditches were dry most of the year, but when they weren't dry, they were roaring. As the snows melted in the hills the ditches began to roar and from somewhere, God knows where, arrived frogs and turtles, water snakes and fish. In the spring of the year the water hurried, and with it the heart, but as the fields changed from green to brown, the blossoms to fruit, the shy warmth to arrogant heat, the ditches slowed down and the heart grew lazy. The first water from the hills was cold, swift, and frightening. It was too cold and busy to invite the naked body of a boy.

Alone, or in a group, a boy would stand on the bank of a ditch and watch the water for many minutes, and then, terribly challenged, fling off his clothes, make a running dive, come up gasping, and swim across to the other side. If the boy was the first of a group to dive, the others would soon follow, in order not to walk home in shame. It wasn't simply that the water was cold. It was more that it had no time for boys. The springtime water was as unfriendly as anything could be.

One day in April I set out for Thompson Ditch with my cousin Mourad and a pal of his named Joe Bettencourt, a Portuguese who loved nothing more than to be free and out-of-doors. A schoolroom made Joe stupid. It embarrassed him. But once out of school, once off the school-grounds, he was as intelligent, as good-natured, casual, sincere, and friendly as anyone could possibly be. As my cousin Mourad said, Joe ain't dumb—he just doesn't want an education.

It was a bright Saturday morning. We had two baloney sandwiches each, and ten cents between the three of us. We decided to walk to the ditch so that we would get there around noon, when the day would be warm. We walked along the railroad tracks to Calwa. Along the state highway to Malaga. And then east through the vineyard country to the ditch. When we said Thompson Ditch, we meant a specific place. It was an intersection of country roads, with a wooden bridge and a headgate. The swimming was south of the bridge. West of the ditch was a big fenced-in pasture, with cows and horses grazing in it. East of the ditch was the country road. The road and the ditch traveled together many miles. The flow was south, and the next bridge was two miles away. In the summertime a day of swimming was in-complete until a boy had gone downstream to the other bridge, rested a moment in the pasture land, and then come back up, against the stream, which was a good workout.

By the time we got out to Thompson Ditch the brightness of morning had changed to a gloom that was unmistakably wintry; in fact, the beginning of a storm. The water was roaring, the sky was gray, growing black, the air was cold and unfriendly, and the landscape seemed lonely and desolate.

Joe Bettencourt said, I came all this way to swim and rain or no rain I'm going to swim.

So am I, I said.

You wait, my cousin Mourad said. Me and Joe will see how it is. If it's all right, you can come in. Can you really swim?

Aw shut up, I said.

This is what I always said when it seemed to me that somebody had unwittingly insulted me.

Well, Joe said, *can* you?

Sure I can swim, I said.

If you ask *him,* my cousin Mourad said, he can do anything. Better than anybody in the world.

Neither of them knew how uncertain I was as to whether or not I could swim well enough to negotiate a dive and a swim across that body of cold roaring water. If the truth were known, when I saw the dark water roaring I was scared, challenged, and insulted.

Aw shut up, I said to the water.

I brought out my lunch and bit into one of the sandwiches. My cousin Mourad whacked my hand and almost knocked the sandwich into the water.

We eat after we swim, he said. Do you want to have cramps?

I had plumb forgotten. It was because I was so challenged and scared.

One sandwich won't give anybody cramps, I said.

It'll taste better after we swim, Joe said.

He was a very kind boy. He knew I was scared and he knew I was bluffing. I knew *he* was scared, but I knew he was figuring everything out a little more wisely than I was.

Let's see, he said. We'll swim across, rest, swim back, get dressed, eat, and unless the storm passes, start for home. Otherwise we'll swim some more.

This storm isn't going to pass, my cousin Mourad said. If we're going to swim, we're going to have to do it in a hurry and start for home.

By this time Joe was taking off his clothes. My cousin Mourad was taking off his, and I was taking off mine. We stood together naked on the bank of the ditch looking at the unfriendly water. It certainly didn't invite a dive, but there was no other honorable way to enter a body of water. If you tried to walk in, you were just naturally not a swimmer. If you jumped in feet first it wasn't exactly a disgrace, it was just bad style. On the other hand, the water was utterly without charm, altogether unfriendly, uninviting, and sinister. It was certainly challenging, though. The swiftness of the water made the distance to the opposite bank seem greater than it was.

Without a word Joe dived in. Without a word my cousin Mourad dived in. The second or two between splashes seemed like long days dreamed in a winter dream because I was not only scared but very cold. With a bookful of unspoken words on my troubled mind, I dived in.

The next thing I knew—and it wasn't more than three seconds later— I was listening to Joe yelling, my cousin Mourad yelling, and myself yelling. What had happened was that we had all dived into mud up to our elbows, had gotten free only with great effort, and had each come up worrying about what had happened to the other two. We were all standing in the cold roaring water, up to our knees in soft mud.

The dives had been standing dives. If they had been running dives we would have stuck in the mud up to our ankles, head first, and remained there until summer, or later.

This scared us a little on the one hand and on the other hand made us feel very lucky to be alive.

The storm broke while we stood in the mud of the ditch.

Well, Joe said, we're going to get caught in the rain anyhow. We might as well stay in a little while anyway.

We were all shivering, but it seemed sensible that we should try our best to make a swim of it. The water wasn't three feet deep; nevertheless, Joe managed to leap out of the mud and swim across, and then back.

We swam for what seemed like a long time, but was probably no more than ten minutes. Then we got out of the water and mud and dressed and, standing under a tree, ate our sandwiches.

Instead of stopping, the rain increased, so we decided to set out for home right away.

We may get a ride, Joe said.

All the way to Malaga the country road was deserted. In Malaga we went into the general store and warmed ourselves at the stove and chipped in and bought a can of beans and a loaf of French bread. The proprietor of the store was a man named Darcous who wasn't a foreigner. He opened the can for us, divided the beans into three parts on three paper plates, gave us each a wooden fork, and sliced the bread for us. He was an old man who seemed funny and young.

Where you been, boys? he said.

Swimming, Joe said.

Swimming? he said.

Sure, Joe said. We showed that river.

Well, I'll be harrowed, the grocer said. How was it?

Not three feet deep, Joe said.

Cold?

Ice-cold.

Well, I'll be cultivated, the grocer said. Did you have fun?

Did we? Joe asked my cousin Mourad.

Joe didn't know whether it had been fun or something else.

I don't know, my cousin Mourad said. When we dived in we got stuck in the mud up to our elbows.

It wasn't easy to get loose from the mud, I said.

Well, I'll be pruned, the grocer said.

He opened a second can of beans, pitched an enormous forkful into his mouth, and then divided the rest onto the three paper plates.

We haven't got any more money, I said.

Now, tell me, boys, the grocer said, what made you do it?

Nothing, Joe said with the finality of a boy who has too many reasons to enumerate at a moment's notice, and his mouth full of beans and French bread.

Well, I'll be gathered into a pile and burned, the grocer said. Now, boys, he said, tell me—of what race are you? Californians, or foreigners?

We're all Californians, Joe said. I was born on G Street in Fresno. Mourad here was born on Walnut Avenue or some place on the other side of the Southern Pacific tracks, I guess, and his cousin somewhere around in that neighborhood, too.

Well, I'll be irrigated, the grocer said. Now, tell me, boys, what sort of educations have you got?

We ain't educated, Joe said.

Well, I'll be picked off a tree and thrown into a box, the grocer said. Now, tell me, boys, what foreign languages do you speak?

I speak Portuguese, Joe said.

You ain't educated? the grocer said. I have a degree from Yale, my boy, and I can't speak Portuguese. And you, son, how about you?

I speak Armenian, my cousin Mourad said.

Well, I'll be cut off a vine and eaten grape by grape by a girl in her teens, the grocer said. I can't speak a word of Armenian and I'm a college graduate, class of 1892. Now, tell me, son, he said. What's *your* name?

Aram Garoghlanian, I said.

I think I can get it, he said. Gar-oghlan-ian. Is that it?

That's it, I said.

Aram, he said.

Yes, sir, I said.

And what strange foreign language do *you* speak? he said.

I speak Armenian, too, I said. That's my cousin. *Mourad* Garoghlanian.

Well, I'll be harrowed, he said, cultivated, pruned, gathered into a pile, burned, picked off a tree, and let me see what else? Thrown into a box, I think it was, cut off a vine and eaten grape by grape by a girl in her teens. Yes, sir. All them things, if this doesn't beat everything. Did you encounter any reptiles?

What's reptiles? Joe said.

Snakes, the grocer said.

We didn't see any, Joe said. The water was black.

Black water, the grocer said. Any fish?

Didn't see any, Joe said.

A Ford stopped in front of the store and an old man got out and came across the wood floor of the porch into the store.

Open me a bottle, Abbott, the man said.

Judge Harmon, the grocer said, I want you to meet three of the most heroic Californians of this great state.

The grocer pointed at Joe, and Joe said, Joseph Bettencourt—I speak Portuguese.

Stephen L. Harmon, the Judge said. I speak a little French.

The grocer pointed at my cousin Mourad and Mourad said, Mourad Garoghlanian.

What do you speak? the Judge said.

Armenian, my cousin Mourad said.

The grocer gave the Judge the opened bottle, the Judge lifted it to his lips, swallowed three swigs, beat his chest, and said, I'm mighty proud to meet a Californian who speaks Armenian.

The grocer pointed at me.

Aram Garoghlanian, I said.

Brothers? the Judge asked.

Cousins, I said.

Same thing, the Judge said. Now, Abbott, if you please, what's the occasion for this banquet and your poetic excitement, if not delirium?

The boys have just come from showing that old river, the grocer said.

The Judge took three more swigs, beat his chest three times slowly and said, Come from *what?*

They've just come from swimming, the grocer said.

Have any of you fevers? the Judge said.

Fever? Joe said. We ain't sick.

The grocer busted out with a roar of laughter.

Sick? he said. Sick? Judge, these boys dived naked into the black water of winter and came up glowing with the warmth of summer.

We finished the beans and the bread. We were thirsty but didn't know if we should intrude with a request for a drink of water. At least *I* didn't know, but Joe apparently didn't stop to consider.

Mr. Abbott, he said, could we have a drink of water?

Water? the grocer said. Water, my boy? Water's for swimming in, not for drinking.

He fetched three paper cups, went to a small barrel with a tap, turned the tap, and filled each cup with a light golden fluid.

Here, boys, he said. Drink. Drink the lovely juice of the golden apple, unfermented.

The Judge poured the grocer a drink out of his bottle, lifted the bottle to his lips, and said, To your health, gentlemen.

Yes, sir, Joe said.

We all drank.

The Judge screwed the top onto the bottle, put the bottle into his back pocket, looked at each of us carefully, as if to remember us for the rest of his life, and said, Good-by, gentlemen. Court opens in a half hour. I must pass sentence on a man who says he *borrowed* the horse, *didn't* steal it. He speaks Mexican. The man who says he *stole* the horse speaks Italian. Good-by.

Good-by, we said.

By this time our clothes were almost dry, but the rain hadn't stopped.

Well, Joe said, thanks very much, Mr. Abbott. We've got to get home.

Not at all, the grocer said. *I* thank you.

The grocer seemed to be in a strange silence for a man who only a moment before had been so noisy with talk.

We left the store quietly and began to walk down the highway. The rain was now so light it didn't seem like rain at all. I didn't know what to make of it. Joe was the first to speak.

That Mr. Abbott, he said, he's some man.

The name on the sign is Darcous, I said. Abbott's first name.

First or last, Joe said, he sure is some man.

That Judge was somebody too, my cousin Mourad said.

Educated, Joe said. I'd learn French myself, but who would I talk to?

We walked along the highway in silence. After a few minutes the black clouds parted, the sun came through, and away over in the east we saw the rainbow over the Sierra Nevadas.

We sure showed that old river, Joe said. Was he crazy?

I don't know, my cousin Mourad said.

It took us another hour to get home. We had all thought about the two men and whether or not the grocer was crazy. Myself, I believed he wasn't, but at the same time it seemed to me he had acted kind of crazy.

So long, Joe said.

So long, we said.

He went down the street. Fifty yards away he turned around and said something almost to himself.

What? my cousin Mourad shouted.

He was, Joe said.

Was what? I shouted.

Crazy, Joe shouted back.

Yeah? I shouted back. How do you know?

How can you be cut off a vine and eaten grape by grape by a girl in her teens? Joe shouted.

Suppose he was crazy? my cousin Mourad said. What of it?

Joe put his hand to his chin and began to consider. The sun was shining for all it was worth now and the world was full of light.

I don't think he was crazy, he shouted.

He went on down the street.

He was pretty crazy, my cousin Mourad said.

Well, I said, maybe he's not always.

We decided to let the matter rest at this point until we went swimming again, at which time we would visit the store again and see what happened.

A month later when, after swimming in the ditch, the three of us went into the store, the man who was in charge was a much younger man than Mr. Abbott Darcous. He wasn't a foreigner either.

What'll it be? he said.

A nickel's worth of baloney, Joe said, and a loaf of French bread.

Where's Mr. Darcous? my cousin Mourad said.

He's gone home, the young man said.

Where's that? I said.

Some place in Connecticut, I think, the young man said.

We made sandwiches of the baloney and French bread and began to eat.

At last Joe asked the question.

Was he crazy? Joe said.

Well, the young man said, that's hard to say. I thought he was crazy at first. Then I decided he wasn't. The way he ran this store made you think he was crazy. He gave away more than he sold. To hear him talk you'd think he was crazy. Otherwise he was all right.

Thanks, Joe said.

The store was all in order now, and a very dull place. We walked out, and began walking home.

He's crazy, Joe said.

Who? I said.

That guy in the store now, Joe said.

That young fellow? I said.

Yeah, Joe said. That new fellow in there that ain't got no education.

I think you're right, my cousin Mourad said.

All the way home we remembered the educated grocer.

Well, I'll be cultivated, Joe said when he left us and walked on down the street.

Well, I'll be picked off a tree and thrown in a box, my cousin Mourad said.

Well, I'll be cut off a vine and eaten grape by grape by a girl in her teens, I said.

He sure was some man. Twenty years later, I decided he had been a poet and had run that grocery store in that little run-down village just for the casual poetry in it instead of the paltry cash.

Questions

1. As evidenced by this story, how does Saroyan apparently feel about life, the boys, and the grocer? What do the boys and the grocer have in common?

2. What kind of life doesn't Saroyan feel good about?

3. Does the Rockwell (p. 106) or Tchelitchew painting best illustrate Saroyan's presentation of boyhood?

4. Tell in your own words the meaning of the last sentence of the story.

5. What is an educated man in your estimation? In Saroyan's estimation?

There Is No Frigate Like a Book*

EMILY DICKINSON

There is no Frigate like a Book
To take us Lands away
Nor any Coursers like a Page
Of prancing Poetry—
This Traverse may the poorest take
Without oppress of Toll—
How frugal is the Chariot
That bears the Human soul.

Questions

1. A ship, horses, and a chariot have what to do with books and poetry?

2. Even the poorest lacks not the funds to do what?

3. The human soul, according to the poet, is moved by (borne by) what? Do you agree with the poet?

4. Is The Tribe in the story "The Way It Spozed To Be" proof that this poem is false?

5. What shaped The Tribe?

---

* From *The Complete Poems of Emily Dickinson* published by Little, Brown and Company. Reprinted by permission.

On Flunking a Nice Boy
Out of School*

JOHN CIARDI

I wish I could teach you how ugly
decency and humility can be when they are not
the election of a contained mind but only
the defenses of an incompetent. Were you taught
meekness as a weapon? Or did you discover,
by chance maybe, that it worked on mother
and was generally a good thing—
at least when all else failed—to get you over
the worst of what was coming? Is that why you bring
these sheep-faces to Tuesday?
                                    They won't do.

It's three months' work I want, and I'd sooner have it
from the brassiest lumpkin in pimpledom, but have it,
than all these martyred repentances from you.

Questions

1. What worked with mother that the student hopes will work with the instructor?

2. In your own words describe "the brassiest lumpkin in pimpledom."

3. What does Ciardi mean by "a contained mind"? In your estimation is the nice boy a hypocrite?

4. Often both the humble excuse bringer and the brassy lumpkin state in humble and brassy tones respectively, "An F (or D or C or B)? But I worked so hard on that paper." Is the instructor justified in striking the student?

5. Instructors usually delight in Ciardi's poem. Students, if they smile, are thin-lipped. Will the instructors mold the student in a new shape, different from the shape the student's mother patted from the clay?

The Purist*

OGDEN NASH

I give you now Professor Twist,
A conscientious scientist.
Trustees exclaimed, "He never bungles!"
And sent him off to distant jungles.
Camped on a tropic riverside,

One day he missed his loving bride.
She had, the guide informed him later,
Been eaten by an alligator.
Professor Twist could not but smile.
"You mean," he said, "a crocodile."

Questions

1. Professor Twist's wife has just been killed. What is the professor's concern?

2. Does the question, "Should the school teach the student more than the words, more than how to tell an alligator from a crocodile?" contain a built-in answer?

3. Is the question, "Should the school from which Professor Twist graduated be proud of him?" a better question?

4. What are the qualities of a good question? Of a good class? Of a good student? Of a good teacher? Of a good society?

Transcendentalism

A STUDENT

You have me confused
Professor Bens
Are you and me
At opposite ends?
I write what I write
and I write what I see
But you exclaim of
morality

---

*Copyright, 1935, by The Curtis Publishing Company. From *Verses From 1929 On* by Ogden Nash, by permission of Little, Brown and Co.

I'm frightened, I'm worried,
Filled with dread
Because of the things
You have said.
I see what I see
an' write what I write
But you 'ole buddy,
Say that ain't right
Be true to my public
and never lie
But I'll tell you,
I'd druther die.
You can say my morals
are extremely rank
But I'll just chuckle
And so will the bank
I'm not intellectual
here we'll agree
But I write what I write
And I write what I see
I like to tell
of high-ball glasses,
half drunk men
makin' passes,
I work pretty hard
a 'writin' my stuff
And what if it is
a lotta guff?
There ain't no gun
in nobody's back
and it ain't my fault
for mental lack!
So if they buy
and if they read
unintellectual
chicken feed
that's their fault
don't blame me.
I write what I write
I write what I see.

Questions

1. This poem was written in a creative writing class. Is the student poet nec-
    essarily describing a real situation? What is the situation he describes?

2. How would you describe the kind of stories the "I" wants to be helped to write?

3. What do you imagine is the morality the "I" claims the teacher exclaims of?

4. The "I" says "I write what I see." Is the "I" honest in that statement?

5. The title "Transcendentalism" perhaps means a truth or reality beyond the
    natural. Do you think the word *transcendentalism* better describes the teacher's
    philosophy or the poet's?

6. Do you imagine the teacher described in the poem refused to aid the student
    in writing what the student wanted to write? What is the school's job? The
    student's job?

The Slave*

JAMES OPPENHEIM

They set the slave free, striking off his chains. . . .
Then he was as much of a slave as ever.

He was still chained to servility,
He was still manacled to indolence and sloth,
He was still bound by fear and superstition,
By ignorance, suspicion, and savagery . . .
His slavery was not in the chains,
But in himself. . . .

They can only set free men free . . .
And there is no need of that:
Free men set themselves free.

Questions

1. The poet says that striking off the chains does not set the slave free. What
    does the poet mean by free?

2. When are young people supposedly set free? Are they free? Explain.

3. Robert Henri in the essay entitled "On Schools" (p. 102) and James Herndon in
    "The Way It Spozed To Be" describe students and a school. Upon graduation
    from their respective schools, which group of students will be free?

---

* By permission of Arthur B. Spingarn, executor.

O World, Thou Choosest Not the Better Part*

GEORGE SANTAYANA

O world, thou choosest not the better part!
It is not wisdom to be only wise,
And on the inward vision close the eyes,
But it is wisdom to believe the heart.
Columbus found a world, and had no chart
Save one that faith deciphered in the skies;
To trust the soul's invincible surmise
Was all his science and his only art.
Our knowledge is a torch of smoky pine
That lights the pathway but one step ahead
Across a void of mystery and dread.
Bid, then, the tender light of faith to shine
By which alone the mortal heart is led
Unto the thinking of the thought divine.

Questions

1. What is the difference between wisdom of the eyes and wisdom of the heart?

2. If science and art represent the wisdom of the eye, what to the poet represents the wisdom of the heart?

3. How does knowledge resulting from the wisdom of the eye light our pathway? What does wisdom of the heart light?

4. What evidence (of the eye) leads you to believe Santayana? To disbelieve? What evidence (of the heart) leads you to believe him? To disbelieve?

5. What has shaped you to take the position on Santayana that you take?

On Schools*

ROBERT HENRI

Some students possess the school they work in. Others are possessed by the school.

Let a student enter the school with this advice:

No matter how good the school is, his education is in his own hands. All education must be self-education.

Let him realize the truth of this, and no school will be a danger to him. The school is a thing of the period. It has the faults and the virtues of the period. It either uses the student for its own success or the self-educating student uses it for his success. This is generally true of all schools and students of our time.

It is up to the student whether he becomes a school-made man or whether he uses the school as a place of experience where there are both good and bad advices, where there are strengths and weaknesses, where there are facilities, and much information to be had from the instructors, and much to be gained by association with the other students. He may learn equally from the strong and the weak students. There are models to work from and a place to work in.

The self-educator judges his own course, judges advices, judges the evidences about him. He realizes that he is no longer an infant. He is already a man: has his own development in process.

No one can lead him. Many can give advices, but the greatest artist in the world cannot point his course for he is a new man. Just what he should know, just how he should proceed can only be guessed at.

A school should be an offering of opportunity, not a direction, and the student should know that the school will be good for him only to the degree that he makes it good. It is a field for activity where he will see much, hear much and where he must be a judge, selecting for his special need, and daily discovering his need.

When we have bred a line of self-educators there will then be no fear of schools. Those who have done distinguished work in the past, who have opened new roadways of vision and invented techniques specific to such visions have done it in spite of environment. They have learned what the schools had to offer, how much, how little. Strengths and weaknesses have alike been material to their progress.

Different men must learn different things. Each man must put himself as far as possible in the way of knowing what is known and he must make his choices. Everything back of him is his heritage to use or to leave. The school is a place of strengths and weaknesses. There are things insisted upon and there are things omitted. There are all sorts of advices, good and bad, and there are advices that will serve one and not another.

The man who goes into a school to educate himself and not to be educated will get somewhere. He should start out a master, master of such as he has, however little that may be. By being master of such as he has in the beginning it is likely he may later be master, after years of study, of much.

He should not enter the school with any preconceived idea of his destiny. In fact he should be open and free. His aim should be to search deeply and work hard and let the outcome be what it may.

The best art the world has ever had is but the impress left by men who have thought less of making great art than of living full and completely with all their faculties in the enjoyment of full play. From these the result is inevitable.

Questions

1. Henri speaks of students who possess the school, and students who are possessed by the school. Does The Tribe ("The Way It Spozed To Be") fit into either category?

2. What kind of school and students does Henri favor?

3. Do most students want the school Henri describes? If not, why? Does the "I" in the poem "Transcendentalism" want such a school?

4. Is Henri describing a school best suited for Oppenheim's slave or free man (see the poem "The Slave")?

5. Discuss the sentence, "The man who goes into a school to educate himself and not to be educated will get somewhere." Where is somewhere?

6. Does Professor Twist teach in Henri's school?

Or Does the Pupil Know More?

(painting—see p. 68)

FRANCISCO DE GOYA Y LUCIENTES

Education Strengthens the Nation

(poster—see p. 69)

NATIONAL EDUCATION ASSOCIATION

Questions

1. What does the poster painter want you to think and feel? Explain.

2. What does Goya apparently want you to feel? How do the symbols differ in the two pictures?

3. Historically Goya's picture had to do with the education of the Queen of Spain's lover. He was a soldier and needed "brushing up" to make him presentable in aristocratic society. Goya apparently did not think much of the soldier or his teachers. Should the picture have been used in this book?

Mass Media and the Popular Arts

The Four Seasons by Norman Rockwell

Courtesy of Norman Rockwell and Brown & Bigelow

Mechanical Man with Pretty Pictures by Mara McAfee

(1963) 51 × 40 in. Courtesy of Mara McAfee

Preliminary Statements for Discussion
and Writing

1. You would not give your body to any passerby to do with as he would. Why do you give your mind?

2. Happiness is the effect of virtue.

3. Popular art preserves, and fine art upsets, the status quo.

4. What appears in the newspapers is food for the public lust.

5. Happiness is the perpetual possession of being well-deceived.

6. Let me write a nation's songs and I do not care what goes on in the legislature.

7. Sentimentality is a coin with two sides; one rose-colored, one dung-colored.

8. If I owned a newspaper, the comics would be my editorial page.

9. If television is the teacher, anticipate a nation of magnificent consumers.

10. You can fool some of the people some of the time and all of the people some of the time, but you cannot fool all of the people all of the time.

11. What is excluded from the newspapers and news programs should be of equal or more interest to the public than what is included.

12. The winds of emotion shape man. Look to the wind-makers.

13. The mass media encourage man to pawn his intellect for a drink.

Night Club*

KATHARINE BRUSH

Promptly at quarter of ten P.M. Mrs. Brady descended the steps of the Elevated. She purchased from the newsdealer in the cubbyhole beneath them a next month's magazine and a to-morrow morning's paper and, with these tucked under one plump arm, she walked. She walked two blocks north on Sixth Avenue; turned and went west. But not far west. Westward half a block only, to the place where the gay green awning marked Club Français paints a stripe of shade across the glimmering sidewalk. Under this awning Mrs. Brady halted briefly, to remark to the six-foot doorman that it looked like rain and to await his performance of his professional duty. When the small green door yawned open, she sighed deeply and plodded in.

The foyer was a blackness, an airless velvet blackness like the inside of a jeweller's box. Four drum-shaped lamps of golden silk suspended from the ceiling gave it light (a very little) and formed the jewels: gold signets, those, or cuff-links for a giant. At the far end of the foyer there were black stairs, faintly dusty, rippling upward toward an amber radiance. Mrs. Brady approached and ponderously mounted the stairs, clinging with one fist to the mangy velvet rope that railed their edge.

From the top, Miss Lena Levin observed the ascent. Miss Levin was the checkroom girl. She had dark-at-the-roots blonde hair and slender hips upon which, in moments of leisure, she wore her hands, like buckles of ivory loosely attached. This was a moment of leisure. Miss Levin waited behind her counter. Row upon row of hooks, empty as yet, and seeming to beckon —wee curved fingers of iron—waited behind her.

"Late," said Miss Levin, "again."

"Go wan!" said Mrs. Brady. "It's only ten to ten. *Whew!* Them *stairs!*"

She leaned heavily, sideways, against Miss Levin's counter, and, applying one palm to the region of her heart, appeared at once to listen and to count. "Feel!" she cried then in a pleased voice.

Miss Levin obediently felt.

"Them stairs," continued Mrs. Brady darkly, "with my bad heart, will be the death of me. Whew! Well, dearie? What's the news?"

"You got a paper," Miss Levin languidly reminded her.

"Yeah!" agreed Mrs. Brady with sudden vehemence. "I got a paper!" She slapped it upon the counter. "An' a lot of time I'll get to *read* my paper, won't I now? On a Saturday night!" She moaned. "Other nights is bad enough, dear knows—but *Saturday* nights! How I dread 'em! Every Saturday

---

night I say to my daughter, I say, 'Geraldine, I can't,' I say, 'I can't go through it again, an' that's all there is to it,' I say. 'I'll *quit!*' I say. An' I *will,* too!" added Mrs. Brady firmly, if indefinitely.

Miss Levin, in defense of Saturday nights, mumbled some vague something about tips.

"Tips!" Mrs. Brady hissed it. She almost spat it. Plainly money was nothing, nothing at all, to this lady. "I just wish," said Mrs. Brady, and glared at Miss Levin, "I just wish *you* had to spend one Saturday night, just one, in that dressing room! Bein' pushed an' stepped on and near knocked down by that gang of hussies, an' them orderin' an' bossin' you 'round like you was *black,* an' usin' your things an' then sayin' they're sorry, they got no change, they'll be back. Yah! They *never* come back!"

"There's Mr. Costello," whispered Miss Levin through lips that, like a ventriloquist's, scarely stirred.

"An' as I was sayin'," Mrs. Brady said at once brightly, "I got to leave you. Ten to ten, time I was on the job."

She smirked at Miss Levin, nodded, and right-about-faced. There, indeed, Mr. Costello was. Mr. Billy Costello, manager, proprietor, monarch of all he surveyed. From the doorway of the big room, where the little tables herded in a ring around the waxen floor, he surveyed Mrs. Brady, and in such a way that Mrs. Brady, momentarily forgetting her bad heart, walked fast, scurried faster, almost ran.

The door of her domain was set politely in an alcove, beyond silken curtains looped up at the sides. Mrs. Brady reached it breathless, shouldered it open, and groped for the electric switch. Lights sprang up, a bright white blaze, intolerable for an instant to the eyes, like sun on snow. Blinking, Mrs. Brady shut the door.

The room was a spotless, white-tiled place, half beauty shop, half dressing room. Along one wall stood washstands, sturdy triplets in a row, with pale-green liquid soap in glass balloons afloat above them. Against the opposite wall there was a couch. A third wall backed an elongated glass-topped dressing table; and over the dressing table and over the washstands long rectangular sheets of mirror reflected lights, doors, glossy tiles, lights multiplied. . . .

Mrs. Brady moved across this glitter like a thick dark cloud in a hurry. At the dressing table she came to a halt, and upon it she laid her newspaper, her magazine, and her purse—a black purse worn gray with much clutching. She divested herself of a rusty black coat and a hat of the mushroom persuasion, and hung both up in a corner cupboard which she opened by means of one of a quite preposterous bunch of keys. From a nook in the cupboard she took down a lace-edged handkerchief with long streamers. She untied the streamers and tied them again around her chunky black alpaca waist. The handkerchief became an apron's baby cousin.

Mrs. Brady relocked the cupboard door, fumbled her keyring over, and unlocked a capacious drawer of the dressing table. She spread a fresh towel on the plate-glass top, in the geometrical centre, and upon the towel she arranged with care a procession of things fished from the drawer. Things for the hair. Things for the complexion. Things for the eyes, the lashes, the brows, the lips, and the finger nails. Things in boxes and things in jars and things in tubes and tins. Also, an ash tray, matches, pins, a tiny sewing kit, a pair of scissors. Last of all, a hand-printed sign, a nudging sort of sign:

NOTICE!

These articles, placed here for your convenience, are the property of the *maid.*

And directly beneath the sign, propping it up against the looking-glass, a china saucer, in which Mrs. Brady now slyly laid decoy money: two quarters and two dimes, in four-leaf-clover formation.

Another drawer of the dressing table yielded a bottle of bromo seltzer, a bottle of aromatic spirits of ammonia, a tin of sodium bicarbonate, and a teaspoon. These were lined up on a shelf above the couch.

Mrs. Brady was now ready for anything. And (from the grim, thin pucker of her mouth) expecting it.

Music came to her ears. Rather, the beat of music, muffled, rhythmic, remote. *Umpa-um, umpa-um, umpa-um-umm*—Mr. "Fiddle" Baer and his band, hard at work on the first foxtrot of the night. It was teasing, foot-tapping music; but the large solemn feet of Mrs. Brady were still. She sat on the couch and opened her newspaper; and for some moments she read uninterruptedly, with special attention to the murders, the divorces, the breaches of promise, the funnies.

Then the door swung inward, admitting a blast of Mr. "Fiddle" Baer's best, a whiff of perfume, and a girl.

Mrs. Brady put her paper away.

The girl was *petite* and darkly beautiful; wrapped in fur and mounted on tall jewelled heels. She entered humming the ragtime song the orchestra was playing, and while she stood near the dressing table, stripping off her gloves, she continued to hum it softly to herself:

> "Oh, I know my baby loves me,
> I can tell my baby loves me."

Here the dark little girl got the left glove off, and Mrs. Brady glimpsed a platinum wedding ring.

> "'Cause there ain't no maybe
> In my baby's
> Eyes."

The right glove came off. The dark little girl sat down in one of the chairs that faced the dressing table. She doffed her wrap, casting it carelessly over the chair back. It had a cloth-of-gold lining, and "Paris" was embroidered in curlicues on the label. Mrs. Brady hovered solicitously near.

The dark little girl, still humming, looked over the articles "placed here for your convenience," and picked up the scissors. Having cut off a very small hangnail with the air of one performing a perilous major operation, she seized and used the manicure buffer, and after that the eyebrow pencil. Mrs. Brady's mind, hopefully calculating the tip, jumped and jumped again like a taximeter.

"Oh, I know my baby loves me—"

The dark little girl applied powder and lipstick belonging to herself. She examined the result searchingly in the mirror and sat back, satisfied. She cast some silver *Klink! Klink!* into Mrs. Brady's saucer, and half rose. Then, remembering something, she settled down again.

The ensuing thirty seconds were spent by her in pulling off her platinum wedding ring, tying it in a corner of a lace handkerchief, and tucking the handkerchief down the bodice of her tight white velvet gown.

"There!" she said.

She swooped up her wrap and trotted toward the door, jewelled heels merrily twinkling.

"'Cause there ain't no maybe—"

The door fell shut.

Almost instantly it opened again, and another girl came in. A blonde, this. She was pretty in a round-eyed, babyish way; but Mrs. Brady, regarding her, mentally grabbed the spirits of ammonia bottle. For she looked terribly ill. The round eyes were dull, the pretty, silly little face was drawn. The thin hands, picking at the fastenings of a specious beaded bag, trembled and twitched.

Mrs. Brady cleared her throat. "Can I do something for you, miss?"

Evidently the blonde girl had believed herself alone in the dressing room. She started violently and glanced up, panic in her eyes. Panic, and something else. Something very like murderous hate—but for an instant only, so that Mrs. Brady, whose perceptions were never quick, missed it altogether.

"A glass of water?" suggested Mrs. Brady.

"No," said the girl, "no." She had one hand in the beaded bag now. Mrs. Brady could see it moving, causing the bag to squirm like a live thing, and the fringe to shiver. "Yes!" she cried abruptly. "A glass of water—please—you get it for me."

She dropped on to the couch. Mrs. Brady scurried to the water cooler in the corner, pressed the spigot with a determined thumb. Water trickled out thinly. Mrs. Brady pressed harder, and scowled, and thought, "Something's wrong with this thing. I mustn't forget, next time I see Mr. Costello————"

When again she faced her patient, the patient was sitting erect. She was thrusting her clenched hand back into the beaded bag again.

She took only a sip of the water, but it seemed to help her quite miraculously. Almost at once colour came to her cheeks, life to her eyes. She grew young again—as young as she was. She smiled up at Mrs. Brady.

"Well!" she exclaimed. "What do you know about that!" She shook her honey-coloured head. "I can't imagine what came over me."

"Are you better now?" inquired Mrs. Brady.

"Yes. Oh, yes. I'm better now. You see," said the blonde girl confidentially, "we were at the theatre, my boy friend and I, and it was hot and stuffy—I guess that must have been the trouble." She paused, and the ghost of her recent distress crossed her face. "God! I thought that last act *never* would end!" she said.

While she attended to her hair and complexion, she chattered gaily to Mrs. Brady, chattered on with scarcely a stop for breath, and laughed much. She said, among other things, that she and her "boy friend" had not known one another very long, but that she was "ga-ga" about him. "He is about me, too," she confessed. "He thinks I'm grand."

She fell silent then, and in the looking-glass her eyes were shadowed, haunted. But Mrs. Brady, from where she stood, could not see the looking-glass; and half a minute later the blonde girl laughed and began again. When she went out she seemed to dance out on little winged feet; and Mrs. Brady, sighing, thought it must be nice to be young . . . and happy like that.

The next arrivals were two. A tall, extremely smart young woman in black chiffon entered first, and held the door open for her companion; and the instant the door was shut, she said, as though it had been on the tip of her tongue for hours, "Amy, what under the sun *happened?*"

Amy, who was brown-eyed, brown-bobbed-haired, and patently annoyed about something, crossed to the dressing table and flopped into a chair before she made reply.

"Nothing," she said wearily then.

"That's nonsense!" snorted the other. "Tell me. Was it something she said? She's a tactless ass, of course. Always was."

"No, not anything she said. It was————" Amy bit her lip. "All right! I'll tell you. Before we left your apartment I just happened to notice that Tom had disappeared. So I went to look for him—I wanted to ask him if he'd remembered to tell the maid where we were going—Skippy's subject to croup, you know, and we always leave word. Well, so I went into the kitchen, thinking Tom might be there mixing cocktails—and there he was —and there *she* was!"

The full red mouth of the other young woman pursed itself slightly. Her arched brows lifted. "Well?"

Her matter-of-factness appeared to infuriate Amy. "He was *kissing* her!" she flung out.

"Well?" said the other again. She chuckled softly and patted Amy's shoulder, as if it were the shoulder of a child. "You're surely not going to let *that* spoil your whole evening? Amy *dear!* Kissing may once have been serious and significant—but it isn't nowadays. Nowadays, it's like shaking hands. It means nothing."

But Amy was not consoled. "I hate her!" she cried desperately. "Red-headed *thing!* Calling me 'darling' and 'honey,' and s-sending me handkerchiefs for C-Christmas—and then sneaking off behind closed doors and k-kissing my h-h-husband . . ."

At this point Amy quite broke down, but she recovered herself sufficiently to add with venom, "I'd like to slap her!"

"Oh, oh, oh," smiled the tall young woman, "I wouldn't do that!"

Amy wiped her eyes with what might well have been one of the Christmas handkerchiefs, and confronted her friend. "Well, what *would* you do, Claire? If you were I?"

"I'd forget it," said Claire, "and have a good time. I'd kiss somebody myself. You've no idea how much better you'd feel!"

"I don't do————" Amy began indignantly; but as the door behind her opened and a third young woman—red-headed, earringed, exquisite—lilted in, she changed her tone. "Oh, hello!" she called sweetly, beaming at the newcomer via the mirror. "We were wondering what had become of you!"

The red-headed girl, smiling easily back, dropped her cigarette on the floor and crushed it out with a silver-shod toe. "Tom and I were talking to 'Fiddle' Baer," she explained. "He's going to play 'Clap Yo' Hands' next, because it's my favourite. Lend me a comb, will you, somebody?"

"There's a comb there," said Claire, indicating Mrs. Brady's business comb.

"But imagine using it!" murmured the red-headed girl. "Amy, darling, haven't you one?"

Amy produced a tiny comb from her rhinestone purse. "Don't forget to bring it when you come," she said, and stood up. "I'm going on out, I want to tell Tom something."

She went.

The red-headed young woman and the tall black-chiffon one were alone, except for Mrs. Brady. The red-headed one beaded her incredible lashes. The tall one, the one called Claire, sat watching her. Presently she said, "Sylvia, look here." And Sylvia looked. Anybody, addressed in that tone, would have.

"There is one thing," Claire went on quietly, holding the other's eyes, "that I want understood. And that is, '*Hands off!*' Do you hear me?"

"I don't know what you mean."

"You do know what I mean!"

The red-headed girl shrugged her shoulders. "Amy told you she saw us, I suppose."

"Precisely. And," went on Claire, gathering up her possessions and rising, "as I said before, you're to keep away." Her eyes blazed sudden white-hot rage. "Because, as you very well know, he belongs to *me*," she said, and departed, slamming the door.

Between eleven o'clock and one Mrs. Brady was very busy indeed. Never for more than a moment during those two hours was the dressing room empty. Often it was jammed, full to overflowing with curled cropped heads, with ivory arms and shoulders, with silk and lace and chiffon, with legs. The door flapped in and back, in and back. The mirrors caught and held— and lost—a hundred different faces. Powder veiled the dressing table with a thin white dust; cigarette stubs, scarlet at the tips, choked the ash-receiver. Dimes and quarters clattered into Mrs. Brady's saucer—and were transferred to Mrs. Brady's purse. The original seventy cents remained. That much, and no more, would Mrs. Brady gamble on the integrity of womankind.

She earned her money. She threaded needles and took stitches. She powdered the backs of necks. She supplied towels for soapy, dripping hands. She removed a speck from a teary blue eye and pounded the heel on a slipper. She curled the straggling ends of a black bob and a gray bob, pinned a velvet flower on a lithe round waist, mixed three doses of bicarbonate of soda, took charge of a shed pink-satin girdle, collected, on hands and knees, several dozen fake pearls that had wept from a broken string.

She served chorus girls and schoolgirls, gay young matrons and gayer young mistresses, a lady who had divorced four husbands, and a lady who had poisoned one, the secret (more or less) sweetheart of a Most Distinguished Name, and the Brains of a bootleg gang. . . . She saw things. She saw a yellow check, with the ink hardly dry. She saw four tiny bruises, such as fingers might make, on an arm. She saw a girl strike another girl, not playfully. She saw a bundle of letters some man wished he had not written, safe and deep in a brocaded handbag.

About midnight the door flew open and at once was pushed shut, and a gray-eyed, lovely child stood backed against it, her palms flattened on the panels at her sides, the draperies of her white chiffon gown settling lightly to rest around her.

There were already five damsels of varying ages in the dressing room. The latest arrival marked their presence with a flick of her eyes and standing just where she was, she called peremptorily, "Maid!"

Mrs. Brady, standing just where *she* was, said, "Yes, miss?"

"Please come here," said the girl.

Mrs. Brady, as slowly as she dared, did so.

The girl lowered her voice to a tense half-whisper. "Listen! Is there any way I can get out of here except through this door I came in?"

Mrs. Brady stared at her stupidly.

"Any window?" persisted the girl. "Or anything?"

Here they were interrupted by the exodus of two of the damsels-of-varying ages. Mrs. Brady opened the door for them—and in so doing caught a glimpse of a man who waited in the hall outside, a debonair, old-young man with a girl's furry wrap hung over his arm, and his hat in his hand.

The door clicked. The gray-eyed girl moved out from the wall, against which she had flattened herself—for all the world like one eluding pursuit in a cinema.

"What about that window?" she demanded, pointing.

"That's all the farther it opens," said Mrs. Brady.

"Oh! And it's the only one—isn't it?"

"It is."

"Damn," said the girl. "Then there's *no* way out?"

"No way but the door," said Mrs. Brady testily.

The girl looked at the door. She seemed to look *through* the door, and to despise and to fear what she saw. Then she looked at Mrs. Brady. "Well," she said, "then I s'pose the only thing to do is to stay in here."

She stayed. Minutes ticked by. Jazz crooned distantly, stopped, struck up again. Other girls came and went. Still the gray-eyed girl sat on the couch, with her back to the wall and her shapely legs crossed, smoking cigarettes, one from the stub of another.

After a long while she said, "Maid!"

"Yes, miss?"

"Peek out that door, will you, and see if there's anyone standing there."

Mrs. Brady peeked, and reported that there was. There was a gentleman with a little bit of a black moustache standing there. The same gentleman, in fact, who was standing there "just after you come in."

"Oh, Lord," sighed the gray-eyed girl. "Well . . . I can't stay here all *night,* that's one sure thing."

She slid off the couch, and went listlessly to the dressing table. There she occupied herself for a minute or two. Suddenly, without a word, she darted out.

Thirty seconds later Mrs. Brady was elated to find two crumpled one-dollar bills lying in her saucer. Her joy, however, died a premature death. For she made an almost simultaneous second discovery. A saddening one. Above all, a puzzling one.

"Now what for," marvelled Mrs. Brady, "did she want to walk off with them *scissors?*"

This at twelve-twenty-five.

At twelve-thirty a quartette of excited young things burst in, babbling madly. All of them had their evening wraps with them; all talked at once.

One of them, a Dresden china girl with a heart-shaped face, was the centre of attention. Around her the rest fluttered like monstrous butterflies; to her they addressed their shrill exclamatory cries. "Babe," they called her.

Mrs. Brady heard snatches: "Not in this state unless . . ." "Well, you can in Maryland, Jimmy says." "Oh, there must be some place nearer than . . ." "Isn't this *marvellous?*" "When did it happen, Babe? When did you decide?"

"Just now," the girl with the heart-shaped face sang softly, "when we were dancing."

The babble resumed, "But listen, Babe, what'll your mother and father . . .?" "Oh, never mind, let's hurry." "Shall we be warm enough with just these thin wraps, do you think? Babe, will you be warm enough? Sure?"

Powder flew and little pocket combs marched through bright marcels. Flushed cheeks were painted pinker still.

"My pearls," said Babe, "are *old*. And my dress and my slippers are *new*. Now, let's see—what can I *borrow?*"

A lace handkerchief, a diamond bar pin, a pair of earrings were proffered. She chose the bar pin, and its owner unpinned it proudly, gladly.

"I've got blue garters!" exclaimed another girl.

"Give me one, then," directed Babe. "I'll trade with you. . . . There! That fixes that."

More babbling, "Hurry! Hurry up!" . . . "Listen, are you *sure* we'll be warm enough? Because we can stop at my house, there's nobody home." "Give me that puff, Babe, I'll powder your back." "And just to think a week ago you'd never even met each other!" "Oh, hurry *up*, let's get *started!*" "I'm ready." "So'm I." "Ready, Babe? You look adorable." "Come on, everybody."

They were gone again, and the dressing room seemed twice as still and vacant as before.

A minute of grace, during which Mrs. Brady wiped the spilled powder away with a damp gray rag. Then the door jumped open again. Two evening gowns appeared and made for the dressing table in a bee line. Slim tubular gowns they were, one silver, one palest yellow. Yellow hair went with the silver gown, brown hair with the yellow. The silver-gowned, yellow-haired girl wore orchids on her shoulder, three of them, and a flashing bracelet on each fragile wrist. The other girl looked less prosperous; still, you would rather have looked at her.

Both ignored Mrs. Brady's cosmetic display as utterly as they ignored Mrs. Brady, producing full field equipment of their own.

"Well," said the girl with the orchids, rouging energetically, "how do you like him?"

"Oh-h—all right."

"Meaning, 'Not any,' hmm? I suspected as much!" The girl with the orchids turned in her chair and scanned her companion's profile with disapproval. "See here, Marilee," she drawled, "are you going to be a damn fool *all* your life?"

"He's fat," said Marilee dreamily. "Fat, and—greasy, sort of. I mean, greasy in his mind. Don't you know what I mean?"

"I know *one* thing," declared the girl with orchids. "I know Who He Is! And if I were you, that's all I'd need to know. *Under the circumstances.*"

The last three words, stressed meaningly, affected the girl called Marilee curiously. She grew grave. Her lips and lashes drooped. For some seconds she sat frowning a little, breaking a black-sheathed lipstick in two and fitting it together again.

"She's worse," she said finally, low.

"Worse?"

Marilee nodded.

"Well," said the girl with orchids, "there you are. It's the climate. She'll never be anything *but* worse, if she doesn't get away. Out West, or some-where."

"I know," murmured Marilee.

The other girl opened a tin of eye shadow. "Of course," she said drily, "suit yourself. She's not *my* sister."

Marilee said nothing. Quiet she sat, breaking the lipstick, mending it, breaking it.

"Oh, well," she breathed finally, wearily, and straightened up. She propped her elbows on the plate-glass dressing-table top and leaned toward the mirror, and with the lipstick she began to make her coral-pink mouth very red and gay and reckless and alluring.

Nightly at one o'clock Vane and Moreno dance for the Club Français. They dance a tango, they dance a waltz; then, by way of encore, they do a Black Bottom, and a trick of their own called the Wheel. They dance for twenty, thirty minutes. And while they dance you do not leave your table—for this is what you came to see. Vane and Moreno. The New York thrill. The sole justification for the five-dollar couvert extorted by Billy Costello.

From one until half-past, then, was Mrs. Brady's recess. She had been looking forward to it all the evening long. When it began—when the opening chords of the tango music sounded stirringly from the room outside—Mrs. Brady brightened. With a right good will she sped the parting guests.

Alone, she unlocked her cupboard and took out her magazine—the maga-zine she had bought three hours before. Heaving a great breath of relief and satisfaction, she plumped herself on the couch and fingered the pages. Im-mediately she was absorbed, her eyes drinking up printed lines, her lips moving soundlessly.

The magazine was Mrs. Brady's favourite. Its stories were true stories, taken from life (so the editor said); and to Mrs. Brady they were live, vivid threads in the dull, drab pattern of her night.

Questions

1. What do Mrs. Brady's waiting for the doorman to do his duty and her expression "like you was *black*" (p. 110) indicate about her?

2. What dramatic events was Mrs. Brady witness to that she did not see? Where was there drama she would give her heart to?

3. What do Gibran's poem "On Work" (p. 181) and Tagore's poem "Where the Mind Is Without Fear" (p. 56) make us see in the lives of the characters in "Night Club"?

4. This story was selected as one of the best stories in the O. Henry Awards of 1927. A work of art is said to be perpetually modern. Does "Night Club" work in your estimation?

Chaos, Disorder and the Late Show*

Warren Miller

I am a certified public accountant and a rational man. More exactly, and putting things in their proper order, I am a rational man first and an accountant second. I insist on order; I like the symbols of order—a blunt, hardy plus sign or a forthright minus delights me. I make lists, I am always punctual, I wear a hat. Maltz believes this has caused my hairline to recede. Maltz is one of my associates at the office. He married too young and he regrets it.

In fact, there is no scientific foundation for his view that wearing a hat causes the hairline to recede. Such things are largely a matter of heredity, although my father has a luxuriant head of hair. But what of my grandfathers? I have no doubt that one of them accounts for my high forehead. Talent, I believe I have read somewhere, often skips a generation or jumps from uncle to nephew. Studies have been made. Naturally there are exceptions. But it provides one with the beginning of an explanation. The notion of having been an adopted child is a fancy I have never indulged. I have never doubted that my parents are my true parents. But I sometimes suspect they think I am not their true son.

Let me say just this about my father: He is a high-school history teacher, and every summer for twenty-five years he has had a three-month vacation. Not once has he ever put this time to any real use. He could have been a counselor at a camp, taught the summer session, clerked at a department store or . . . any number of things. I recall that he spent one entire summer lying on the sofa, reading. Some years he goes to the beach. Once he went to Mexico. His income is, to be sure, adequate, but I am certain that one major illness would wipe out his savings. I have tried to speak to him about preplanning; he listens, but he does not seem to hear.

My mother—I think this one example will suffice—my mother believes that Leslie Howard, who was a Hollywood actor killed in the war, is still alive. My father merely smiles when she speaks of Leslie Howard—I believe he actually enjoys it—but I have brought home almanacs and circled references in *Harper's* and other magazines attesting to the fact that Leslie Howard is, in fact and in truth, dead. Definitive proof.

Not that I care; not that I care very deeply. It is a harmless-enough delusion; but it is sloppy. I believe that the world tends naturally to chaos and that we all have to make our daily—even hourly—contribution toward order. My parents, in my opinion, are unwilling to shoulder their share of this responsibility.

I have, once or twice, discussed the matter with Maltz, whose wife has proved to be unreliable in some ways and who has a sympathy in matters of this kind. Maltz agrees that my father is mistaken in his indulgent attitude; on the other hand, he believes it would, perhaps, be better psychologically if I ignored my mother's pitiful little delusion—as he called it.

But it is like a pebble in my shoe or loose hair under my shirt collar. Chaos and disorder in the world, in the natural scheme of things, is bad enough; one does not want to have to put up with it at home too. The subways are dirty and unreliable; the crosstown buses are not properly spaced; clerks in stores never know where their stock is.

The extent of the breakdown is incredible. Every year at this time I rent an empty store on upper Broadway and help people with their income-tax returns. These people keep no records! They have no receipts! They lose their canceled checks! They guess! The year just past is, to them, a fast-fading and already incomplete collection of snapshots. It was full of medical and business expenses and deductions for entertaining, yet they remember nothing. Believe me, the chaos of subways and crosstown buses and our traffic problems is as nothing compared to the disorder in the heads of *people*. Every year I am struck with this anew.

This extra-time work continues for three months and becomes more intense as deadline time draws near. It is amazing how many people wait until the last possible moment. Often I am there until nearly midnight.

At the beginning of March I hire Maltz and pay him by the head. He is not as fast as I would like, but he is reliable and, because of his wife and her extravagances, he needs the money. "It would embarrass me," he says, "if I had to tell you how much she spends every week on magazines alone."

Poor guy.

I live with my parents. The store I rent is near their apartment, a matter of three blocks, walking distance. It is a neighborhood of small shops and large supermarkets which once were movie houses; their marquees now advertise turkeys and hams. Maltz occasionally will walk me to my door.

That night, the night of the incident, it was snowing. It had been snowing all day. No one had cleaned his sidewalk, and it made walking treacherous. I almost slipped twice.

"Isn't there a city ordinance about people cleaning their sidewalks? Isn't it mandatory?" I asked.

Maltz said, "There is such an ordinance, Norman, but it is more honored in the breach than in the practice."

The sadness of his marriage has given Maltz a kind of wisdom. The next time he slipped I took his arm, and I thought, Here is a man who might one day be my friend. The loneliness of the mismated is a terrible thing to see. It touches me. I believe I understand it. At the door of my building I said good night and I watched for a moment as Maltz proceeded reluctantly toward home.

The elevator was out of order again. When a breakdown occurs, tenants must use the freight elevator at the rear of the lobby. I had to ring for it three times and wait more than five minutes; then I had to ride up with two open garbage cans. It was not very pleasant. The elevator man said, "How's business, Mr. Whitehead?"

"Very good, thank you, Oscar," I said.

"I'll be in to see you real soon, Mr. Whitehead."

I nodded. I knew he'd wait, as he did last year, until the last possible moment. I tried to shrug it off. It's no good trying to carry the next man's share on your own shoulders, I told myself. Forget it, I thought.

Because I had come up in the freight elevator, I therefore entered our apartment by way of the kitchen. I took off my rubbers and carried them in with me, my briefcase in the other hand. As a result the door slammed shut, since I had no free hand to close it slowly.

"Is it you?" my mother called.

She was at the kitchen table having her midnight cup of tea; she said it calmed her and made sleeping easier to have tea before bed. I have tried to explain to her that tea has a higher percentage of caffeine than coffee, but she continues to drink it.

She was smiling.

"What is it?" I said.

"Mr. Know-it-all, come here and I would like to show you something."

She had a newspaper on the table. I did not move. "What is it?" I asked.

"Come here and I will show you, Norman," she said, still smiling.

At this point my father shouted something unintelligible from their bedroom.

"What did you say, dear? What?"

"Bette Davis on the late show. *Dark Victory!*"

My mother put her hand to her heart. "I remember the day I saw it," she said. "At the Rivoli, with Millie Brandon." She sat there, staring at nothing; she had forgotten all about me.

"What was it you wanted, Mother?" I said.

"Twenty-five cents if you got there before noon, would you believe it," she said.

I looked at the newspaper. I was astonished to see that she had brought such a newspaper into the house. There it was, beside her teacup, one of those weekly papers that always has headlines such as: MOTHER POISONS HER FIVE BABIES or TAB HUNTER SAYS "I AM LONELY." The inside pages, I have been told, are devoted to racing news.

"Mr. Know-it-all," she said and began to smile again.

"What are you doing with *that* paper, Mother?"

"Millie called me this afternoon and I ran out and bought it. Look!" she cried, and with an all-too-typical dramatic flourish she unfolded it and showed me the front page. The headline read: LESLIE HOWARD STILL ALIVE.

"So much for your almanacs and your definitive proof," she said. "Now what have you got to say, my dear?"

"Two minutes, dear," my father called in to her. "Commercial on now."

"Coming," she called back.

"Mother," I said, "you know very well what kind of paper this is."

"Why should they pick this subject?" she said, tapping the headline with her fingernail. "Why should they pick this particular subject right out of the blue? I would like to ask you that."

"Did you read the article itself, Mother? Is there one iota of hard fact in it?"

"There are facts, and there are facts, my dear boy."

I was very patient with her. "Mother," I said, "he is dead. It is well known that he is dead. He went down at sea in a transport plane. . . ."

"First of all, Mr. Smart One, it was not a transport. It was a Spitfire. He always flew Spitfires. He and David Niven."

"Well, then, Mother, just tell me this," I said. "If he's alive, where is he? Where is he?"

"It's starting, dear," my father called.

"The loveliest man who ever walked this earth," she said.

"I have never had the pleasure of seeing him, Mother."

"Steel-rimmed glasses. A pipe. Tweed jackets."

"Well, where is he, Mother?"

"So gentle. Gentle, yet dashing. If everybody was like Leslie Howard, wouldn't this be one beautiful world. Oh, what a beautiful world it would be!"

"Under no circumstances would I trust that particular newspaper," I said.

"This newspaper, my dear boy, is like every other newspaper. It is sometimes right."

I put my rubbers under the sink.

"The year you were born I saw him in *Intermezzo*, Ingrid Bergman's first American movie. Produced by Selznick, who was then still married, I believe, to Louis B. Mayer's daughter Irene." She sipped her tea and looked at the headline. She said, "These days they don't even name boys Leslie anymore. *Girls* are now named Leslie. Before the war people had such lovely names. Leslie, Cary, Myrna, Fay, Claudette. What has happened?"

She looked at me as if it were all my fault. "*I* don't know what's happened, Mother," I said, perhaps a little testily.

"It's your world, my dear; therefore you should know," she said. "Nowadays they even name them after the days of the week."

"I have named no one after any day of the week, Mother," I said, but she was not listening.

"You could always find a parking place. People were polite. Self-service was unheard of. Frozen food was something to be avoided at all costs."

"I can put no confidence at all in that particular newspaper," I said. "Absolutely none."

"Then I am sorry for you and I pity you," she said in a manner that I thought entirely uncalled for.

"Why? Why should you be sorry for me and pity me?" I asked.

I waited for her to answer, but she went back to sipping her tea and reading the headline.

"I have a good job," I said, "and I am doing the work I like."

"Nevertheless, Norman, I feel sorry for you."

I had not even taken off my overcoat, and I was forced to put up with an attack of this nature! I was struck by the unfairness of it. I said, "You *know* what a silly newspaper that is, Mother. What is the matter with you? You know he is dead. I know you know it. Everybody knows that he is dead."

She banged down her cup. "He is not!" she said. "He is not dead! He is not!"

"What's going on in there?" my father called.

"He is alive!"

"Then where is he?" I demanded, and I raised my voice, too; I admit that I raised my voice. "Where is he?"

"Oh," she said as if she were completely disgusted with me. "Oh, Mr. Born Too Late, I'll tell you where he is," she said, getting up from her chair, the newspaper in her hand. And she began to hit me on the head with it. She hit me on the head with it. Every time she mentioned a name she hit me. "I'll tell you where he is, I'll tell you where he is. He is with Carole Lombard and Glenn Miller and Will Rogers and Franklin . . ."

I ran out of the room. Why argue? She has a harmless delusion. From now on I will try to ignore her when she gets on this particular subject. Maltz may be right about this. I hung up my coat. Fortunately it is only when I stand at my closet door that I can hear the sound of their television set, which often goes on until three in the morning. Once I shut that door, however, my room is perfectly silent.

Questions

1. Why is telling the story so well suited to the young man?

2. What do the buses' lack of schedule and the failure of people to shovel the snow off their sidewalks prove to Norman? What other failures in the story are further proof to Norman?

3. Does the author want us to sympathize with Norman or his mother? Where are your sympathies?

4. Why does Norman's mother hit him on the head?

5. Are Norman, his mother, and his father three of the main types that make up the world?

6. Is the father in the story "The Knife" (p. 10) shaping a Norman, a Norman's mother, or a Norman's father?

The Outcasts of Poker Flat*

Bret Harte

Mr. Oakhurst's calm, handsome face betrayed small concern in these indications. Whether he was conscious of any predisposing cause was another question. "I reckon they're after somebody," he reflected; "likely it's me." He returned to his pocket the handkerchief with which he had been whipping away the red dust of Poker Flat from his neat boots, and quietly discharged his mind of any further conjecture.

In point of fact, Poker Flat was "after somebody." It had lately suffered the loss of several thousand dollars, two valuable horses, and a prominent citizen. It was experiencing a spasm of virtuous reaction, quite as lawless and ungovernable as any of the acts that had provoked it. A secret committee had determined to rid the town of all improper persons. This was done permanently in regard of two men who were then hanging from the boughs of a sycamore in the gulch, and temporarily in the banishment of certain other objectionable characters. I regret to say that some of these were ladies. It is but due to the sex, however, to state that their impropriety was professional, and it was only in such easily established standards of evil that Poker Flat ventured to sit in judgment.

Mr. Oakhurst was right in supposing that he was included in this category. A few of the committee had urged hanging him as a possible example and a sure method of reimbursing themselves from his pockets of the sums he had won from them. "It's agin justice," said Jim Wheeler, "to let this yer young man from Roaring Camp—an entire stranger—carry away our money." But a crude sentiment of equity residing in the breasts of those who had been fortunate enough to win from Mr. Oakhurst overruled this narrower local prejudice.

Mr. Oakhurst received his sentence with philosophic calmness, none the less coolly that he was aware of the hesitation of his judges. He was too much of a gambler not to accept fate. With him life was at best an uncertain game, and he recognized the usual percentage in favor of the dealer.

A body of armed men accompanied the deported wickedness of Poker Flat to the outskirts of the settlement. Besides Mr. Oakhurst, who was known to be a coolly desperate man, and for whose intimidation the armed escort was intended, the expatriated party consisted of a young woman familiarly known as "The Duchess;" another who had won the title of "Mother Shipton;" and "Uncle Billy," a suspected sluice-robber and confirmed drunkard. The cavalcade provoked no comments from the spectators, nor was any word uttered by the escort. Only when the gulch which marked the uttermost limit of Poker

---

° Courtesy of Houghton Mifflin Company, original publishers of *Bret Harte's Works*.

Flat was reached, the leader spoke briefly and to the point. The exiles were forbidden to return at the peril of their lives.

As the escort disappeared, their pent-up feelings found vent in a few hysterical tears from the Duchess, some bad language from Mother Shipton, and a Parthian volley of expletives from Uncle Billy. The philosophic Oakhurst alone remained silent. He listened calmly to Mother Shipton's desire to cut somebody's heart out, to the repeated statements of the Duchess that she would die in the road, and to the alarming oaths that seemed to be bumped out of Uncle Billy as he rode forward. With the easy good humor characteristic of his class, he insisted upon exchanging his own riding-horse, "Five-Spot," for the sorry mule which the Duchess rode. But even this act did not draw the party into any closer sympathy. The young woman readjusted her somewhat draggled plumes with a feeble, faded coquetry; Mother Shipton eyed the possessor of "Five-Spot" with malevolence, and Uncle Billy included the whole party in one sweeping anathema.

The road to Sandy Bar—a camp that, not having as yet experienced the regenerating influences of Poker Flat, consequently seemed to offer some invitation to the emigrants—lay over a steep mountain range. It was distant a day's severe travel. In that advanced season the party soon passed out of the moist, temperate regions of the foothills into the dry, cold, bracing air of the Sierras. The trail was narrow and difficult. At noon the Duchess, rolling out of her saddle upon the ground, declared her intention of going no farther, and the party halted.

The spot was singularly wild and impressive. A wooded amphitheatre, surrounded on three sides by precipitous cliffs of naked granite, sloped gently toward the crest of another precipice that overlooked the valley. It was, undoubtedly, the most suitable spot for a camp, had camping been advisable. But Mr. Oakhurst knew that scarcely half the journey to Sandy Bar was accomplished, and the party were not equipped or provisioned for delay. This fact he pointed out to his companions curtly, with a philosophic commentary on the folly of "throwing up their hand before the game was played out." But they were furnished with liquor, which in this emergency stood them in place of food, fuel, rest, and prescience. In spite of his remonstrances, it was not long before they were more or less under its influence. Uncle Billy passed rapidly from a bellicose state into one of stupor, the Duchess became maudlin, and Mother Shipton snored. Mr. Oakhurst alone remained erect, leaning against a rock, calmly surveying them.

Mr. Oakhurst did not drink. It interfered with a profession which required coolness, impassiveness, and presence of mind, and, in his own language, he "couldn't afford it." As he gazed at his recumbent fellow exiles, the loneliness begotten of his pariah trade, his habits of life, his very vices, for the first time seriously oppressed him. He bestirred himself in dusting his black clothes, washing his hands and face, and other acts characteristic of his studiously neat habits, and for a moment forgot his annoyance. The thought of deserting his weaker and more pitiable companions never perhaps occurred to him. Yet he could not help feeling the want of that excitement which, singularly enough, was most conducive to that calm equanimity for which he was notorious. He looked at the gloomy walls that rose a thousand feet sheer above the circling pines around him, at the sky ominously clouded, at the valley below, already deepening into shadow; and, doing so, suddenly he heard his own name called.

A horseman slowly ascended the trail. In the fresh, open face of the new-comer Mr. Oakhurst recognized Tom Simson, otherwise known as "The Innocent," of Sandy Bar. He had met him some months before over a "little game," and had, with perfect equanimity, won the entire fortune—amounting to some forty dollars—of that guileless youth. After the game was finished, Mr. Oakhurst drew the youthful speculator behind the door and thus addressed him: "Tommy, you're a good little man, but you can't gamble worth a cent. Don't try it over again." He then handed him his money back, pushed him gently from the room, and so made a devoted slave of Tom Simson.

There was a remembrance of this in his boyish and enthusiastic greeting of Mr. Oakhurst. He had started, he said, to go to Poker Flat to seek his fortune. "Alone?" No, not exactly alone; in fact (a giggle), he had run away with Piney Woods. Didn't Mr. Oakhurst remember Piney? She that used to wait on the table at the Temperance House? They had been engaged a long time, but old Jake Woods had objected, and so they had run away, and were going to Poker Flat to be married, and here they were. And they were tired out, and how lucky it was they had found a place to camp, and company. All this the Innocent delivered rapidly, while Piney, a stout, comely damsel of fifteen, emerged from behind the pine-tree, where she had been blushing unseen, and rode to the side of her lover.

Mr. Oakhurst seldom troubled himself with sentiment, still less with propriety; but he had a vague idea that the situation was not fortunate. He retained, however, his presence of mind sufficiently to kick Uncle Billy, who was about to say something, and Uncle Billy was sober enough to recognize in Mr. Oakhurst's kick a superior power that would not bear trifling. He then endeavored to dissuade Tom Simson from delaying further, but in vain. He even pointed out the fact that there was no provision, nor means of making a camp. But, unluckily, the Innocent met this objection by assuring the party that he was provided with an extra mule loaded with provisions, and by the discovery of a rude attempt at a log house near the trail. "Piney can stay with Mrs. Oakhurst," said the Innocent, pointing to the Duchess, "and I can shift for myself."

Nothing but Mr. Oakhurst's admonishing foot saved Uncle Billy from bursting into a roar of laughter. As it was, he felt compelled to retire up the cañon until he could recover his gravity. There he confided the joke to the tall pine-trees, with many slaps of his leg, contortions of his face, and the usual profanity. But when he returned to the party, he found them seated by a fire—for the air had grown strangely chill and the sky overcast—in apparently amicable conversation. Piney was actually talking in an impulsive girlish fashion to the Duchess, who was listening with an interest and animation she had not shown for many days. The Innocent was holding forth, apparently with equal effect, to Mr. Oakhurst and Mother Shipton, who was actually relaxing into amiability. "Is this yer a d—d picnic?" said Uncle Billy, with inward scorn, as he surveyed the sylvan group, the glancing firelight, and the tethered animals in the foreground. Suddenly an idea mingled with the alcoholic fumes that disturbed his brain. It was apparently of a jocular nature, for he felt impelled to slap his leg again and cram his fist into his mouth.

As the shadows crept slowly up the mountain, a slight breeze rocked the tops of the pine-trees and moaned through their long and gloomy aisles. The ruined cabin, patched and covered with pine boughs, was set apart for the ladies. As the lovers parted, they unaffectedly exchanged a kiss, so honest and sincere that it might have been heard above the swaying pines. The frail Duchess and the malevolent Mother Shipton were probably too stunned to remark upon this last evidence of simplicity, and so turned without a word to the hut. The fire was replenished, the men lay down before the door, and in a few minutes were asleep.

Mr. Oakhurst was a light sleeper. Toward morning he awoke benumbed and cold. As he stirred the dying fire, the wind, which was now blowing strongly, brought to his cheek that which caused the blood to leave it,—snow!

He started to his feet with the intention of awakening the sleepers, for there was no time to lose. But turning to where Uncle Billy had been lying, he found him gone. A suspicion leaped to his brain, and a curse to his lips. He ran to the spot where the mules had been tethered—they were no longer there. The tracks were already rapidly disappearing in the snow.

The momentary excitement brought Mr. Oakhurst back to the fire with his usual calm. He did not waken the sleepers. The Innocent slumbered peacefully, with a smile on his good-humored, freckled face; the virgin Piney slept beside her frailer sisters as sweetly as though attended by celestial guardians; and Mr. Oakhurst, drawing his blanket over his shoulders, stroked his mustaches and waited for the dawn. It came slowly in a whirling mist of snow-flakes that dazzled and confused the eye. What could be seen of the landscape appeared magically changed. He looked over the valley, and summed up the present and future in two words, "Snowed in!"

A careful inventory of the provisions, which, fortunately for the party, had been stored within the hut, and so escaped the felonious fingers of Uncle Billy, disclosed the fact that with care and prudence they might last ten days longer. "That is," said Mr. Oakhurst *sotto voce* to the Innocent, "if you're willing to board us. If you ain't—and perhaps you'd better not—you can wait till Uncle Billy gets back with provisions." For some occult reason, Mr. Oakhurst could not bring himself to disclose Uncle Billy's rascality, and so offered the hypothesis that he had wandered from the camp and had accidentally stampeded the animals. He dropped a warning to the Duchess and Mother Shipton, who of course knew the facts of their associate's defection. "They'll find out the truth about us *all* when they find out anything," he added significantly, "and there's no good frightening them now."

Tom Simson not only put all his worldly store at the disposal of Mr. Oakhurst, but seemed to enjoy the prospect of their enforced seclusion. "We'll have a good camp for a week, and then the snow'll melt, and we'll all go back together." The cheerful gayety of the young man and Mr. Oakhurst's calm infected the others. The Innocent, with the aid of pine boughs, extemporized a thatch for the roofless cabin, and the Duchess directed Piney in the rearrangement of the interior with a taste and tact that opened the blue eyes of that provincial maiden to their fullest extent. "I reckon now you're used to fine things at Poker Flat," said Piney. The Duchess turned away sharply to conceal something that reddened her cheeks through their professional tint, and Mother Shipton requested Piney not to "chatter." But when Mr. Oakhurst returned from a weary search for the trail, he heard the sound of happy laughter echoed from the rocks. He stopped in some alarm, and his thoughts first·naturally reverted to the whiskey, which he had prudently cachéd. "And yet it don't somehow sound like whiskey," said the gambler. It was not until he caught sight of the blazing fire through the still blinding storm, and the group around it, that he settled to the conviction that it was "square fun."

Whether Mr. Oakhurst had cachéd his cards with the whiskey as something debarred the free access of the community, I cannot say. It was certain that, in Mother Shipton's words, he "didn't say 'cards' once" during that evening. Haply the time was beguiled by an accordion, produced somewhat ostentatiously by Tom Simson from his pack. Notwithstanding some difficulties attending the manipulation of this instrument, Piney Woods managed to pluck several reluctant melodies from its keys, to an accompaniment by the Innocent on a pair of bone castanets. But the crowning festivity of the evening was reached in a rude camp-meeting hymn, which the lovers, joining hands, sang with great earnestness and vociferation. I fear that a certain defiant tone and Covenanter's swing to its chorus, rather than any devotional quality, caused it speedily to infect the others, who at last joined in the refrain:

> "I'm proud to live in the service of the Lord,
> And I'm bound to die in His army."

The pines rocked, the storm eddied and whirled above the miserable group, and the flames of their altar leaped heavenward, as if in token of the vow.

At midnight the storm abated, the rolling clouds parted, and the stars glittered keenly above the sleeping camp. Mr. Oakhurst, whose professional habits had enabled him to live on the smallest possible amount of sleep, in dividing the watch with Tom Simson somehow managed to take upon himself the greater part of that duty. He excused himself to the Innocent by say-

ing that he had "often been a week without sleep." "Doing what?" asked
Tom. "Poker!" replied Oakhurst sententiously. "When a man gets a streak
of luck,—nigger-luck,—he don't get tired. The luck gives in first. Luck," continued the gambler reflectively, "is a mighty queer thing. All you know about
it for certain is that it's bound to change. And it's finding out when it's going
to change that makes you. We've had a streak of bad luck since we left Poker
Flat,—you come along, and slap you get into it, too. If you can hold your
cards right along you're all right. For," added the gambler, with cheerful
irrelevance—

"I'm proud to live in the service of the Lord,
And I'm bound to die in His army."

The third day came, and the sun, looking through the white-curtained
valley, saw the outcasts divide their slowly decreasing store of provisions for
the morning meal. It was one of the peculiarities of that mountain climate
that its rays diffused a kindly warmth over the wintry landscape, as if in re-
gretful commiseration of the past. But it revealed drift on drift of snow piled
high around the hut,—a hopeless, uncharted, trackless sea of white lying below
the rocky shores to which the castaways still clung. Through the marvelously
clear air the smoke of the pastoral village of Poker Flat rose miles away. Mother
Shipton saw it, and from a remote pinnacle of her rocky fastness hurled in
that direction a final malediction. It was her last vituperative attempt, and
perhaps for that reason was invested with a certain degree of sublimity. It did
her good, she privately informed the Duchess. "Just you go out there and cuss,
and see." She then set herself to the task of amusing "the child," as she and
the Duchess were pleased to call Piney. Piney was no chicken, but it was a
soothing and original theory of the pair thus to account for the fact that she
didn't swear and wasn't improper.

When night crept up again through the gorges, the reedy notes of the
accordion rose and fell in fitful spasms and long-drawn gasps by the flickering
campfire. But music failed to fill entirely the aching void left by insufficient
food, and a new diversion was proposed by Piney,—story-telling. Neither Mr.
Oakhurst nor his female companions caring to relate their personal experiences,
this plan would have failed too, but for the Innocent. Some months before
he had chanced upon a stray copy of Mr. Pope's ingenious translation of the
Iliad. He now proposed to narrate the principal incidents of that poem—
having thoroughly mastered the argument and fairly forgotten the words—in
the current vernacular of Sandy Bar. And so for the rest of that night the
Homeric demigods again walked the earth. Trojan bully and wily Greek wrestled in the winds, and the great pines in the cañon seemed to bow to the
wrath of the son of Peleus. Mr. Oakhurst listened with quiet satisfaction.
Most especially was he interested in the fate of "Ash-heels," as the Innocent
persisted in denominating the "swiftfooted Achilles."

So, with small food and much of Homer and the accordion, a week passed over the heads of the outcasts. The sun again forsook them, and again from leaden skies the snowflakes were sifted over the land. Day by day closer around them drew the snowy circle, until at last they looked from their prison over drifted walls of dazzling white, that towered twenty feet above their heads. It became more and more difficult to replenish their fires, even from the fallen trees beside them, now half hidden in the drifts. And yet no one complained. The lovers turned from the dreary prospect and looked into each other's eyes, and were happy. Mr. Oakhurst settled himself coolly to the losing game before him. The Duchess, more cheerful than she had been, assumed the care of Piney. Only Mother Shipton—once the strongest of the party—seemed to sicken and fade. At midnight on the tenth day she called Oakhurst to her side. "I'm going," she said, in a voice of querulous weakness, "but don't say anything about it. Don't waken the kids. Take the bundle from under my head, and open it." Mr. Oakhurst did so. It contained Mother Shipton's rations for the last week, untouched. "Give 'em to the child," she said, pointing to the sleeping Piney. "You've starved yourself," said the gambler. "That's what they call it," said the woman querulously, as she lay down again, and, turning her face to the wall, passed quietly away.

The accordion and the bones were put aside that day, and Homer was forgotten. When the body of Mother Shipton had been committed to the snow, Mr. Oakhurst took the Innocent aside, and showed him a pair of snow-shoes, which he had fashioned from the old pack-saddle. "There's one chance in a hundred to save her yet," he said, pointing to Piney; "but it's there," he added, pointing toward Poker Flat. "If you can reach there in two days she's safe." "And you?" asked Tom Simson. "I'll stay here," was the curt reply.

The lovers parted with a long embrace. "You are not going, too?" said the Duchess, as she saw Mr. Oakhurst apparently waiting to accompany him. "As far as the cañon," he replied. He turned suddenly and kissed the Duchess, leaving her pallid face aflame, and her trembling limbs rigid with amazement.

Night came, but not Mr. Oakhurst. It brought the storm again and the whirling snow. Then the Duchess, feeding the fire, found that some one had quietly piled beside the hut enough fuel to last a few days longer. The tears rose to her eyes, but she hid them from Piney.

The women slept but little. In the morning, looking into each other's faces, they read their fate. Neither spoke, but Piney, accepting the position of the stronger, drew near and placed her arm around the Duchess's waist. They kept this attitude for the rest of the day. That night the storm reached its greatest fury, and, rending asunder the protecting vines, invaded the very hut.

Toward morning they found themselves unable to feed the fire, which gradually died away. As the embers slowly blackened, the Duchess crept closer to Piney, and broke the silence of many hours: "Piney, can you pray?" "No, dear," said Piney simply. The Duchess, without knowing exactly why, felt relieved, and, putting her head upon Piney's shoulder, spoke no more. And so reclining, the younger and purer pillowing the head of her soiled sister upon her virgin breast, they fell asleep.

The wind lulled as if it feared to waken them. Feathery drifts of snow, shaken from the long pine boughs, flew like white-winged birds, and settled about them as they slept. The moon through the rifted clouds looked down upon what had been the camp. But all human stain, all trace of earthly travail, was hidden beneath the spotless mantle mercifully flung from above.

They slept all that day and the next, nor did they waken when voices and footsteps broke the silence of the camp. And when pitying fingers brushed the snow from their wan faces, you could scarcely have told from the equal peace that dwelt upon them which was she that had sinned. Even the law of Poker Flat recognized this, and turned away, leaving them still locked in each other's arms.

But at the head of the gulch, on one·of the largest pine-trees, they found the deuce of clubs pinned to the bark with a bowie-knife. It bore the following, written in pencil in a firm hand:

BENEATH THIS TREE

LIES THE BODY

OF

JOHN OAKHURST,

WHO STRUCK A STREAK OF BAD LUCK

ON THE 23D OF NOVEMBER, 1850,

AND

HANDED IN HIS CHECKS

ON THE 7TH DECEMBER, 1850.

And pulseless and cold, with a Derringer by his side and a bullet in his heart, though still calm as in life, beneath the snow lay he who was at once the strongest and yet the weakest of the outcasts of Poker Flat.

Questions

1. For what undesirable professions were the outcasts cast out of the town of Poker Flat?

2. What did Mother Shipton do for Piney, "the child"?

3. How does Tom Simson's and Piney's method of entertaining themselves and the group make us feel about Tom and Piney?

4. Burlesque humor is humor carried to a ridiculous degree—the club is too big, the pie is too custardy, the shoes are too big, the pants are too baggy. How does Harte want you to feel at the close of his story? How many devices does he set up to make you feel this way? Is number 4 a loaded item?

5. Does Bret Harte want you to feel about his leading characters the same way Katharine Brush ("Night Club") wants you to feel about her leading character?

6. Give directions to the actor and actresses playing the leading roles in a movie to be made of the Bret Harte story. Is Norman in "Chaos, Disorder and the Late Show" the opposite of the characters in the Harte story? Would Norman's mother enjoy the Harte story?

7. Which stories in this section are examples of popular art, and which are attacks on the popular arts?

8. The story was written between the years 1868 and 1870. The time of the story is 1850. From your knowledge of American history, discuss the "authenticity" of the story.

Story for the Slicks*

ELINOR GOULDING SMITH

Carol Saunders brushed her thick mop of chestnut hair off her forehead with long, nervous white fingers. *How am I going to tell Jim?* she thought. *How can I tell him?* She thought of Jim's long, lean jaw, his dark tousled hair, and his crooked grin. *Oh, Jim, Jim*—(Opening paragraph plunges you right into the story with all its intense passion and suspense.)

But I mustn't think about that now. I'm so tired, she thought wearily, and the thin fingers twined nervously in the thick hair. She stood up suddenly and went into the bathroom, and she noticed dully that the faucet was still dripping. *I'll have to get Jim to fix it,* she thought automatically. (The homey touch.)

Determinedly, she turned on the cold water full force and let its clean sparkling freshness flow over her thin white wrists, and then she leaned over and dipped up the water with her slim hands and felt the sharp cold on her hot face. She dipped pads of absorbent cotton in the water and bathed her burning eyes, and she brushed out her hair with long, soothing, rhythmic strokes, away from her forehead. (Beauty hints.)

She surveyed herself in the mirror. She saw the white, pointed face and the hair that seemed almost too heavy for the slim neck. It hung round her shoulders in a thick mass. "It's as soft to touch as a spaniel's ears," Jim always said. The lashes around the wide gray eyes were stuck together in dark points with little beads of the cold water still clinging to them. And the lower lip of the full crimson mouth was quivering. (Important that heroine be described, but not too specifically. Sprinkle liberally with "slim" wherever possible. Helpful if heroine can be made to whip in and out of tight sweaters.)

Tomorrow, she thought wearily, twisting and untwisting the long, nervous fingers. *Let tomorrow be time enough to tell him. I'm so tired today.* (There has to be at least one sentence starting with "let.")

She moved swiftly, with the easy flowing walk that Jim loved, and stood awkwardly for a moment in the living room. The late afternoon sun made a brilliant, warm golden splash on the center of the soft green carpet. *It's so quiet,* she thought, *and it seems almost strange to be here, in this house, now.* (This doesn't mean a thing, but it almost sounds as though it does, doesn't it?)

She thought suddenly that it was getting late, and Jim would be home soon. She went into the kitchen and leaned on the cool enamel table. The kitchen was bright and sunny with yellow walls and crisp curtains with appliquéd tulips. (Interior decorating hints are absolutely necessary.)

---

*Copyright © 1958 by Elinor Goulding Smith from the book, *Confessions of Mrs. Smith: Reckless Recollections True and Otherwise* published by Harcourt, Brace & World, Inc. Reprinted by permission of McIntosh and Otis, Inc.

She caught herself humming a tune—"Star Dust," she realized suddenly. Their song. *Oh, Jim, Jim,* she thought, *remember how it was that night on the top of the bus, and it was so cold and clear, and I could feel the roughness of your coat against my cheek!* (Stir in a little nostalgia.)

And you were laughing because the clean cold wind kept whipping my hair across your face. Ah, we had fun. (Always change paragraphs at every possible opportunity, regardless of the meaning. Be sure heroine talks and thinks like a heroine, as opposed to a human being.)

And suddenly the small white face was down on the cold enamel table and bitter sobs shook the slim shoulders. (Got another "slim" in. Good!)

Then she straightened up with determination. *That's enough of that, Carol Saunders,* she thought, and she threw back the slim shoulders and lifted the little pointed chin. (A little pointed chin is always good too—tears at the heartstrings.)

I think I'll make some blueberry torte, she decided, and she glanced at the clock to see if there would be enough time before dinner. There would be, and she started working swiftly; she thought happily, *Jim always loves blueberry torte.* (Always be specific about food. A good recipe never hurts either.)

She deftly creamed a quarter of a cup of rich yellow butter and a tablespoon of sugar in the blue bowl, and added one egg yolk and a little salt and flour. (This is the most complicated recipe I could find in the Settlement Cook Book—it ought to be a killer.) She patted and pressed the dough in the shining greased pan (or spring form) with her slim quick fingers till it was a quarter of an inch thick, and placed it in the gleaming refrigerator overnight. Then she filled it with any desired Fruit Mixture, and baked.

Then, still humming to herself, having lined the bottom and sides of a spring form with Muerbe Teig No. 1, page 377, she sprinkled it with bread crumbs, added one quart of blueberries (*How ripe the berries are!* she thought, and she ate one, slowly savoring its sweetness), sprinkled it with one quarter of a cup of sugar (*How white the sugar is!* she thought unexpectedly), and cinnamon and two tablespoons of lemon juice. Over all she dripped the yolk of an egg beaten with three tablespoons of rich yellow cream. She baked it in the hot oven for fifteen minutes, then reduced the heat to three hundred and twenty-five degrees Fahrenheit.

This time she baked it till the crust was golden brown. *Jim loves it with the crust nice and brown,* she thought.

She sniffed the heavenly smell of the Muerbe Teig No. 1, page 377, and her face was flushed from the heat of the stove and her eyes were shining. She beat four egg whites until they were stiff and stood up in little white crusty peaks, and added powdered sugar. When the torte was ready, crust nicely browned, she spread the beaten eggs and sugar over it, returned it quickly to the oven, and baked it fifteen minutes more at three hundred degrees Fahrenheit. (I wonder if anybody ever tried this.)

While she was waiting for it to be ready, she realized suddenly that she was famished, and she thought, *I'll make pickled herring with lots of sour cream, just the way Jim loves it, and chicken soup with matzos balls, and creplach. And pot roast with potato latkes.* (Always give menus. Memo: Remember to get other cook book. Feel certain this is not the right cook book for magazine fiction writer.)

Carol didn't hear Jim's key turning in the lock, and he strode in and stood for a moment in the kitchen doorway, looking at her. Her face was flushed, and one tendril of hair had separated from the chestnut mass and curled over one cheek. (A loose tendril is always good.)

Suddenly she felt his presence, and she turned quickly. He was standing there, grinning that crooked grin that always made her heart turn over. (Crooked grin absolutely essential.) He was at her side with one step, and then he was crushing her to him, and her little white face was pressed tight against the warm roughness of his tweed shoulder. He buried his hands in the thick mass of her hair, and then he lifted her face up to kiss her. *She's so little,* he thought. He was always surprised at how little she was. (This establishes that he is of the necessary height and breadth for a proper hero.)

"Jim, darling," Carol said, "let me get my breath." (*He mustn't suspect,* she thought. *I'll tell him tomorrow.*) "And darling," she said, "you'd better hurry and wash—dinner's ready."

When they sat down to dinner, she was quite composed again. The tall glasses sparkled against the deep blue linen table mats that she had made from that old blue linen dress, and trimmed with the oyster-white cotton fringe that made a happy design against the polished mahogany. (More housekeeping hints.) The lovely old silver that she had got from Grandmother Stanford on her wedding day gleamed softly. She kept the silver polished with reverent care, and its soft sheen never failed to remind her of Grandmother Stanford's shining white hair that she had carried bravely, like a banner. (Bravely, like a banner—isn't that *good?*) If only she could be as brave, if only she could have the strength that Grandmother had had.

Not that Carol Saunders hadn't been brave. She'd been brave the day that Jim had come home from the Army induction center, rejected. She had been strong then. She remembered how he had come home that day, his shoulders bent, his gray eyes smouldering with helpless rage. "It's no good," he had said, "they won't have me—that ankle—" Carol had known about his ankle—that time it had been broken, but he'd fought on to make his touchdown before he collapsed and was carried from the field. That ankle would never be right—she had known that. And she had been strong. (Naturally, there has to be a football injury.)

But this—this was different.

They finished dinner, and Jim helped her to clear away the dishes.

"Darling," she said, blinking back the tears, "I don't feel like washing the dishes tonight—let's just stack them in the sink, and I'll do them in the morning." She pushed her hair back from her forehead with the funny little gesture that Jim loved.

"Sure, honey," he said, "if you say so. It's certainly no hardship for me."

Carol laughed uncertainly. And then suddenly she knew that she had to tell him. Now.

"Come in the living room," she said. Her heart pounded painfully, and she could feel the pulse beating in the soft part of her neck. "I want to talk to you."

Jim looked puzzled, but he followed Carol into the living room. He sank down on the big soft couch covered with deep red frieze and trimmed with a looped woolen fringe of the palest gray. Carol came and sat close to him. She linked her thin fingers, and sat there a moment, looking down at her hands. *I have to tell him now,* she thought. But still she sat there, silently, twining and untwining the long, thin fingers.

Jim sat as still as death, waiting. Suddenly he leaned forward and caught both her hands in his big ones. "What is it, Carol?" he said, his deep voice vibrant with sympathy. "What is it?" he said again. "Darling," he added softly, "remember that I love you."

Carol looked up gratefully, and her wide gray eyes filled with tears.

She felt fear, like a cold hand laid across her heart.

And then suddenly she thought of Grandmother Stanford. And she knew then, deep within her, that she could be strong too. She held her little head high, and the gray eyes were shining.

"Jim," she said, "I'm going to tell you straight. I—I—" Her voice broke, but she swallowed and went on bravely in a clear voice. (Now, I believe, if I have learned the method properly, we are at the crux of the story. It just so happens I don't have a good crux on hand at the moment, but I can think one up later. It hardly matters, for the denouement is the same in any case.)

Jim stared at her a moment, unbelief in his honest eyes, his long jaw rigid. She saw a tiny muscle quivering in his temple. The room was very still, and somewhere off in the distance they heard the plaintive cry of a train rushing through the night.

Finally Jim spoke. "Carol," he said, and his voice shook a little.

"Carol—we'll be all right. We'll start over, you and I, together."

"Jim!" Carol cried. "Oh, Jim!" She started to cry, and he wrapped her in his strong arms till she was quiet again. "Oh, darling," she said then. "Darling."

Suddenly she sat up straight. "Jim," she said. "Let's wash the dishes *now.*"

Questions

1. In the book *The Writer's Market,* which is published yearly, notice the various kinds and levels of magazines. What is a slick magazine?

2. How does a "story for the slicks" differ from a story for the so-called quality magazines?

3. List a number of ingredients that the author feels a "story for the slicks" must have.

4. Why doesn't the author bother to tell us what Carol tells Jim?

5. Suggest several titles for the story about Carol and Jim.

6. This story makes fun of the stories that often appear in magazines designed to appeal to housewives. What are some of the stock ingredients in the magazine stories that are written to appeal to the housewife's husband?

7. Why aren't "stories for the slicks" included in this text? How is the text apparently trying to shape you?

8. Are these popular stories "bad"? Explain.

9. What would be the reaction of Mrs. Brady in "Night Club" to "Story for the Slicks"?

Ad*

KENNETH FEARING

WANTED: Men;
Millions of men are WANTED AT ONCE in a big new field;
NEW, TREMENDOUS, THRILLING, GREAT.

If you've ever been a figure in the chamber of horrors,
If you've ever escaped from the psychiatric ward,
If you thrill at the thought of throwing poison into wells, have heavenly
                          visions of people, by the thousands, dying in flames—

YOU ARE THE VERY MAN WE WANT
We mean business and our business is YOU
WANTED: A race of brand-new men.

Apply: Middle Europe;
No skill needed;
No ambition required; no brains wanted and no character allowed;

TAKE A PERMANENT JOB IN THE COMING PROFESSION
Wages: DEATH.

Questions

1. "Ad" is short for *advertisement*. Who or what is wanted?

---

*By permission of the estate of Kenneth Fearing.

2. If you delight in doing _____, you will like this job.

3. What qualities are not needed or desired of the applicants?

4. What are the wages?

5. In your estimation should a newspaper, or a television station, or a magazine accept or refuse such an ad?

My Creed*

EDGAR A. GUEST

To live as gently as I can;
To be, no matter where, a man;
To take what comes of good or ill
And cling to faith and honor still;
To do my best, and let that stand
The record of my brain and hand;
And then, should failure come to me,
Still work and hope for victory.

To have no secret place wherein
I stoop unseen to shame or sin;
To be the same when I'm alone
As when my every deed is known;
To live undaunted, unafraid
Of any step that I have made;
To be without pretense or sham
Exactly what men think I am.

To leave some simple mark behind
To keep my having lived in mind;
If enmity to aught I show,
To be an honest, generous foe,
To play my little part, nor whine
That greater honors are not mine.
This, I believe, is all I need
For my philosophy and creed.

Questions

1. Are "Don'ts" and "My Creed" the opposite of one another?

2. What do the following mean? To be a man; to cling to faith and honor; to be exactly what men think I am; and to be an honest, generous foe.

° By permission of Reilly & Lee Company, Chicago.

3. Should Edgar Guest be praised for setting high standards for us or is he the Sunday School version of Mickey Spillane, shaping us not to goodness but to hypocrisy? Does society give its rewards to those who have Edgar Guest's creed or belief? What are society's rewards?

Four Preludes
on Playthings of the Wind*
"The Past Is a Bucket of Ashes"

CARL SANDBURG

1

The woman named Tomorrow
sits with a hairpin in her teeth
and takes her time
and does her hair the way she wants it
and fastens at last the last braid and coil
and puts the hairpin where it belongs
and turns and drawls: Well, what of it?
My grandmother, Yesterday, is gone.
What of it? Let the dead be dead.

2

The doors were cedar
and the panel strips of gold
and the girls were golden girls
and the panels read and the girls chanted:
     We are the greatest city,
     and the greatest nation:
     nothing like us ever was.

The doors are twisted on broken hinges,
Sheets of rain swish through on the wind
     where the golden girls ran and the panels read:
     We are the greatest city,
     the greatest nation,
     nothing like us ever was.

3

It has happened before.
Strong men put up a city and got
     a nation together,

And paid singers to sing and women
　　to warble: We are the greatest city,
　　　　the greatest nation,
　　　　nothing like us ever was.

And while the singers sang
and the strong men listened
and paid the singers well,
　　　　there were rats and lizards who listened
　　　　. . . and the only listeners left now
　　　　. . . are . . . the rats . . . and the lizards.
　　And there are black crows
　　crying, "Caw, caw,"
　　bringing mud and sticks
　　building a nest
　　over the words carved
　　on the doors where the panels were cedar
　　and the strips on the panels were gold
　　and the golden girls came singing:
　　　　We are the greatest city,
　　　　the greatest nation:
　　　　nothing like us ever was.

The only singers now are crows crying, "Caw, caw,"
And the sheets of rain whine in the wind and doorways.
And the only listeners now are . . . the rats . . . and the lizards.

　　　　4
The feet of the rats
scribble on the doorsills;
the hieroglyphs of the rat footprints
chatter the pedigrees of the rats
and babble of the blood
and gabble of the breed
of the grandfathers and the great-grandfathers
of the rats.

And the wind shifts
and the dust on a doorsill shifts
and even the writing of the rat footprints
tells us nothing, nothing at all
about the greatest city, the greatest nation
where the strong men listened
and the women warbled: Nothing like us ever was.

Questions

1. Leaves, old newspapers, and weeds might be thought of as the playthings of
    the wind. What does Sandburg make the plaything of the wind?

2. The woman named Tomorrow is or is not upset that Yesterday is gone? Is
    Sandburg upset?

3. In the story by Ray Bradbury, "There Will Come Soft Rains," an atomic ex-
    plosion apparently accounted for the disaster. What brought about the change
    in Sandburg's greatest nation?

4. Bradbury perhaps indicates that man could shape himself a certain way and
    save himself from man-made destruction. What does Sandburg imply about this?

Island Magic*

LEONARD BERNSTEIN

DINAH: What a movie!
        What a terrible, awful movie!
        It's a crime what they put on the screen!
        Do they think we're a lot of children?
        It would bore any four-year-old!
        What drivel! What nonsense!
        What escapist Technicolor twaddle!!
        "Trouble in Tahiti", indeed!
        "Trouble in Tahiti", imagine!
        There she is in her inch or two of sarong,
        F-loating, f-loat-ing, f-loat-ing, all among the f-loat-ing f-low'rs . . .
        Then she sees him, the handsome American;
        (I must say he's really a man:
        Six feet tall, and each foot just incredible!)
        Well, they're madly in love,
        But, there's trouble ahead:
        There's a legend:
        (*In a "South Pacific" accent*)
        "If a princess marry white man, and rain fall that day,
        Then the white man shall be sacrifice without delay."
        Sure enough, on the night of their wedding day,
        There's a storm like nothing on earth;
        Tidal waves and siroccos and hurricanes;
        And to top it all off,
        The volcano erupts,

---

*Copyright 1953 by G. Schirmer, Inc. Reprinted by permission.

As the natives sing:
"Ah! Ah! Ah! Olé!"
They go crazy with the drumming and the chanting and
ritual dance,
While the lovers sing a ballad of South Sea romance:
It's so lovely, I wish I could think of it:
Da da dee da da dee da da. It was called "Island Magic".
I think it was. Oh, a beautiful song!
I remember it now:
"Island magic.
Where the midnight breezes caress us,
And the stars above seem to bless us,
That's island magic.
Island magic . . ."
Well, in any case, the hero is tied to a tree.
(Did I tell you he's a flyer who got lost at sea?)
Anyway, all the natives are crazy now,
Running wild with lances and knives:
Then they pile up the wood for the sacrifice,
And a witch-doctor comes,
And he sets it on fire.
As the natives sing:
"Ah! Ah! Ah! Olé!"
But at this point
Comes the good old U.S. Navy, a-singin' a song;
They come swarming down in parachutes, a thousand strong!
Ev'ryone is happy as pie:
And they all do a great Rhumba version of "Island Magic",
of course!

It's a dazzling sight;
With the sleek brown native women
Dancing with the U.S. Navy boys,
And a hundred-piece symphony orchestra:
(*Dinah is swept away completely by the story and begins dancing all
over the stage.*)

DINAH;   "Island magic!
and TRIO: Where the palm-trees whisper together,
And it's always mid-summer weather,
That's island magic,
Island magic,
That's island magic!
With the one I love very near;
Island magic,
That's island magic!

Whisp'ring native words in my ear.
Island magic,
Island magic!
Only you my darling, could weave it,
And I never ever will leave it,
And I simply cannot believe
It really is mine!
It really is mine!
Island magic!
Island ma . . ."
(Dinah comes to her senses.)

DINAH: What a terrible, awful movie!

Dinah describes a Technicolor movie she has seen, called "Trouble in Tahiti." Dinah
and her husband are extremely unhappy and cannot communicate with one another.
Although they are well-to-do, have a child, and are intelligent, they exist rather
than live. Because they have no magic of their own, they go to the movies and try
to lose themselves in the "bought and paid for magic . . . on a super-silver screen."

Questions

1. What is the plot of the movie "Trouble in Tahiti"?

2. Why is Dinah so upset about the film?

3. The island in the South Seas is part of the daydream of many humans. Which
    is easier, to attack or to defend the daydream?

4. These lyrics are taken from Bernstein's opera *Trouble in Tahiti*. Can you imagine
    why Bernstein gave the opera the same title as the movie?

The Fiddler of Dooney*

WILLIAM BUTLER YEATS

When I play on my fiddle in Dooney,
Folk dance like a wave of the sea;
My cousin is priest in Kilvarnet,
My brother in Mocharabuiee.[1]

---

[1] Pronounced as if spelled "Mockrabwee."

I passed my brother and cousin:
They read in their books of prayer;
I read in my book of songs
I bought at the Sligo fair.

When we come at the end of time
To Peter sitting in state,
He will smile on the three old spirits,
But call me first through the gate;

For the good are always the merry,
Save by an evil chance,
And the merry love the fiddle,
And the merry love to dance:

And when the folk there spy me,
They will all come up to me,
With 'Here is the fiddler of Dooney!'
And dance like a wave of the sea.

Questions

1. The fiddler of Dooney has a cousin and a brother who are not fiddlers. What do they do when he reads his book of songs?

2. Who, according to the fiddler, will St. Peter call first through the gate of heaven when the cousin, the brother, and the fiddler arrive? Why?

3. The fiddler, the priest, or the poet—who is the strongest in shaping you to the ways of God? Explain.

What Is News?*

DUANE BRADLEY

What is news? It is the honest and unbiased and complete account of events of interest and concern to the public.

A typical metropolitan daily may receive approximately 8 million words of copy each day from its staff, wire services, feature syndicates, correspondents and special writers. Of this, only about 100,000 can be used in the paper.

Local stories are gathered by staff reporters and correspondents. Each reporter is responsible for certain types of news and some have what are called "beats." One may cover the city offices, another the police court and state police, someone else the society news. Correspondents from neighborhood areas and surrounding towns write or telephone news from their localities.

A reporter on his beat will make notes of various stories he encounters, then return to the office and write them. On a larger paper, or during an emergency when time is precious, he may phone them in to the "desk" where a rewrite man will take them.

Other people also telephone in stories or suggestions for stories. No newspaper has enough reporters to cover every spot where news may break, nor can it possibly keep up with all of the activities in any town. Members of the public and town officials frequently notify a paper when an important issue is coming up in a town meeting, when a deer has wandered into a suburban neighborhood, or when a certain couple is planning to celebrate a golden wedding anniversary.

Public relations and publicity people for all sorts of individuals and organizations regularly send stories to newspapers. Some of these stories are legitimate news, and some are merely designed to keep clients in the spotlight of public attention.

Foreign and out-of-state news stories often carry a set of initials in the dateline which indicates that they were supplied by one of the wire services. AP means Associated Press. UPI means United Press International. Such a story from New York, for instance, was covered by a wire service staff member at the spot where it occurred and phoned in to the New York office. It was handled by a rewrite man, then edited and teletyped to subscribing New York bureaus and to regional bureau offices throughout the country. At each regional office it was again edited before being teletyped to subscribing newspapers in the area. This editing is done to fit the needs of out-of-town papers which will not want as long a story as those near the area where the event happened. At the local paper, a city editor or news editor evaluated the story

* Reprinted from *The Newspaper: Its Place in a Democracy* by Duane Bradley. By permission of D. Van Nostrand Company, Inc.

and decided where it was to be used in his paper. He then passed it to the copy desk where it was again refined, pared to a specific length, and headlined. It was scrutinized by an editorial board before being sent to the composing room. A newspaper which subscribes to a wire service may edit stories to fit its needs but may not change the content or slant them without removing the wire service identification.

All news stories, once written, are edited and designated for particular spots in the paper. Their length, their position and whether or not news photos accompany them will depend on their importance compared to other news in the same issue.

There is a well-known truism about news that defines it as something out of the ordinary. It says that if a dog bites a man it is not news, but that if a man bites a dog, it *is* news. Anyone who reads the average newspaper will realize that this hardly applies to a large per cent of what is presented to him as news. Much space in all newspapers is devoted to ordinary, expected, and not particularly surprising events:

The Elks have a picnic, the PTA holds a reception for new members, the League of Women Voters offers transportation to the polls, the Little League wins a game, ten speeders are fined in police court—these stories, multiplied a thousand-fold, appear daily in newspapers all across America.

Seemingly even less important and exciting than these are what are called "meet-the-train" items. "Mr. and Mrs. Joseph Smith were dinner guests at the home of Mr. and Mrs. Sam Brown on Thursday, March 19." "Miss Jane Brown has returned home from Chatham College, where she has just completed her junior year." Newspapers value these stories more than you might suppose because they are so important to those whose names are mentioned.

The "big" stories, the hurricane that demolishes a town, the child lost in the woods, the bank robbery, the escaped criminal, do not happen so often, and may well be called "man bites dog" stories.

The type of story that is hardest to get and offers the most potential danger to a paper is the one kept hidden from the public. The good reporter and the good editor are never content with routine news and regular "hand-outs" from official sources, but are always on the alert for what is not easy to see.

A city plans a huge new park in a residential area. It is much needed to provide recreation facilities for large numbers of children. On the other hand, who now owns the land where it will be located, and when did they buy it? (Did the plans leak from certain city officials so that relatives and friends could buy the land at a low price, to resell later at a profit?) How much will be paid for the land, and who decides on its value? How are the contracts for the necessary work to be awarded? Who has written the specifications for construction and will everything be of the best quality? The alert paper seeking this information will have no difficulty if all city officials are honest, but a crooked administration will resent a public scrutiny of its affairs. The paper that battles dishonest public officials is asking for trouble, but many a good paper has brought about great social reforms by doing just that.

News in American newspapers is supposed to be honest, accurate, concise, and easy to understand. It should not be written to serve any special interests, groups, or individuals. Most reporters and editors pride themselves on living up to these standards. It is much more difficult than it might seem to be sure that this is always done.

News which gives a one-sided impression is "slanted." A reporter or editor can, consciously or unconsciously, slant news in many different ways.

The selection of which stories to print may slant the news. Some Southern newspapers have carried almost no news about racial difficulties in their areas, which may have given the impression that such things did not exist there. Some Northern newspapers have ignored stories of racial difficulties in the North, but headlined those in the South, which may have given the impression that it was a purely regional problem. During a presidential campaign, partisan Republican papers may print countless stories about the huge crowds attending speeches made by the Republican candidate and hardly mention the same sort of crowds present to hear the Democratic candidate. Partisan Democratic papers may run stories showing the popularity of their candidate, and select those which show a lack of popularity on the part of his opponent.

When done deliberately, this sort of slanting defeats the purpose of giving the public a clear and balanced picture of current events. It is often done, in a minor way, with no such intention. The editor who is an avid sports fan is apt to have a larger sports section than the one who is uninterested in sports but deeply involved in politics. The reporter who is fascinated by the business growth of the city will see more stories there than in its schools.

Responsible editors are aware that they often "create" news by selecting it for their columns. There are dozens of different departments in any state government, and news is apt to be in the making in all of them most of the time. The highway department is planning new roads, the department of employment is devising new tests for prospective employees, the treasurer has a report on the state's financial condition, the state promotion department is running a contest to choose a state flower, the state police department is reorganizing, the governor is making a speech, the welfare department reports an unusually heavy case load, the state park authority wants to create a new park in land reclaimed by a flood control project. Most of these matters are routine and might ordinarily be handled by routine news treatment.

Suppose that the newspaper editor decides that the matter of reclaimed land is of the utmost importance to the state, either because he thinks it should be a park or because he thinks it should be left untouched and used for a wild life refuge. He can put a good reporter on the story, set him to work digging up background and similar situations in other states, and run a series of front page stories which treat the matter as if it were the only really vital thing going on in the state. He could do the same with any one of the listed stories and give it importance at the expense of other news.

The attempt to make a paper interesting and exciting can slant news. Some newspapers fill their columns with stories of crime, tragedy, and corruption in order to attract readers; this makes it seem that these are the only noteworthy things happening. Other papers, wishing to help their communities by keeping everyone happy, err on the other side and rarely print anything unpleasant.

The position of a particular news story on the page and the page on which it appears, the number of words used for it, whether or not it is illustrated, and the way in which it is headlined can slant news.

Remember our fictitious governor who was involved in a traffic accident? Let us assume that it was snowing, that he was driving down a hill where children were sliding on the sidewalk, and that his car went out of control, narrowly missed another one, and crashed into a tree. He was examined by a doctor but was found to be uninjured. Think of the different headlines that could be written for such a story: "Governor Escapes Death in Accident," "Governor to Face Court Charges in Accident," "Children Uninjured by Governor's Accident, Is Claim"—and so on.

News may be slanted by lack of time and manpower to pursue it thoroughly. A newspaper may get a tip that a Mr. Peter Smith has been victimized by the state highway department. A reporter is sent to investigate the incident.

He finds Mr. Smith, aged 79, living near a new highway but unable to have a driveway built between it and his house. He had previously lived at another location, but his land was confiscated by the highway department to make room for the new highway. Being too poor to hire a lawyer, he had taken the price offered for his land by the state. A neighbor had interceded with the state on his behalf and helped him buy back his original home, which had then been moved to its present spot. Once settled, he had planted a garden, bought a cow, built a henhouse, and *then* had found that the state would not allow him to build the necessary driveway. His only access to the outside world is a path a quarter of a mile long which leads to a secondary road. He cannot afford to turn this into a proper driveway because the only money he has is the amount the state paid him for his former property.

The reporter finds this a heart-rending story and returns to his office to write it. His editor looks it over carefully. It is interesting, the public should know about it if it is a typical incident, and it is true in the sense that it is reported exactly as Mr. Smith told it. If it turns out not to be the complete truth, the paper is not in danger of a libel suit, because the state cannot bring such a suit. (In our country, the government *is* the people, and we cannot sue ourselves. If a story accuses a specific government official of something that may harm his reputation, he can bring suit as an individual on the basis of personal injury.)

The editor suggests that the reporter telephone the proper state official and get the state's side of the story. The reporter makes the call and is connected with a man who has a desk full of important work and no inclination to talk. The official says he is sick and tired of hearing about Mr. Smith and of the way newspaper reporters distort facts. Here is another angle to the story. "State official angered by questions, has no sympathy for Mr. Smith, and accuses newspapers of distorting the truth." It becomes more colorful by the minute.

A good reporter does not stop there. He should insist on his right to know the facts and should explain that the story is going to be printed and he would like to make it as accurate as possible. (Most state officials and others in public life realize it is always better to talk to the press than to refuse to, no matter what they may happen to think of the individual reporter or newspaper concerned.)

A subsequent interview will present new facts. The state is involved in a large-scale operation of highway construction, and the property of Mr. Smith is one of many it has purchased. All such property has been evaluated by professional appraisers to determine its true value. Mr. Smith was informed, by letter, that he could buy back his original home at a modest price, as were all uprooted home owners. He was further advised, again by letter, that the property to which he had his house moved would not be allowed access to the new highway. Most new highways, such as this one, have limited side access in order to prevent dangerous cross traffic.

The state official might eventually become more friendly with the reporter and advise him that Mr. Smith is a well-known crank who has caused endless trouble. He may suggest that it would be wise to drop the whole story, since it is obviously not a case of right or wrong, but of a man who can get along with no one.

This changes the story entirely, and the reporter and the paper have now spent considerable time on it—time which would otherwise have gone to other stories. Is this the end?

Not yet. The reporter should check the official records and interview other state officials and those whose property has been purchased for the same highway. Out of all this time and effort may come a story that uncovers wrong-doing on the part of the state, or a story that is hardly worth writing and printing. Few newspapers have the facilities for following up every suggested story to this extent. *A story that is incomplete may be slanted because it omits some of the facts.*

Some stories may be both true and important, but misleading. Some years ago the late Senator Joseph McCarthy undertook a crusade to rid the government, schools, and churches of people whom he considered sympathetic to Communism. Speaking in the Senate (where his senatorial immunity made him safe from libel suits), he began to name people whom he said were Communists, Communist sympathizers, or "soft on Communism." Many of them were prominent people whose names were as newsworthy as the senator's.

It is news when any government official makes such statements. Many thoughtful editors did not believe the charges were true but they could not ignore their news value nor express their opinions in the news stories themselves. In order to handle the matter in what they considered the proper perspective, they printed their opinions on the editorial page, made a consistent effort to follow up on all of the accusations and give their readers the facts. Some published interviews with those accused giving their background and stature and with people who opposed Senator McCarthy's project.

To return to our original definition, news is an honest, unbiased, and complete account of events of interest or concern to the public. Professor George H. Morris of Florida Southern University, who was a newspaperman for many years before he became a teacher, characterizes news as "history in a hurry." He says "Read several papers, day after day, and eventually the truth will emerge."

No newspaper, because of the limitations of time and space, can print all of the facts that make the news in any one issue. No reader can understand what is happening by scanning any one issue of any one paper.

It is difficult for even the best newspaper to do a good job of gathering and writing the news. The good reader will evaluate it by reading carefully day after day and comparing the way identical stories are covered in papers with different viewpoints.

Questions

1. "All the News That's Fit to Print" is the motto of *The New York Times*. In your estimation, what is and is not fit to print?

2. Compare a copy of another newspaper with *The New York Times* for the same date. Does the geographic location of the newspapers account for their differences?

3. What is the author's definition of news? Does he explain what is of "concern and interest to the public"?

4. According to the author, what does a newspaper have to do before it may change the content, or slant a story from the wire services? Is the wire service story "truth"?

5. Slanting, creating, and censoring—can a newspaper do anything else to the news?

The Trumpeter Taken Prisoner*

ÆSOP

A Trumpeter, being taken prisoner in battle, begged hard for quarter, declared his innocence and protested that he neither had, nor could kill any man since he bore no arms and carried only his trumpet which he was obliged to sound at the word of command. "For that reason," replied his enemies, "we are determined not to spare you; for though you yourself never fight, yet with that wicked instrument of yours, you blow up hatred between other people and so become the occasion of much bloodshed."

Questions

1. Why according to the trumpeter shouldn't he be put to death?

2. What was the logic of the conquerors?

3. A fable is a parable. Who or what is the trumpeter or shaper of society? Is this fable properly located in the text?

The Four Seasons

(*painting—see p. 106*)

NORMAN ROCKWELL

Questions

1. How does Rockwell establish the four seasons?

2. As a result of the painting, how do you feel about the boy, the dog, and the seasons? Explain what the artist did to make you feel this way.

3. Pictures by Norman Rockwell are extremely popular in America. Pictures by Ivan Albright (see "And God Created Man in His Own Image") have not achieved such popularity. On the basis of these two paintings, what qualities make a painting popular?

4. How would you reply to a person who said that Norman Rockwell paints falsehood? That he paints truth?

5. How might some of the fictional characters in the text react to "The Four Seasons"? Give examples.

Mechanical Man with Pretty Pictures

(*painting—see p. 107*)

MARA MCAFEE

Questions

1. A mechanical man does not have to be made of metal. Why do you imagine the artist calls the figure "mechanical man"?

2. "Pretty Pictures"—what makes the framed pictures pretty, and why does the artist repeat the one picture?

3. Why didn't the artist use the Reginald Marsh painting "High Yaller" (p. 194) or the Albright painting (p. 35) or the Milles' statue (p. 34) for his background?

4. The pictures of the child are similar to the paintings of a very popular painter. Were you that painter, how might you respond to the Mara McAfee painting? How would various fictional characters in the text respond?

5. Do the four preceding questions slant you to feel the way the editor of the text feels about the painting? If the questions do not slant you, if they are unbiased, write two or three questions about the painting that *are* slanted or biased. If the editor's questions are biased, write several that are not.

Peers and Environment

The Feast of Pure Reason by Jack Levine

(1937) Oil on canvas, 42 × 48 in. On extended loan to The Museum of Modern Art, New York, from the United States WPA Art Program.

Handball by Ben Shahn

(1939) Tempera on paper over composition board, 22¾ × 31¼ in. Collection, The Museum of Modern Art, New York. Abby Aldrich Rockefeller Fund.

Preliminary Statements for Discussion
and Writing

1. Mediocrity is the reward of pleasing our friends.

2. Properly speaking, all true work is religion.

3. Environment has everything or nothing to do with man.

4. It is never too late to give up your prejudices.

5. A tie ball game is like kissing your sister.

6. I do not expect a soldier to think.

7. Man is born free, and everywhere he is in chains.

8. Society does not give its rewards to its critics.

9. There are no small parts, only small actors.

10. A man should *be* upright, not be *kept* upright.

11. One should immediately re-evaluate his thinking when he finds himself in the camp of the majority. The people—no.

12. And God made man in His own image.

13. Some men are only passages for food.

14. Family, school, church, and art are insignificant when a brass band plays.

15. Because you are virtuous, should there be no more cakes and ale?

Black Is My Favorite Color*

Bernard Malamud

Charity Sweetness sits in the toilet eating her two hardboiled eggs while I'm
having my ham sandwich and coffee in the kitchen. That's how it goes only
don't get the idea of ghettoes. If there's a ghetto I'm the one that's in it.
She's my cleaning woman from Father Divine and comes in once a week to
my small three-room apartment on my day off from the liquor store. "Peace,"
she says to me, "Father reached on down and took me right up in Heaven."
She's a small person with a flat body, frizzy hair, and a quiet face that the
light shines out of, and Mama had such eyes before she died. The first time
Charity Sweetness came in to clean, a little more than a year and a half, I
made the mistake to ask her to sit down at the kitchen table with me and
eat her lunch. I was still feeling not so hot after Ornita left but I'm the kind
of a man—Nat Lime, forty-four, a bachelor with a daily growing bald spot
on the back of my head, and I could lose frankly fifteen pounds—who enjoys
company so long as he has it. So she cooked up her two hardboiled eggs and
sat down and took a small bite out of one of them. But after a minute she
stopped chewing and she got up and carried the eggs in a cup in the bathroom, and since then she eats there. I said to her more than once, "Okay,
Charity Sweetness, so have it your way, eat the eggs in the kitchen by yourself and I'll eat when you're done," but she smiles absentminded, and eats
in the toilet. It's my fate with colored people.

Although black is still my favorite color you wouldn't know it from my
luck except in short quantities even though I do all right in the liquor store
business in Harlem, on Eighth Avenue between 110th and 111th. I speak with
respect. A large part of my life I've had dealings with Negro people, most on
a business basis but sometimes for friendly reasons with genuine feeling on
both sides. I'm drawn to them. At this time of my life I should have one or
two good colored friends but the fault isn't necessarily mine. If they knew
what was in my heart towards them, but how can you tell that to anybody
nowadays? I've tried more than once but the language of the heart either is
a dead language or else nobody understands it the way you speak it. Very few.
What I'm saying is, personally for me there's only one human color and that's
the color of blood. I like a black person if not because he's black, then because I'm white. It comes to the same thing. If I wasn't white my first choice
would be black. I'm satisfied to be white because I have no other choice.
Anyway, I got an eye for color. I appreciate. Who wants everybody to be
the same? Maybe it's like some kind of a talent. Nat Lime might be a liquor
dealer in Harlem, but once in the jungle in New Guinea in the Second War,

I got the idea when I shot at a running Jap and missed him, that I had some kind of a talent, though maybe it's the kind where you have a marvelous idea now and then but in the end what do they come to? After all, it's a strange world.

Where Charity Sweetness eats her eggs makes me think about Buster Wilson when we were both boys in the Williamsburg section of Brooklyn. There was this long block of run-down dirty frame houses in the middle of a not-so-hot white neighborhood full of pushcarts. The Negro houses looked to me like they had been born and died there, dead not long after the beginning of the world. I lived on the next street. My father was a cutter with arthritis in both hands, big red knuckles and swollen fingers so he didn't cut, and my mother was the one who went to work. She sold paper bags from a second-hand pushcart in Ellery Street. We didn't starve but nobody ate chicken unless we were sick or the chicken was. This was my first acquaintance with a lot of black people and I used to poke around on their poor block. I think I thought, brother, if there can be like this, what can't there be? I mean I caught an early idea what life was about. Anyway I met Buster Wilson there. He used to play marbles by himself. I sat on the curb across the street, watching him shoot one marble lefty and the other one righty. The hand that won picked up the marbles. It wasn't so much of a game but he didn't ask me to come over. My idea was to be friendly, only he never encouraged, he discouraged. Why did I pick him out for a friend? Maybe because I had no others then, we were new in the neighborhood, from Manhattan. Also I liked his type. Buster did everything alone. He was a skinny kid and his brothers' clothes hung on him like worn-out potato sacks. He was a beanpole boy, about twelve, and I was then ten. His arms and legs were burnt out matchsticks. He always wore a brown wool sweater, one arm half unraveled, the other went down to the wrist. His long and narrow head had a white part cut straight in the short woolly hair, maybe with a ruler there, by his father, a barber but too drunk to stay a barber. In those days though I had little myself I was old enough to know who was better off, and the whole block of colored houses made me feel bad in the daylight. But I went there as much as I could because the street was full of life. In the night it looked different, it's hard to tell a cripple in the dark. Sometimes I was afraid to walk by the houses when they were dark and quiet. I was afraid there were people looking at me that I couldn't see. I liked it better when they had parties at night and everybody had a good time. The musicians played their banjos and saxophones and the houses shook with the music and laughing. The young girls, with their pretty dresses and ribbons in their hair, caught me in my throat when I saw them through the windows.

But with the parties came drinking and fights. Sundays were bad days after the Saturday night parties. I remember once that Buster's father, also long and loose, always wearing a dirty gray Homburg hat, chased another black man in the street with a half-inch chisel. The other one, maybe five feet high, lost his shoe and when they wrestled on the ground he was already bleeding through his suit, a thick red blood smearing the sidewalk. I was frightened by the blood and wanted to pour it back in the man who was bleeding from the chisel. On another time Buster's father was playing in a crap game with two big bouncy red dice, in the back of an alley between two middle houses. Then about six men started fist-fighting there, and they ran out of the alley and hit each other in the street. The neighbors, including children, came out and watched, everybody afraid but nobody moving to do anything. I saw the same thing near my store in Harlem, years later, a big crowd watching two men in the street, their breaths hanging in the air on a winter night, murdering each other with switch knives, but nobody moved to call a cop. I didn't either. Anyway, I was just a young kid but I still remember how the cops drove up in a police paddy wagon and broke up the fight by hitting everybody they could hit with big nightsticks. This was in the days before LaGuardia. Most of the fighters were knocked out cold, only one or two got away. Buster's father started to run back in his house but a cop ran after him and cracked him on his Homburg hat with a club, right on the front porch. Then the Negro men were lifted up by the cops, one at the arms and the other at the feet, and they heaved them in the paddy wagon. Buster's father hit the back of the wagon and fell, with his nose spouting very red blood, on top of three other men. I personally couldn't stand it, I was scared of the human race so I ran home, but I remember Buster watching without any expression in his eyes. I stole an extra fifteen cents from my mother's pocketbook and I ran back and asked Buster if he wanted to go to the movies. I would pay. He said yes. This was the first time he talked to me.

So we went more than once to the movies. But we never got to be friends. Maybe because it was a one-way proposition—from me to him. Which includes my invitations to go with me, my (poor mother's) movie money, Hershey chocolate bars, watermelon slices, even my best Nick Carter and Merriwell books that I spent hours picking up in the junk shops, and that he never gave me back. Once he let me go in his house to get a match so we could smoke some butts we found, but it smelled so heavy, so impossible, I died till. I got out of there. What I saw in the way of furniture I won't mention—the best was falling apart in pieces. Maybe we went to the movies all together five or six matinees that spring and in the summertime, but when the shows were over he usually walked home by himself.

"Why don't you wait for me, Buster?" I said. "We're both going in the same direction."

But he was walking ahead and didn't hear me. Anyway he didn't answer.

One day when I wasn't expecting it he hit me in the teeth. I felt like crying but not because of the pain. I spit blood and said, "What did you hit me for? What did I do to you?"

"Because you a Jew bastard. Take your Jew movies and your Jew candy and shove them up your Jew ass."

And he ran away.

I thought to myself how was I to know he didn't like the movies. When I was a man I thought, you can't force it.

Years later, in the prime of my life, I met Mrs. Ornita Harris. She was standing by herself under an open umbrella at the bus stop, crosstown 110th, and I picked up her green glove that she had dropped on the wet sidewalk. It was in the end of November. Before I could ask her was it hers, she grabbed the glove out of my hand, closed her umbrella, and stepped in the bus. I got on right after her.

I was annoyed so I said, "If you'll pardon me, Miss, there's no law that you have to say thanks, but at least don't make a criminal out of me."

"Well, I'm sorry," she said, "but I don't like white men trying to do me favors."

I tipped my hat and that was that. In ten minutes I got off the bus but she was already gone.

Who expected to see her again but I did. She came into my store about a week later for a bottle of scotch.

"I would offer you a discount," I told her, "but I know you don't like a certain kind of a favor and I'm not looking for a slap in the face."

Then she recognized me and got a little embarrassed.

"I'm sorry I misunderstood you that day."

"So mistakes happen."

The result was she took the discount. I gave her a dollar off.

She used to come in about every two weeks for a fifth of Haig and Haig. Sometimes I waited on her, sometimes my helpers, Jimmy or Mason, also colored, but I said to give the discount. They both looked at me but I had nothing to be ashamed. In the spring when she came in we used to talk once in a while. She was a slim woman, dark but not the most dark, about thirty years I would say, also well built, with a combination nice legs and a good-size bosom that I like. Her face was pretty, with big eyes and high cheek bones, but lips a little thick and nose a little broad. Sometimes she didn't feel like talking, she paid for the bottle, less discount, and walked out. Her eyes were tired and she didn't look to me like a happy woman.

I found out her husband was once a window cleaner on the big buildings, but one day his safety belt broke and he fell fifteen stories. After the funeral she got a job as a manicurist in a Times Square barber shop. I told her I was a bachelor and lived with my mother in a small three-room apartment on West Eighty-third near Broadway. My mother had cancer, and Ornita said she was very sorry.

One night in July we went out together. How that happened I'm still not so sure. I guess I asked her and she didn't say no. Where do you go out with a Negro woman? We went to the Village. We had a good dinner and walked in Washington Square Park. It was a hot night. Nobody was surprised when they saw us, nobody looked at us like we were against the law. If they looked maybe they saw my new lightweight suit that I bought yesterday and my shiny bald spot when we walked under a lamp, also how pretty she was for a man of my type. We went in a movie on West Eighth Street. I didn't want to go in but she said she had heard about the picture. We went in like strangers and we came out like strangers. I wondered what was in her mind and I thought to myself, whatever is in there it's not a certain white man that I know. All night long we went together like we were chained. After the movie she wouldn't let me take her back to Harlem. When I put her in a taxi she asked me, "Why did we bother?"

For the steak, I wanted to say. Instead I said, "You're worth the bother."

"Thanks anyway."

Kiddo, I thought to myself after the taxi left, you just found out what's what, now the best thing is forget her.

It's easy to say. In August we went out the second time. That was the night she wore a purple dress and I thought to myself, my God, what colors. Who paints that picture paints a masterpiece. Everybody looked at us but I had pleasure. That night when she took off her dress it was in a furnished room I had the sense to rent a few days before. With my sick mother, I couldn't ask her to come to my apartment, and she didn't want me to go home with her where she lived with her brother's family on West 115th near Lenox Avenue. Under her purple dress she wore a black slip, and when she took that off she had white underwear. When she took off the white underwear she was black again. But I know where the next white was, if you want to call it white. And that was the night I think I fell in love with her, the first time in my life though I have liked one or two nice girls I used to go with when I was a boy. It was a serious proposition. I'm the kind of a man when I think of love I'm thinking of marriage. I guess that's why I am a bachelor.

That same week I had a holdup in my place, two big men—both black—with revolvers. One got excited when I rang open the cash register so he could take the money and he hit me over the ear with his gun. I stayed in the hospital a couple of weeks. Otherwise I was insured. Ornita came to see me. She sat on a chair without talking much. Finally I saw she was uncomfortable so I suggested she ought to go home.

"I'm sorry it happened," she said.

"Don't talk like it's your fault."

When I got out of the hospital my mother was dead. She was a wonderful person. My father died when I was thirteen and all by herself she kept the family alive and together. I sat shive for a week and remembered how she sold paper bags on her pushcart. I remembered her life and what she tried to teach me. Nathan, she said, if you ever forget you are a Jew a goy will remind you. Mama, I said, rest in peace on this subject. But if I do something you don't like, remember, on earth it's harder than where you are. Then when my week of mourning was finished, one night I said, "Ornita, let's get married.

We're both honest people and if you love me like I love you it won't be such a bad time. If you don't like New York I'll sell out here and we'll move someplace else. Maybe to San Francisco where nobody knows us. I was there for a week in the Second War and I saw white and colored living together."

"Nat," she answered me, "I like you but I'd be afraid. My husband woulda killed me."

"Your husband is dead."

"Not in my memory."

"In that case I'll wait."

"Do you know what it'd be like—I mean the life we could expect?"

"Ornita," I said, "I'm the kind of a man, if he picks his own way of life he's satisfied."

"What about children? Were you looking forward to half-Jewish polka dots?"

"I was looking forward to children."

"I can't," she said.

Can't is can't. I saw she was afraid and the best thing was not to push. Sometimes when we met she was so nervous that whatever we did she couldn't enjoy it. At the same time I still thought I had a chance. We were together more and more. I got rid of my furnished room and she came to my apartment—I gave away Mama's bed and bought a new one. She stayed with me all day on Sundays. When she wasn't so nervous she was affectionate, and if I know what love is, I had it. We went out a couple of times a week, the same way—usually I met her in Times Square and sent her home in a taxi, but I talked more about marriage and she talked less against it. One night she told me she was still trying to convince herself but she was almost convinced. I took an inventory of my liquor stock so I could put the store up for sale.

Ornita knew what I was doing. One day she quit her job, the next day she took it back. She also went away a week to visit her sister in Philadelphia for a little rest. She came back tired but said maybe. Maybe is maybe so I'll wait. The way she said it it was closer to yes. That was the winter two years ago. When she was in Philadelphia I called up a friend of mine from the Army, now CPA, and told him I would appreciate an invitation for an evening. He knew why. His wife said yes right away. When Ornita came back we went there. The wife made a fine dinner. It wasn't a bad time and they told us to come again. Ornita had a few drinks. She looked relaxed, wonderful. Later, because of a twenty-four hour taxi strike I had to take her home on the subway. When we got to the 116th Street station she told me to stay on the train, and she would walk the couple of blocks to her house. I didn't like a woman walking alone on the streets at that time of the night. She said she never had any trouble but I insisted nothing doing. I said I would walk to her stoop with her and when she went upstairs I would go back to the subway.

On the way there, on 115th in the middle of the block before Lenox, we were stopped by three men—maybe they were boys. One had a black hat with a half-inch brim, one a green cloth hat, and the third wore a black leather cap. The green hat was wearing a short coat and the other two had long ones. It was under a street light but the leather cap snapped a six-inch switchblade open in the light.

"What you doin' with this white son of a bitch?" he said to Ornita.

"I'm minding my own business," she answered him, "and I wish you would too."

"Boys," I said, "we're all brothers. I'm a reliable merchant in the neighborhood. This young lady is my dear friend. We don't want any trouble. Please let us pass."

"You talk like a Jew landlord," said the green hat. "Fifty a week for a single room."

"No charge fo' the rats," said the half-inch brim.

"Believe me, I'm no landlord. My store is 'Nathan's Liquors' between Hundred Tenth and Eleventh. I also have two colored clerks, Mason and Jimmy, and they will tell you I pay good wages as well as I give discounts to certain customers."

"Shut your mouth, Jewboy," said the leather cap, and he moved the knife back and forth in front of my coat button. "No more black pussy for you."

"Speak with respect about this lady, please."

I got slapped on my mouth.

"That ain't no lady," said the long face in the half-inch brim, "that's black pussy. She deserve to have evvy bit of her hair shave off. How you like to have evvy bit of your hair shave off, black pussy?"

"Please leave me and this gentleman alone or I'm gonna scream long and loud. That's my house three doors down."

They slapped her. I never heard such a scream. Like her husband was falling fifteen stories.

I hit the one that slapped her and the next I knew I was lying in the gutter with a pain in my head. I thought, goodbye, Nat, they'll stab me for sure, but all they did was take my wallet and run in three different directions.

Ornita walked back with me to the subway and she wouldn't let me go home with her again.

"Just get home safely."

She looked terrible. Her face was gray and I still remembered her scream. It was a terrible winter night, very cold February, and it took me an hour and ten minutes to get home. I felt bad for leaving her but what could I do?

We had a date downtown the next night but she didn't show up, the first time.

In the morning I called her in her place of business.

"For God's sake, Ornita, if we got married and moved away we wouldn't have that kind of trouble that we had. We wouldn't come in that neighborhood any more."

"Yes, we would. I have family there and don't want to move anyplace else. The truth of it is I can't marry you, Nat. I got troubles enough of my own."

"I coulda sworn you love me."

"Maybe I do but I can't marry you."

"For God's sake, why?"

"I got enough trouble of my own."

I went that night in a cab to her brother's house to see her. He was a quiet man with a thin mustache. "She gone," he said, "left for a long visit to some close relatives in the South. She said to tell you she appreciate your intentions but didn't think it will work out."

"Thank you kindly," I said.

Don't ask me how I got home.

Once on Eighth Avenue, a couple of blocks from my store, I saw a blind man with a white cane tapping on the sidewalk. I figured we were going in the same direction so I took his arm.

"I can tell you're white," he said.

A heavy colored woman with a full shopping bag rushed after us.

"Never mind," she said, "I know where he live."

She pushed me with her shoulder and I hurt my leg on the fire hydrant. That's how it is. I give my heart and they kick me in my teeth.

"Charity Sweetness—you hear me?—come out of that goddamn toilet!"

Questions

1. Although black is his favorite color, what has been Nathan Lime's experience with Negroes? Can you list four experiences?

2. The love scene and the hoodlum scene are quite explicit. How do you distinguish between explicitness and obscenity?

3. What prejudice is evident on the part of the Negro hoodlums?

4. What does the author accomplish by opening and closing the story in much the same way?

5. Whose side is the author on concerning the marriage? What are your own thoughts on the subject?

6. What are the possibilities that Nathan will achieve oneness with Negroes? Will the poem "The Slave," page 100, aid you?

7. Does Malamud answer question 5 by the title of the collection of short stories that includes "Black Is My Favorite Color"? He calls the collection *Idiots First.*

The Chrysanthemums*

JOHN STEINBECK

The high gray-flannel fog of winter closed the Salinas Valley from the sky and from all the rest of the world. On every side it sat like a lid on the mountains and made of the great valley a closed pot. On the broad, level land floor the gang plows bit deep and left the black earth shining like a metal where the shares had cut. On the foothill ranches across the Salinas River the yellow stubble fields seemed to be bathed in pale cold sunshine; but there was no sunshine in the valley now in December. The thick willow scrub along the river flamed with sharp and positive yellow leaves.

It was a time of quiet and of waiting. The air was cold and tender. A light wind blew up from the southwest so that the farmers were mildly hopeful of a good rain before long; but fog and rain do not go together.

Across the river, on Henry Allen's foothill ranch there was little work to be done, for the hay was cut and stored and the orchards were plowed up to receive the rain deeply when it should come. The cattle on the higher slopes were becoming shaggy and rough-coated.

Elisa Allen, working in her flower garden, looked down across the yard and saw Henry, her husband, talking to two men in business suits. The three of them stood by the tractor shed, each man with one foot on the side of the Little Fordson. They smoked cigarettes and studied the machine as they talked.

Elisa watched them for a moment and then went back to her work. She was thirty-five. Her face was lean and strong and her eyes were as clear as water. Her figure looked blocked and heavy in her gardening costume, a man's black hat pulled low down over her eyes, clodhopper shoes, a figured print dress almost completely covered by a big corduroy apron with four big pockets to hold the snips, the trowel and scratcher, the seeds and the knife she worked with. She wore heavy leather gloves to protect her hands while she worked.

She was cutting down the old year's chrysanthemum stalks with a pair of short and powerful scissors. She looked down toward the men by the tractor shed now and then. Her face was eager and mature and handsome; even her work with the scissors was overeager, overpowerful. The chrysanthemum stems seemed too small and easy for her energy.

She brushed a cloud of hair out of her eyes with the back of her glove, and left a smudge of earth on her cheek in doing it. Behind her stood the neat white farmhouse with red geraniums close-banked round it as high as the windows. It was a hard-swept looking little house, with hard-polished windows, and a clean mat on the front steps.

Elisa cast another glance toward the tractor shed. The stranger men were getting into their Ford coupe. She took off a glove and put her strong fingers down into the forest of new green chrysanthemum sprouts that were growing round the old roots. She spread the leaves and looked down among the close-growing stems. No aphids were there, no sow bugs nor snails nor cutworms. Her terrier fingers destroyed such pests before they could get started.

Elisa started at the sound of her husband's voice. He had come near quietly and he leaned over the wire fence that protected her flower garden from cattle and dogs and chickens.

"At it again," he said. "You've got a strong new crop coming."

Elisa straightened her back and pulled on the gardening glove again. "Yes. They'll be strong this coming year." In her tone and on her face there was a little smugness.

"You've got a gift with things," Henry observed. "Some of those yellow chrysanthemums you had last year were ten inches across. I wish you'd work out in the orchard and raise some apples that big."

Her eyes sharpened. "Maybe I could do it too. I've a gift with things all right. My mother had it. She could stick anything in the ground and make it grow. She said it was having planters' hands that knew how to do it."

"Well, it sure works with flowers," he said.

"Henry, who were those men you were talking to?"

"Why, sure, that's what I came to tell you. They were from the Western Meat Company. I sold those thirty head of three-year-old steers. Got nearly my own price too."

"Good," she said. "Good for you."

"And I thought," he continued, "I thought how it's Saturday afternoon, and we might go into Salinas for dinner at a restaurant and then to a picture show—to celebrate, you see."

"Good," she repeated. "Oh, yes. That will be good."

Henry put on his joking tone. "There's fights tonight. How'd you like to go to the fights?"

"Oh, no," she said breathlessly. "No, I wouldn't like fights."

"Just fooling, Elisa. We'll go to a movie. Let's see. It's two now. I'm going to take Scotty and bring down those steers from the hill. It'll take us maybe two hours. We'll go in town about five and have dinner at the Cominos Hotel. Like that?"

"Of course I'll like it. It's good to eat away from home."

"All right then. I'll go get up a couple of horses."

She said, "I'll have plenty of time to transplant some of these sets, I guess."

She heard her husband calling Scotty down by the barn. And a little later she saw the two men ride up the pale-yellow hillside in search of the steers.

There was a little square sandy bed kept for rooting the chrysanthemums. With her trowel she turned the soil over and over and smoothed it and patted it firm. Then she dug ten parallel trenches to receive the sets. Back at the chrysanthemum bed she pulled out the little crisp shoots, trimmed off the leaves of each one with her scissors, and laid it on a small orderly pile.

A squeak of wheels and plod of hoofs came from the road. Elisa looked up. The country road ran along the dense bank of willows and cottonwoods that bordered the river, and up this road came a curious vehicle, curiously drawn. It was an old spring-wagon, with a round canvas top on it like the cover of a prairie schooner. It was drawn by an old bay horse and a little gray-and-white burro. A big stubble-bearded man sat between the cover flaps and drove the crawling team. Underneath the wagon, between the hind wheels, a lean and rangy mongrel dog walked sedately. Words were painted on the canvas in clumsy crooked letters. "Pots, pans, knives, sisors, lawn mores, Fixed." Two rows of articles, and the triumphantly definitive "Fixed" below. The black paint had run down in little sharp points beneath each letter.

Elisa, squatting on the ground, watched to see the crazy loose-jointed wagon pass by. But it didn't pass. It turned into the farm road in front of her house, crooked old wheels skirling and squeaking. The rangy dog darted from beneath the wheels and ran ahead. Instantly the two ranch shepherds flew out at him. Then all three stopped, and with stiff and quivering tails, with taut straight legs, with ambassadorial dignity, they slowly circled, sniffing daintily. The caravan pulled up to Elisa's wire fence and stopped. Now the newcomer dog, feeling outnumbered, lowered his tail and retired under the wagon with raised hackles and bared teeth.

The man on the wagon seat called out, "That's a bad dog in a fight when he gets started."

Elisa laughed. "I see he is. How soon does he generally get started?"

The man caught up her laughter and echoed it heartily. "Sometimes not for weeks and weeks," he said. He climbed stiffly down over the wheel. The horse and the donkey drooped like unwatered flowers.

Elisa saw that he was a very big man. Although his hair and beard were graying, he did not look old. His worn black suit was wrinkled and spotted with grease. The laughter had disappeared from his face and eyes the moment his laughing voice ceased. His eyes were dark and they were full of the brooding that gets in the eyes of teamsters and of sailors. The calloused hands he rested on the fence were cracked, and every crack was a black line. He took off his battered hat.

"I'm off my general road, ma'am," he said. "Does this dirt road cut over across the river to the Los Angeles highway?"

Elisa stood up and shoved the thick scissors in her apron pocket. "Well, yes, it does, but it winds around and then fords the river. I don't think your team could pull through the sand."

He replied with some asperity, "It might surprise you what them beasts can pull through."

"When they get started?" she asked.

He smiled for a second. "Yes. When they get started."

"Well," said Elisa, "I think you'll save time if you go back to the Salinas road and pick up the highway there."

He drew a big finger down the chicken wire and made it sing. "I ain't in any hurry, ma'am. I go from Seattle to San Diego and back every year. Takes all my time. About six months each way. I aim to follow nice weather."

Elisa took off her gloves and stuffed them in the apron pocket with the scissors. She touched the under edge of her man's hat, searching for fugitive hairs. "That sounds like a nice kind of a way to live," she said.

He leaned confidentially over the fence. "Maybe you noticed the writing on my wagon. I mend pots and sharpen knives and scissors. You got any of them things to do?"

"Oh, no," she said quickly. "Nothing like that." Her eyes hardened with resistance.

"Scissors is the worst thing," he explained. "Most people just ruin scissors trying to sharpen 'em, but I know how. I got a special tool. It's a little bobbit kind of thing and patented. But it sure does the trick."

"No. My scissors are all sharp."

"All right then. Take a pot," he continued earnestly, "a bent pot or a pot with a hole. I can make it like new so you don't have to buy no new ones. That's a saving for you."

"No," she said shortly. "I tell you I have nothing like that for you to do."

His face fell to an exaggerated sadness. His voice took on a whining undertone. "I ain't had a thing to do today. Maybe I won't have no supper tonight. You see I'm off my regular road. I know folks on the highway clear from Seattle to San Diego. They save their things for me to sharpen up because they know I do it so good and save them money."

"I'm sorry," Elisa said irritably. "I haven't anything for you to do."

His eyes left her face and fell to searching the ground. They roamed about until they came to the chrysanthemum bed where she had been working. "What's them plants, ma'am?"

The irritation and resistance melted from Elisa's face. "Oh, those are chrysanthemums, giant whites and yellows. I raise them every year, bigger than anybody around here."

"Kind of a long-stemmed flower? Looks like a quick puff of colored smoke?" he asked.

"That's it. What a nice way to describe them."

"They smell kind of nasty till you get used to them," he said.

"It's a good bitter smell," she retorted, "not nasty at all."

He changed his tone quickly. "I like the smell myself."

"I had ten-inch blooms this year," she said.

The man leaned farther over the fence. "Look, I know a lady down the road a piece has got the nicest garden you ever seen. Got nearly every kind of flower but no chrysanthemums. Last time I was mending a copper-bottom wash tub for her (that's a hard job but I do it good), she said to me, 'If you ever run acrost some nice chrysanthemums I wish you'd try to get me a few seeds.' That's what she told me."

Elisa's eyes grew alert and eager. "She couldn't have known much about chrysanthemums. You *can* raise them from seed, but it's much easier to root the little sprouts you see there."

"Oh," he said. "I s'pose I can't take none to her then."

"Why yes, you can," Elisa cried. "I can put some in damp sand, and you can carry them right along with you. They'll take root in the pot if you keep them damp. And then she can transplant them."

"She'd sure like to have some, ma'am. You say they're nice ones?"

"Beautiful," she said. "Oh, beautiful." Her eyes shone. She tore off the battered hat and shook out her dark pretty hair. "I'll put them in a flowerpot, and you can take them right with you. Come into the yard."

While the man came through the picket gate Elisa ran excitedly along the geranium-bordered path to the back of the house. And she returned carrying a big red flowerpot. The gloves were forgotten now. She kneeled on the ground by the starting bed and dug up the sandy soil with her fingers and scooped it into the bright new flowerpot. Then she picked up the little pile of shoots she had prepared. With her strong fingers she pressed them into the sand and tamped round them with her knuckles. The man stood over her. "I'll tell you what to do," she said. "You remember so you can tell the lady."

"Yes, I'll try to remember."

"Well, look. These will take root in about a month. Then she must set them out, about a foot apart in good rich earth like this, see?" She lifted a handful of dark soil for him to look at. "They'll grow fast and tall. Now remember this. In July tell her to cut them down, about eight inches from the ground."

"Before they bloom?" he asked.

"Yes, before they bloom." Her face was tight with eagerness. "They'll grow right up again. About the last of September the buds will start."

She stopped and seemed perplexed. "It's the budding that takes the most care," she said hesitantly. "I don't know how to tell you." She looked deep into his eyes searchingly. Her mouth opened a little, and she seemed to be listening. "I'll try to tell you," she said. "Did you ever hear of planting hands?"

"Can't say I have, ma'am."

"Well, I can only tell you what it feels like. It's when you're picking off the buds you don't want. Everything goes right down into your fingertips. You watch your fingers work. They do it themselves. You can feel how it is. They pick and pick the buds. They never make a mistake. They're with the plant. Do you see? Your fingers and the plant. You can feel that, right up your arm. They know. They never made a mistake. You can feel it. When yor're like that you can't do anything wrong. Do you see that? Can you understand that?"

She was kneeling on the ground looking up at him. Her breast swelled passionately.

The man's eyes narrowed. He looked away self-consciously. "Maybe I know," he said. "Sometimes in the night in the wagon there——"

Elisa's voice grew husky. She broke in on him. "I've never lived as you do, but I know what you mean. When the night is dark—the stars are sharp-pointed, and there's quiet. Why, you rise up and up!"

Kneeling there, her hand went out toward his legs in the greasy black trousers. Her hesitant fingers almost touched the cloth. Then her hand dropped to the ground.

He said, "It's nice, just like you say. Only when you don't have no dinner it ain't."

She stood up then, very straight, and her face was ashamed. She held the flowerpot out to him and placed it gently in his arms. "Here. Put it in your wagon, on the seat, where you can watch it. Maybe I can find something for you to do."

At the back of the house she dug in the can pile and found two old and battered aluminum saucepans. She carried them back and gave them to him, "Here, maybe you can fix these."

His manner changed. He became professional. "Good as new I can fix them." At the back of his wagon he set a little anvil, and out of an oily toolbox dug a small machine hammer. Elisa came through the gate to watch him while he pounded out the dents in the kettles. His mouth grew sure and knowing. At a difficult part of the work he sucked his underlip.

"You sleep right in the wagon?" Elisa asked.

"Right in the wagon, ma'am. Rain or shine I'm dry as a cow in there."

"It must be nice," she said. "It must be very nice. I wish women could do such things."

"It ain't the right kind of a life for a woman."

Her upper lip raised a little, showing her teeth. "How do you know? How can you tell?" she said.

"I don't know, ma'am," he protested. "Of course I don't know. Now here's you kettles, done. You don't have to buy no new ones."

"How much?"

"Oh, fifty cents'll do. I keep my prices down and my work good. That's why I have all them satisfied customers up and down the highway."

Elisa brought him a fifty-cent piece from the house and dropped it in his hand. "You might be surprised to have a rival sometime. I can sharpen scissors too. And I can beat the dents out of little pots. I could show you what a woman might do."

He put his hammer back in the oily box and shoved the little anvil out of sight. "It would be a lonely life for a woman, ma'am, and a scary life, too, with animals creeping under the wagon all night." He climbed over the singletree, steadying himself with a hand on the burro's white rump. He settled himself in the seat, picked up the lines. "Thank you kindly, ma'am," he said. "I'll do like you told me; I'll go back and catch the Salinas road."

"Mind," she called, "if you're long in getting there, keep the sand damp."

"Sand, ma'am?—Sand? Oh, sure. You mean around the chrysanthemums. Sure I will." He clucked his tongue. The beasts leaned luxuriously into their collars. The mongrel dog took his place between the back wheels. The wagon turned and crawled out the entrance road and back the way it had come, along the river.

Elisa stood in front of her wire fence watching the slow progress of the caravan. Her shoulders were straight, her head thrown back, her eyes half-closed, so that the scene came vaguely into them. Her lips moved silently, forming the words "Good-by—good-by." Then she whispered, "That's a bright direction. There's a glowing there." The sound of her whisper startled her. She shook herself free and looked about to see whether anyone had been listening. Only the dogs had heard. They lifted their heads toward her from their sleeping in the dust, and then stretched out their chins and settled asleep again. Elisa turned and ran hurriedly into the house.

In the kitchen she reached behind the stove and felt the water tank. It was full of hot water from the noonday cooking. In the bathroom she tore off her soiled clothes and flung them into the corner. And then she scrubbed herself with a little block of pumice, legs and thighs, loins and chest and arms, until her skin was scratched and red. When she had dried herself she stood in front of a mirror in her bedroom and looked at her body. She tightened her stomach and threw out her chest. She turned and looked over her shoulder at her back.

After a while she began to dress slowly. She put on her newest underclothing and her nicest stockings and the dress which was the symbol of her prettiness. She worked carefully on her hair, penciled her eyebrows, and rouged her lips.

Before she was finished she heard the little thunder of hoofs and the shouts of Henry and his helper as they drove the red steers into the corral. She heard the gate bang shut and set herself for Henry's arrival.

His step sounded on the porch. He entered the house calling, "Elisa, where are you?"

"In my room, dressing. I'm not ready. There's hot water for your bath. Hurry up. It's getting late."

When she heard him splashing in the tub, Elisa laid his dark suit on the bed, and shirt and socks and tie beside it. She stood his polished shoes on the floor beside the bed. Then she went to the porch and sat primly and stiffly down. She looked toward the river road where the willow-lane was still yellow with frosted leaves so that under the high gray fog they seemed a thin band of sunshine. This was the only color in the gray afternoon. She sat unmoving for a long time.

Henry came banging out of the door, shoving his tie inside his vest as he came. Elisa stiffened and her face grew tight. Henry stopped short and looked at her. "Why—why, Elisa. You look so nice!"

"Nice? You think I look nice? What do you mean by 'nice'?"

Henry blundered on. "I don't know. I mean you look different, strong and happy."

"I am strong? Yes, strong. What do you mean 'strong'?"

He looked bewildered. "You're playing some kind of a game," he said helplessly. "It's a kind of play. You look strong enough to break a calf over your knees, happy enough to eat it like a watermelon."

For a second she lost her rigidity. "Henry! Don't talk like that. You didn't know what you said." She grew complete again. "I am strong," she boasted. "I never knew before how strong."

Henry looked down toward the tractor shed, and when he brought his eyes back to her, they were his own again. "I'll get out the car. You can put on your coat while I'm starting."

Elisa went into the house. She heard him drive to the gate and idle down his motor, and then she took a long time to put on her hat. She pulled it here and pressed it there. When Henry turned the motor off she slipped into her coat and went out.

The little roadster bounced along on the dirt road by the river, raising the birds and driving the rabbits into the brush. Two cranes flapped heavily over the willow-line and dropped into the river-bed.

Far ahead on the road Elisa saw a dark speck in the dust. She suddenly felt empty. She did not hear Henry's talk. She tried not to look; she did not want to see the little heap of sand and green shoots, but she could not help herself. The chrysanthemums lay in the road close to the wagon tracks. But not the pot; he had kept that. As the car passed them she remembered the good bitter smell, and a little shudder went through her. She felt ashamed of her strong planter's hands, that were no use, lying palms up in her lap.

The roadster turned a bend and she saw the caravan ahead. She swung full round toward her husband so that she could not see the little covered wagon and the mismatched team as the car passed.

In a moment they had left behind them the man who had not known or needed to know what she said, the bargainer. She did not look back.

To Henry she said loudly, to be heard above the motor. "It will be good, tonight, a good dinner."

"Now you're changed again," Henry complained. He took one hand from the wheel and patted her knee. "I ought to take you in to dinner oftener. It would be good for both of us. We get so heavy out on the ranch."

"Henry," she asked, "could we have wine at dinner?"

"Sure. Say! That will be fine."

She was silent for a while; then she said, "Henry, at those prize fights do the men hurt each other very much?"

"Sometimes a little, not often. Why?"

"Well, I've read how they break noses, and blood runs down their chests. I've read how the fighting gloves get heavy and soggy with blood."

He looked round at her. "What's the matter, Elisa? I didn't know you read things like that." He brought the car to a stop, then turned to the right over the Salinas River bridge.

"Do any women ever go to the fights?" she asked.

"Oh, sure, some. What's the matter, Elisa? Do you want to go? I don't think you'd like it, but I'll take you if you really want to go."

She relaxed limply in the seat. "Oh, no. I don't want to go. I'm sure I don't." Her face was turned away from him "It will be enough if we can have wine. It will be plenty." She turned up her coat collar so he could not see that she was crying weakly—like an old woman.

Questions

1. How did the peddler shape Elisa? Was he justified in what he did?

2. What clues to Elisa's feeling of incompleteness does Steinbeck give us? Elisa is almost immediately attracted to the peddler. Can her reaching toward the peddler be interpreted entirely as a sexual allusion?

3. She is at peace when the peddler leaves. How does her husband describe her "look"? Would Norman in "Chaos, Disorder and the Late Show" be a good husband for Elisa?

4. Relate the Gibran poem "On Work" (p. 181) to Elisa. Relate it to the peddler.

5. Will Elisa find what she wants in the prizefight and wine?

The Day the Dam Broke*

JAMES THURBER

My memories of what my family and I went through during the 1913 flood
in Ohio I would gladly forget. And yet neither the hardships we endured nor
the turmoil and confusion we experienced can alter my feeling toward my
native state and city. I am having a fine time now and wish Columbus were
here, but if anyone ever wished a city was in hell it was during that frightful
and perilous afternoon in 1913 when the dam broke, or, to be more exact,
when everybody in town *thought* that the dam broke. We were both ennobled
and demoralized by the experience. Grandfather especially rose to magnificent
heights which can never lose their splendor for me, even though his reactions
to the flood were based upon a profound misconception; namely, that Nathan
Bedford Forrest's cavalry was the menace we were called upon to face. The
only possible means of escape for us was to flee the house, a step which
grandfather sternly forbade, brandishing his old army sabre in his hand. "Let
the sons— ————come!" he roared. Meanwhile hundreds of people were
streaming by our house in wild panic, screaming "Go east! Go east!" We
had to stun grandfather with the ironing board. Impeded as we were by the
inert form of the old gentleman—he was taller than six feet and weighed
almost a hundred and seventy pounds—we were passed, in the first half-mile,
by practically everybody else in the city. Had grandfather not come to, at
the corner of Parsons Avenue and Town Street, we would unquestionably
have been overtaken and engulfed by the roaring waters—that is, if there had
been any roaring waters. Later when the panic had died down and people had
gone rather sheepishly back to their homes and their offices, minimizing the
distances they had run and offering various reasons for running, city engineers
pointed out that even if the dam had broken, the water level would not
have risen more than two additional inches in the West Side. The West Side
was, at the time of the dam scare, under thirty feet of water—as, indeed,
were all Ohio river towns during the great spring floods of twenty years ago.
The East Side (where we lived and where all the running occurred) had
never been in any danger at all. Only a rise of some ninety-five feet could have
caused the flood waters to flow over High Street—the thoroughfare that
divided the east side of town from the west—and engulf the East Side.

The fact that we were all as safe as kittens under a cookstove did not,
however, assuage in the least the fine despair and the grotesque desperation
which seized upon the residents of the East Side when the cry spread like a
grass fire that the dam had given way. Some of the most dignified, staid,

cynical, and clear-thinking men in town abandoned their wives, stenographers, homes, and offices and ran east. There are few alarms in the world more terrifying than "The dam has broken!" There are few persons capable of stopping to reason when that clarion cry strikes upon their ears, even persons who live in towns no nearer than five hundred miles to a dam.

The Columbus, Ohio, broken-dam rumor began, as I recall it, about noon of March 12, 1913. High Street, the main canyon of trade, was loud with the placid hum of business and the buzzing of placid businessmen arguing, computing, wheedling, offering, refusing, compromising. Darius Conningway, one of the foremost corporation lawyers in the Middle-West, was telling the Public Utilities Commission in the language of Julius Caesar that they might as well try to move the Northern star as to move him. Other men were making their little boasts and their little gestures. Suddenly somebody began to run. It may be that he had simply remembered, all of a moment, an engagement to meet his wife, for which he was now frightfully late. Whatever it was, he ran east on Broad Street (probably toward the Maramor Restaurant, a favorite place for a man to meet his wife). Somebody else began to run, perhaps a newsboy in high spirits. Another man, a portly gentleman of affairs, broke into a trot. Inside of ten minutes, everybody on High Street, from the Union Depot to the Courthouse was running. A loud mumble gradually crystallized into the dread word "dam." "The dam has broke!" The fear was put into words by a little old lady in an electric, or by a traffic cop, or by a small boy: nobody knows who, nor does it now really matter. Two thousand people were abruptly in full flight. "Go east!" was the cry that arose—east away from the river, east to safety. "Go east! Go east! Go east!"

Black streams of people flowed eastward down all the streets leading in that direction; these streams, whose headwaters were in the drygoods stores, office buildings, harness shops, movie theatres, were fed by trickles of housewives, children, cripples, servants, dogs, and cats slipping out of the houses past which the main stream flowed, shouting and screaming. People ran out leaving fires burning and food cooking and doors wide open. I remember, however, that my mother turned out all the fires and that she took with her a dozen eggs and two loaves of bread. It was her plan to make Memorial Hall, just two blocks away, and take refuge somewhere in the top of it, in one of the dusty rooms where war veterans met and where old battle flags and stage scenery were stored. But the seething throngs, shouting "Go east!," drew her along and the rest of us with her. When grandfather regained full consciousness, at Parsons Avenue, he turned upon the retreating mob like a vengeful prophet and exhorted the men to form ranks and stand off the Rebel dogs, but at length he, too, got the idea that the dam had broken and, roaring "Go east!" in his powerful voice, he caught up in one arm a small child and in the other a slight clerkish man of perhaps forty-two and we slowly began to gain on those ahead of us.

A scattering of firemen, policemen, and army officers in dress uniforms —there had been a review at Fort Hayes, in the northern part of town— added color to the surging billows of people. "Go east!" cried a little child in a piping voice, as she ran past a porch on which drowsed a lieutenant-colonel of infantry. Used to quick decisions, trained to immediate obedience, the officer bounded off the porch and running at full tilt, soon passed the child, bawling "Go east!" The two of them emptied rapidly the houses of the little street they were on. "What is it? What is it?" demanded a fat, waddling man who intercepted the colonel. The officer dropped behind and asked the little child what it was. "The dam has broke!" gasped the girl. "The dam has broke!" roared the colonel. "Go east! Go east! Go east!" He was soon leading, with the exhausted child in his arms, a fleeing company of three hundred persons who had gathered around him from living-rooms, shops, garages, backyards, and basements.

Nobody has ever been able to compute with any exactness how many people took part in the great rout of 1913, for the panic, which extended from the Winslow Bottling Works in the south end to Clintonville, six miles north, ended as abruptly as it began and the bobtail and ragtag and velvet-gowned groups of refugees melted away and slunk home, leaving the streets peaceful and deserted. The shouting, weeping, tangled evacuation of the city lasted not more than two hours in all. Some few people got as far east as Reynoldsburg, twelve miles away; fifty or more reached the Country Club, eight miles away; most of the others gave up, exhausted, or climbed trees in Franklin Park, four miles out. Order was restored and fear dispelled finally by means of militiamen riding about in motor lorries bawling through megaphones: "The dam has *not* broken!" At first this tended only to add to the confusion and increase the panic, for many stampeders thought the soldiers were bellowing "The dam has now broken!," thus setting an official seal of authentication on the calamity.

All the time, the sun shone quietly and there was nowhere any sign of oncoming waters. A visitor in an airplane, looking down on the straggling, agitated masses of people below, would have been hard put to it to divine a reason for the phenomenon. It must have inspired, in such an observer, a peculiar kind of terror, like the sight of the *Marie Celeste,* abandoned at sea, its galley fires peacefully burning, its tranquil decks bright in the sunlight.

An aunt of mine, Aunt Edith Taylor, was in a movie theatre on High Street when, over and above the sound of the piano in the pit (a W. S. Hart picture was being shown), there rose the steadily increasing tromp of running feet. Persistent shouts rose above the tromping. An elderly man, sitting near my aunt, mumbled something, got out of his seat, and went up the aisle at a dogtrot. This started everybody. In an instant the audience was jamming the aisles. "Fire!" shouted a woman who always expected to be burned up in a theatre; but now the shouts outside were louder and coherent. "The dam has broke!" cried somebody. "Go east!" screamed a small woman in front of my aunt. And east they went, pushing and shoving and clawing, knocking women and children down, emerging finally into the street, torn and sprawling. Inside the theatre, Bill Hart was calmly calling some desperado's bluff and the brave girl at the piano played "Row! Row! Row!" loudly and then "In My Harem." Outside, men were streaming across the Statehouse yard, others were climbing trees, a woman managed to get up onto the "These Are My Jewels" statue, whose bronze figures of Sherman, Stanton, Grant, and Sheridan watched with cold unconcern the going to pieces of the capital city.

"I ran south to State Street, east on State to Third, south on Third to Town, and out east on Town," my Aunt Edith has written me. "A tall spare woman with grim eyes and a determined chin ran past me down the middle of the street. I was still uncertain as to what was the matter, in spite of all the shouting. I drew up alongside the woman with some effort, for although she was in her late fifties, she had a beautiful easy running form and seemed to be in excellent condition. 'What is it?' I puffed. She gave me a quick glance and then looked ahead again, stepping up her pace a trifle. 'Don't ask me, ask God!' she said.

"When I reached Grant Avenue, I was so spent that Dr. H. R. Mallory —you remember Dr. Mallory, the man with the white beard who looks like Robert Browning?—well, Dr. Mallory, whom I had drawn away from at the corner of Fifth and Town, passed me. 'It's got us!' he shouted, and I felt sure that whatever it was *did* have us, for you know what conviction Dr. Mallory's statements always carried. I didn't know at the time what he meant, but I found out later. There was a boy behind him on rollerskates, and Dr. Mallory mistook the swishing of the skates for the sound of rushing water. He eventually reached the Columbus School for Girls, at the corner of Parsons Avenue and Town Street, where he collapsed, expecting the cold frothing waters of the Scioto to sweep him into oblivion. The boy on the skates swirled past him and Dr. Mallory realized for the first time what he had been running from. Looking back up the street, he could see no signs of water, but nevertheless, after resting a few minutes, he jogged on east again. He caught up with me at Ohio Avenue, where we rested together. I should say that about seven hundred people passed us. A funny thing was that all of them were on foot. Nobody seemed to have had the courage to stop and start his car; but as I remember it, all cars had to be cranked in those days, which is probably the reason."

The next day, the city went about its business as if nothing had happened, but there was no joking. It was two years or more before you dared treat the breaking of the dam lightly. And even now, twenty years after, there are a few persons, like Dr. Mallory, who will shut up like a clam if you mention the Afternoon of the Great Run.

Questions

1. What shaped the people of Columbus to do what they did?

2. Why did Thurber not simply say people climbed up on the statue of Sheridan, Grant, Stanton, and Sherman to escape the flood waters? What did Thurber say? Why?

3. If you are familiar with a number of Thurber's writings and Norman Rockwell's paintings, what similarities and differences can you point out?

4. "The Day the Dam Broke" is obviously meant to delight the reader. Is Thurber describing Carl Milles' figure or Ivan Albright's? For which figure, Milles' or Albright's, is Thurber writing?

5. Is Thurber to be condemned that he did not write of serious mob action of the early 1900s?

Yonder See the Morning Blink*

A. E. HOUSMAN

Yonder see the morning blink:
    The sun is up, and up must I,
To wash and dress and eat and drink
And look at things and talk and think
    And work, and God knows why.

Oh often have I washed and dressed
    And what's to show for all my pain?
Let me lie abed and rest:
Ten thousand times I've done my best
    And all's to do again.

Questions

1. What has shaped us to get up and "wash and dress and eat and drink and look at things and talk and think and work"?

2. How would Housman probably describe the lives of most men? Are most people Nathan Lime in "Black Is My Favorite Color" or the mother in "All the Years of Her Life"?

---

3. What would be Housman's probable reaction to the person who writes the "stories for the slicks"?

4. If the "I" is the poet Housman, does Housman seem to anticipate his poems will shape anyone?

On Work*

KAHLIL GIBRAN

Then a ploughman said, Speak to us of Work.

And he answered, saying:

You work that you may keep pace with the earth and the soul of the earth.

For to be idle is to become a stranger unto the seasons, and to step out of life's procession, that marches in majesty and proud submission towards the infinite.

When you work you are a flute through whose heart the whispering of the hours turns to music.

Which of you would be a reed, dumb and silent, when all else sings together in unison?

Always you have been told that work is a curse and labour a misfortune.

But I say to you that when you work you fulfil a part of earth's furthest dream, assigned to you when that dream was born,

And in keeping yourself with labour you are in truth loving life,

And to love life through labour is to be intimate with life's inmost secret.

But if you in your pain call birth an affliction and the support of the flesh a curse written upon your brow, then I answer that naught but the sweat of your brow shall wash away that which is written.

You have been told also that life is darkness, and in your weariness you echo what was said by the weary.

And I say that life is indeed darkness save when there is urge,

And all urge is blind save when there is knowledge,

And all knowledge is vain save when there is work,

And all work is empty save when there is love;

And when you work with love you bind yourself to yourself, and to one another, and to God.

And what is it to work with love?

It is to weave the cloth with threads drawn from your heart, even as if your beloved were to wear that cloth.

It is to build a house with affection, even as if your beloved were to dwell in that house.

It is to sow seeds with tenderness and reap the harvest with joy, even as if your beloved were to eat the fruit.

It is to charge all things you fashion with a breath of your own spirit,

And to know that all the blessed dead are standing about you and watching.

Often have I heard you say, as if speaking in sleep, "He who works in marble, and finds the shape of his own soul in the stone, is nobler than he who ploughs the soil.

And he who seizes the rainbow to lay it on a cloth in the likeness of man, is more than he who makes the sandals for our feet."

But I say, not in sleep but in the overwakefulness of noontide, that the wind speaks not more sweetly to the giant oaks than to the least of all the blades of grass;

And he alone is great who turns the voice of the wind into a song made sweeter by his own loving.

Work is love made visible.

And if you cannot work with love but only with distaste, it is better that you should leave your work and sit at the gate of the temple and take alms of those who work with joy.

For if you bake bread with indifference, you bake a bitter bread that feeds but half man's hunger.

And if you grudge the crushing of the grapes, your grudge distils a poison in the wine.

And if you sing though as angels, and love not the singing, you muffle man's ears to the voices of the day and the voices of the night.

Questions

1. What do bitter bread, poisoned wine, and muffled song result from according to the poet Gibran?

2. Do most people believe that work is a curse and labor a misfortune?

3. Work minus love minus knowledge minus urge equals darkness in life. What does urge plus knowledge plus work plus love equal?

4. What does Gibran attempt to prove with the words "the wind speaks not more sweetly to the giant oaks than to the least of all the blades of grass"?

5. What fictional characters in this text have Gibran's philosophy on work?

6. If Gibran's philosophy is desirable, how is it to be communicated to and made a part of the lives of the children?

7. How does the world of advertising shape one in regard to work?

8. What might Gibran reply to someone who says, "Why should I look on work this way (Gibran's way) when no one else will?"

The Man with the Hoe*

EDWIN MARKHAM

God made man in His own image,
in the image of God made He him.
GENESIS.

Bowed by the weight of centuries he leans
Upon his hoe and gazes on the ground,
The emptiness of ages in his face,
And on his back the burden of the world.
Who made him dead to rapture and despair,
A thing that grieves not and that never hopes,
Stolid and stunned, a brother to the ox?
Who loosened and let down this brutal jaw?

Whose was the hand that slanted back this brow?
Whose breath blew out the light within this brain?

Is this the Thing the Lord God made and gave
To have dominion over sea and land;
To trace the stars and search the heavens for power;
To feel the passion of Eternity?
Is this the Dream He dreamed who shaped the suns
And pillared the blue firmament with light?
Down all the stretch of Hell to its last gulf
There is no shape more terrible than this—
More tongued with censure of the world's blind greed—
More filled with signs and portents for the soul—
More fraught with menace to the universe.

° Written after seeing Millet's world-famous painting.

What gulfs between him and the seraphim!
Slave of the wheel of labor, what to him
Are Plato and the swing of Pleiades?
What the long reaches of the peaks of song,
The rift of dawn, the reddening of the rose?
Through this dread shape the suffering ages look;
Time's tragedy is in that aching stoop;
Through this dread shape humanity betrayed,
Plundered, profaned and disinherited,
Cries protest to the Judges of the World,
A protest that is also prophecy.

O masters, lords and rulers in all lands,
Is this the handiwork you give to God,
This monstrous thing distorted and soul-quenched?
How will you ever straighten up this shape;
Touch it again with immortality;
Give back the upward looking and the light;
Rebuild in it the music and the dream;
Make right the immemorial infamies,
Perfidious wrongs, immedicable woes?

O masters, lords and rulers in all lands,
How will the Future reckon with this Man?
How answer his brute question in that hour
When whirlwinds of rebellion shake the world?
How will it be with kingdoms and with kings—
With those who shaped him to the thing he is—
When this dumb Terror shall reply to God,
After the silence of the centuries?

Questions

1. Who is the man with the hoe, and why does Markham call him a brother to the ox? Is Markham describing the young men in "Street Corner College" (p. 185)?

2. What question does Markham ask repeatedly through line 16?

3. Can you relate lines 22–26 to Davies' poem "Leisure" (p. 186)?

4. Do the pictures in the section entitled "Religion and Fate" parallel Markham's poem?

5. Who does Markham make responsible for the condition of the man with the hoe?

6. Who or what shaped those who shaped the man with the hoe?

Street Corner College*

KENNETH PATCHEN

Next year the grave grass will cover us.
We stand now, and laugh;
Watching the girls go by;
Betting on slow horses; drinking cheap gin.
We have nothing to do; nowhere to go; nobody.

Last year was a year ago; nothing more.
We weren't younger then; nor older now.

We manage to have the look that young men have;
We feel nothing behind our faces, one way or other.

We shall probably not be quite dead when we die.
We were never anything all the way; not even soldiers.

We are the insulted, brother, the desolate boys.
Sleepwalkers in a dark and terrible land,
Where solitude is a dirty knife at our throats.
Cold stars watch us, chum,
Cold stars and the whores.

Questions

1. What does the street corner college teach?

2. The Patchen poem was written in the depression era. Is the poem dated, or does it have meaning today? Is the poet Patchen describing a modern man with the hoe?

3. If young people are the gold coin of a country's future, what is Patchen telling us of the future?

4. Would the hoodlums who robbed Nathan Lime and Ornita Harris see the application of "Street Corner College" to their own lives?

Leisure*

WILLIAM HENRY DAVIES

What is this life if, full of care,
We have no time to stand and stare.

No time to stand beneath the boughs
And stare as long as sheep or cows.

No time to see, when woods we pass,
Where squirrels hide their nuts in grass.

No time to see, in broad daylight,
Streams full of stars, like stars at night.

No time to turn at Beauty's glance,
And watch her feet, how they can dance.

No time to wait till her mouth can
Enrich that smile her eyes began.

A poor life this if, full of care,
We have no time to stand and stare.

Questions

1. What would the poet Davies have us stare at and why?

2. Haven't the young men in "Street Corner College" the very leisure that Davies speaks of? Explain.

3. Are poems such as "Leisure" a waste of time? The Normans ("Chaos, Disorder and the Late Show") have no time for them, and the young men in "Street Corner College" would undoubtedly hoot at Davies' sentiments.

Ozymandias

PERCY BYSSHE SHELLEY (1792–1822)

I met a traveller from an antique land
Who said: Two vast and trunkless legs of stone
Stand in the desert . . . Near them, on the sand,
Half sunk, a shattered visage lies, whose frown,
And wrinkled lip, and sneer of cold command,
Tell that its sculptor well those passions read
Which yet survive, stamped on these lifeless things,
The hand that mocked them and the heart that fed:
And on the pedestal these words appear:
"My name is Ozymandias, king of kings:
Look on my works, ye Mighty, and despair!"
Nothing beside remains. Round the decay
Of that colossal wreck, boundless and bare
The lone and level sands stretch far away.

Questions

1. What is left of the statue besides the shattered visage or face?

2. What is the look on the face?

3. What is carved on the pedestal or base?

4: How would you describe a person who made such a claim? What comment does the poet make?

An Age When One Must Be an Editor*

RALPH J. GLEASON

It may be an expanding universe as the scientists say, but it's a small world. I said that.

And what I mean is that Sonny Rollins makes a record in New York and within two weeks kids are listening to it in Leningrad as well as Lima and in Boston as well as Bangkok. The electronic age has made communication almost instant and France had to wait weeks to learn that Touissant had led a revolt in Haiti.

Now one of the main effects of the speed-up in communication is a wild cross-pollination in all sorts of feedbacks. There is so much information on almost every subject that no one can handle it, much less know several fields. A professor I know talks of a time when there will be an information computer center in someplace like Denver and everything will be stored there and the questions fed to it from all over.

We have a plethora of records, books, movies and everything. And, as folksinger Pete Seeger recently pointed out, people are not prepared to be editors themselves yet.

Yet, in the face of all this music, learning, painting and the rest, one has to be an editor. Thus the problem of censorship which has cropped up not only with Lenny Bruce but with LeRoi Jones' plays, "Dutchman" and "the toilet." To refuse to carry their ads in a paper is a form of censorship.

Seeger sees all this in an interesting light. "The problems we are having are no more than the whole rest of the world is having," he says.

"Now that the world is getting so mixed up, different cultures and different ways of thinking are being tangled together. Naturally what's right with one is wrong with another. In the old days one could count on one's government to censor out the objectionable from our lives. Now it is obviously not possible for any government to do this and still give freedom of choice to its citizens.

"So," Seeger says, "everybody has to be his own editor. We have to get used to the idea that what somebody else likes, may be absolutely shocking to us but as long as he likes it, he's got a right to it—as long as it doesn't hurt anyone else. As Thomas Jefferson said: 'If I don't like somebody else's opinion it may hurt my feelings but still that man's opinion doesn't rob my pocket or burn my house down.'"

I think Seeger has hold of a good point here. Take the episode of the Mime Troupe in the park. Even if what the actors were saying was deemed

*By permission of Ralph Gleason. Reprinted from the *San Francisco Chronicle*, September 26, 1965.

objectionable as profanity (and I don't agree that it was), no one makes you stand there and listen to it. If we arrested everyone who ever used a four-letter word in Golden Gate Park, we'd be busting cops, firemen, truck drivers, athletes, laborers, street repair men and almost everyone. Do we call the cops when a road gang member yells out a four-letter word to his fellow workers? Hell, no. We walk on by. And that is what Seeger seems to me to be suggesting.

It's more moral to walk on by in this sense than to impose your concepts of right and wrong on somebody else whose concepts are different from yours.

Questions

1. Is John H. Bens the author or editor of this text? What is the difference in the terms?
2. What is the result if a person will not be his own editor?
3. According to Gleason, when was the time when every man did not have to be his own editor?
4. When one becomes his own editor he has become an adult. Do you agree with the statement?
5. In this era, why must one be his own editor?
6. It has been said that man fears nothing so much as freedom. Are the chances good that every man will become his own editor?
7. Is Gleason in agreement with Robert Henri ("On Schools")? Can you be taught to be your own editor?
8. Which fictional characters in this text seem incapable of becoming their own editors?

The Fable of the Corporation Director and the Mislaid Ambition*

GEORGE ADE

One of the Most Promising Boys in a Graded School had a Burning Ambition to be a Congressman. He loved Politics and Oratory. When there was a Rally in Town he would carry a Torch and listen to the Spellbinder with his Mouth open.

The Boy wanted to grow up and wear a Black String Tie and a Bill Cody Hat and walk stiff-legged, with his Vest unbuttoned at the Top, and be Distinguished.

°Reprinted by permission of George Ade Davis.

On Friday Afternoons he would go to School with his Face scrubbed
to a shiny pink and his Hair roached up on one side, and he would Recite
the Speeches of Patrick Henry and Daniel Webster and make Gestures.

When he Graduated from the High School he delivered an Oration on
"The Duty of the Hour," calling on all young Patriots to leap into the
Arena and with the Shield of Virtue quench the rising Flood of Corruption.
He said that the Curse of Our Times was the Greed for Wealth, and he pleaded
for Unselfish Patriotism among those in High Places.

He boarded at Home for a while without seeing a chance to jump into
the Arena, and finally his Father worked a Pull and got him a Job with a
Steel Company. He proved to be a Handy Young Man, and the Manager
sent Him out to make Contracts. He stopped roaching his Hair, and he
didn't give the Arena of Politics any serious Consideration except when the
Tariff on Steel was in Danger.

In a little while he owned a few Shares, and after that he became a
Director. He joined several Clubs and began to enjoy his Food. He drank a
Small Bottle with his Luncheon each Day, and he couldn't talk Business
unless he held a Scotch High Ball in his Right Hand.

With the return of Prosperity and the Formation of the Trust and the
Whoop in all Stocks he made so much Money that he was afraid to tell
the Amount.

His Girth increased—he became puffy under the Eyes—you could see
the little blue Veins on his Nose.

He kept his Name out of the Papers as much as possible, and he never
gave Congress a Thought except when he talked to his Lawyer of the Probable
Manner in which they would Evade any Legislation against Trusts. He took
two Turkish Baths every week and wore Silk Underwear. When an Eminent
Politician would come to his Office to shake him down he would send out
Word by the Boy in Buttons that he had gone to Europe. That's what he
thought of Politics.

One day while rummaging in a lower Drawer in his Library, looking for
a Box of Poker Chips, he came upon a Roll of Manuscript and wondered
what it was. He opened it and read how it was the Duty of all True Americans to hop into the Arena and struggle unselfishly for the General Good.
It came to him in a Flash—this was his High School Oration!

Then suddenly he remembered that for several Years of his Life his con-
suming Ambition had been—to go to Congress!

With a demoniacal Shriek he threw himself at full length on a Leather
Couch and began to Laugh.

He rolled off the Sofa and tossed about on a $1,200 Rug in a Paroxysm
of Merriment.

His Man came running into the Library and saw the Master in Convul-
sions. The poor Trust Magnate was purple in the Face.

They sent for a Great Specialist, who said that his Dear Friend had ruptured one of the smaller Arteries, and also narrowly escaped Death by Apoplexy.

He advised Rest and Quiet and the avoidance of any Great Shock.

So they took the High School Oration and put it on the Ice, and the Magnate slowly recovered and returned to his nine-course Dinners.

MORAL: *Of all Sad Words of Tongue or Pen, the Saddest are these, "It Might Have Been."*

Questions

1. What was the subject and philosophy of the high school speech?

2. What shaped the main character to a different philosophy? What was the new philosophy?

3. If Oakhurst, the gambler, or the Duchess, or Mother Shipton (see "The Outcasts of Poker Flat"), had written high school speeches, what would have been their reaction if they had found them years later? What was the corporation director's reaction?

4. George Ade and Bret Harte tell stories to shape you. The plots of the stories are different, of course. How else do the stories differ?

The Feast of Pure Reason

(*painting—see p. 156*)

JACK LEVINE

Handball

(*painting—see p. 157*)

BEN SHAHN

Questions

1. What does the advertisement for the Shirley Temple film do for Shahn?

2. What do the small figures against the wall do for the artist?

3. Would the painting be used by the Boy Scouts of America or the YMCA or the Chamber of Commerce as an advertisement? Explain.

4. What is the difference in Guest's ("My Creed") and Shahn's messages?

5. Who or what is depicted by each of the figures in the Levine painting?

6. What do the framed painting, the clipboard, the statue, the election sign, and the liquor decanter contribute?

7. How would you differentiate the painting styles of Levine, Tchelitchew (Section One), and Rockwell (Section Four)? What does each do to shape the viewer?

8. Why would D. H. Lawrence ("Don'ts") applaud, and Guest ("My Creed") decry, the Levine painting?

SECTION SIX

Fine Arts

High Yaller by Reginald Marsh

Property of Mr. and Mrs. Alfred Easton Poor

Connoisseurs of Prints by John Sloan

Etching, 4¼ × 6¹¹/₁₆ in. Courtesy of the Achenbach Foundation for Graphic Arts, California Palace of the Legion of Honor.

*Preliminary Statements for Discussion
and Writing*

1. Man is most godlike when he is creating works of art.

2. Who will tell you what a work of art means, is no friend, no teacher, and no artist.

3. Art is the language of the inner world, and speech the language of the outer.

4. Outside his own art, the artist has feet of clay.

5. A man would do nothing if he waited until he could do it so well that no one would find fault with what he has done.

6. Fine art is the only teacher except torture.

7. When love and skill work together, expect a masterpiece.

8. The winning chariot racer gives you the illusion of happiness. The gadfly questioner gives you the reality of happiness.

9. Architecture is frozen music.

10. An artist is the conscience of a people.

The Listener*

JOHN BERRY

Once there was a puny little Czech concert violinist named Rudolf, who lived in Sweden. Some of his friends thought he was not the best of musicians because he was restless; others thought he was restless because he was not the best of musicians. At any rate, he hit upon a way of making a living, with no competitors. Whether by choice or necessity, he used to sail about Scandinavia in his small boat, all alone, giving concerts in little seaport towns. If he found accompanists, well and good; if not, he played works for unaccompanied violin; and it happened once or twice that he wanted a piano so badly that he imagined one, and then he played whole sonatas for violin and piano, with no piano in sight.

One year Rudolf sailed all the way out to Iceland and began working his way around that rocky coast from one town to another. It was a hard, stubborn land; but people in those difficult places do not forget the law of hospitality to the stranger—for their God may decree that they too shall become strangers on the face of the earth. The audiences were small, and even if Rudolf had been really first-rate, they would not have been very demonstrative. From ancient times their energy had gone, first of all, into earnest toil. Sometimes they were collected by the local schoolteacher, who reminded them of their duty to the names of Beethoven and Bach and Mozart and one or two others whose music perhaps was not much heard in those parts. Too often people sat stolidly watching the noisy little fiddler, and went home feeling gravely edified. But they paid.

As Rudolf was sailing from one town to the next along a sparsely settled shore, the northeast turned black and menacing. A storm was bearing down upon Iceland. Rudolf was rounding a bleak, dangerous cape, and his map told him that the nearest harbor was half a day's journey away. He was starting to worry when he saw, less than a mile offshore, a lighthouse on a tiny rock island. At the base of the lighthouse was a deep, narrow cove, protected by cliffs. With some difficulty, in the rising seas, he put in there and moored to an iron ring that hung from the cliff. A flight of stairs, hewn out of the rock, led up to the lighthouse. On top of the cliff, outlined against the scudding clouds, stood a man.

"You are welcome!" the voice boomed over the sound of the waves that were already beginning to break over the island.

Darkness fell quickly. The lighthouse keeper led his guest up the spiral stairs to the living room on the third floor, then busied himself in preparation for the storm. Above all, he had to attend to the great lamp in the tower, that dominated the whole region. It was a continuous light, intensified by reflectors, and eclipsed by shutters at regular intervals. The duration of light was equal to that of darkness.

The lighthouse keeper was a huge old man with a grizzled beard that came down over his chest. Slow, deliberate, bearlike, he moved without wasted motion about the limited world of which he was the master. He spoke little, as if words had not much importance compared to the other forces that comprised his life. Yet he was equable, as those elements were not.

After the supper of black bread and boiled potatoes, herring, cheese and hot tea, which they took in the kitchen above the living room, the two men sat and contemplated each other's presence. Above them was the maintenance room, and above that the great lamp spoke majestic, silent messages of light to the ships at sea. The storm hammered like a battering ram on the walls of the lighthouse. Rudolf offered tobacco, feeling suddenly immature as he did so. The old man smiled a little as he declined it by a slight movement of the head; it was as if he knew well the uses of tobacco and the need for offering it, and affirmed it all, yet—here he, too, was halfway apologetic—was self-contained and without need of anything that was not already within his power or to which he did not relinquish his power. And he sat there, gentle and reflective, his great workman hands resting on outspread thighs.

It seemed to Rudolf that the lighthouse keeper was entirely aware of all the sounds of the storm and of its violent impact upon the lighthouse, but he knew them so well that he did not have to think about them; they were like the involuntary movements of his own heart and blood. In the same way, beneath the simple courtesy that made him speak and listen to his guest in specific ways, he was already *calmly* and mysteriously a part of him, as surely as the mainland was connected with the little island, and all the islands with one another, so commodiously, under the ocean.

Gradually Rudolf drew forth the sparse data of the old man's life: He had been born in this very lighthouse eighty-three years before, when his father was the lighthouse keeper. His mother—the only woman he had ever known—had taught him to read the Bible, and he read it daily. He had no other books.

As a musician, Rudolf had not had time to read much either—but then, he had lived in cities. He reached down and took his beloved violin out of its case.

"What do you make with that, sir?" the old man asked.

For a second Rudolf thought his host might be joking; but the serenity of the other's expression reassured him. There was not even curiosity about the instrument, but rather a whole interest in him, the person, that included his "work." In most circumstances Rudolf would have found it hard to believe that there could exist someone who did not know what a violin was; yet now he had no inclination to laugh. He felt small and inadequate.

"I make—music with it," he stammered in a low voice.

"Music," the old man said ponderously. "I have heard of it. But I have never seen music."

"One does not see music. One hears it."

"Ah, yes," the lighthouse keeper consented, as it were with humility. This too was in the Nature of Things where in all works were wonders, and all things were known eternally and were poignant in their transiency. His wide gray eyes rested upon the little fiddler and conferred upon him all the importance of which any individual is capable.

Then something in the storm and the lighthouse and the old man exalted Rudolf, filled him with compassion and love and a spaciousness infinitely beyond himself. He wanted to strike a work of fire and stars into being for the old man. And, with the storm as his accompanist, he stood and began to play—the Kreutzer Sonata of Beethoven.

The moments passed, moments that were days in the creation of that world of fire and stars: abysses and heights of passionate struggle, the Idea of Order, and the resolution of these in the greatness of the human spirit. Never before had Rudolf played with such mastery—or with such an accompanist. Waves and wind beat the tower with giant hands. Steadily above them the beacon blazed in its sure cycles of darkness and light. The last note ceased and Rudolf dropped his head on his chest, breathing hard. The ocean seethed over the island with a roar as of many voices.

The old man had sat unmoving through the work, his broad, gnarled hands resting on his thighs, his head bowed, listening massively. For some time he continued to sit in silence. Then he looked up, lifted those hands calmly, judiciously, and nodded his head.

"Yes," he said. "That is true."

Questions

1. How did Rudolf, the violinist, earn his living?

2. The author says Rudolf's audiences were seldom very demonstrative. Was their lack of applause and excitement completely due to Rudolf's failure to be first rate?

3. How does the author prevent your smiling or laughing at the old man at the story's close?

4. What did the old man mean by his last remark? Why does his use of the word *true* come as a surprise to most of us?

Seibei's Gourds*

SHIGA NAOYA

This is the story of a young boy called Seibei, and of his gourds. Later on Seibei gave up gourds, but he soon found something to take their place: he started painting pictures. It was not long before Seibei was as absorbed in his paintings as he once had been in his gourds.

Seibei's parents knew that he often went out to buy himself gourds. He got them for a few sen and soon had a sizable collection. When he came home, he would first bore a neat hole in the top of the gourd and extract the seeds. Next he applied tea leaves to get rid of the unpleasant gourd smell. He then fetched the saké which he had saved up from the dregs in his father's cup and carefully polished the surface.

Seibei was passionately interested in gourds. One day as he was strolling along the beach, absorbed in his favorite subject, he was startled by an unusual sight: he caught a glimpse of the bald, elongated head of an old man hurrying out of one of the huts by the beach. "What a splendid gourd!" thought Seibei. The old man disappeared from sight, wagging his bald pink pate. Only then did Seibei realize his mistake and he stood there laughing loudly to himself. He laughed all the way home.

Whenever he passed a grocery, a curio shop, a confectioner's, or in fact any place that sold gourds, he stood for minutes on end, his eyes glued to the window, appraising the precious fruit.

Seibei was twelve years old and still at primary school. After class, instead of playing with the other children, he usually wandered about the town looking for gourds. Then in the evening he would sit cross-legged in the corner of the living room working on his newly acquired fruit. When he had finished treating it, he poured in a little saké, inserted a cork stopper which he had fashioned himself, wrapped it in a towel, put this in a tin especially kept for the purpose and finally placed the whole thing on the charcoal footwarmer. Then he went to bed.

As soon as he woke the next morning, he would open the tin and examine the gourd. The skin would be thoroughly damp from the overnight treatment. Seibei would gaze adoringly at his treasure before tying a string round the middle and hanging it in the sun to dry. Then he set out for school.

Seibei lived in a harbor town. Although it was officially a city, one could walk from one end to the other in a matter of twenty minutes. Seibei was

* Seibei's Gourds (Seibei to Hyotan) by Shiga Naoya, as it appeared in Modern Japanese Stories translated by Ivan Morris. By permission of the author and the publisher Charles E. Tuttle Co., Inc.

always wandering about the streets and had soon come to know every place that sold gourds and to recognize almost every gourd on the market.

He did not care much about the old, gnarled, peculiarly formed gourds usually favored by collectors. The type that appealed to Seibei was even and symmetrical.

"That youngster of yours only seems to like the ordinary looking ones," said a friend of his father's who had come to call. He pointed at the boy, who was sitting in the corner busily polishing a plain, round gourd.

"Fancy a lad spending his time playing around like that with gourds!" said his father, giving Seibei a disgusted look.

"See here, Seibei my lad," said the friend, "there's no use just collecting lots of those things. It's not the quantity that counts, you know. What you want to do is to find one or two really unusual ones."

"I prefer this kind," said Seibei and let the matter drop.

Seibei's father and his friend started talking about gourds.

"Remember that Bakin gourd they had at the agricultural show last spring?" said his father. "It was a real beauty, wasn't it?"

"Yes, I remember. That big, long one. . . ."

As Seibei listened to their conversation, he was laughing inwardly. The Bakin gourd had made quite a stir at the time, but when he had gone to see it (having no idea, of course, who the great poet Bakin might be) he had found it rather a stupid-looking object and had walked out of the show.

"I didn't think so much of it," interrupted Seibei. "It's just a clumsy great thing."

His father opened his eyes wide in surprise and anger.

"What's that?" he shouted. "When you don't know what you're talking about, you'd better shut up!"

Seibei did not say another word.

One day when he was walking along an unfamiliar back street he came upon an old woman with a fruit stall. She was selling dried persimmons and oranges; on the shutters of the house behind the stall she had hung a large cluster of gourds.

"Can I have a look?" said Seibei and immediately ran behind the stall and began examining the gourds. Suddenly he caught sight of one which was about five inches long and at first sight looked quite commonplace. Something about it made Seibei's heart beat faster.

"How much is this one?" he asked, panting out the words.

"Well," said the old woman, "since you're just a lad, I'll let you have it for ten sen."

"In that case," said Seibei urgently, "please hold it for me, won't you? I'll be right back with the money."

He dashed home and in no time at all was back at the stall. He bought the gourd and took it home.

From that time on, he was never separated from his new gourd. He even took it along to school and used to polish it under his desk during class time. It was not long before he was caught at this by one of the teachers, who was particularly incensed because it happened to take place in an ethics class.

This teacher came from another part of Japan and found it most offensive that children should indulge in such effeminate pastimes as collecting gourds. He was forever expounding the classical code of the samurai, and when Kumoemon, the famous Naniwabushi performer, came on tour and recited brave deeds of ancient times, he would attend every single performance, though normally he would not deign to set foot in the disreputable amusement area. He never minded having his students sing Naniwabushi ballads, however raucously. Now, when he found Seibei silently polishing his gourd, his voice trembled with fury.

"You're an idiot!" he shouted. "There's absolutely no future for a boy like you." Then and there he confiscated the gourd on which Seibei had spent so many long hours of work. Seibei stared straight ahead and did not cry.

When he got home, Seibei's face was pale. Without a word, he put his feet on the warmer and sat looking blankly at the wall.

After a while the teacher arrived. As Seibei's father was not yet home from the carpenter's shop where he worked, the teacher directed his attack at Seibei's mother.

"This sort of thing is the responsibility of the family," he said in a stern voice. "It is the duty of you parents to see that such things don't happen." In an agony of embarrassment, Seibei's mother muttered some apology.

Meanwhile, Seibei was trying to make himself as inconspicuous as possible in the corner. Terrified, he glanced up at his vindictive teacher and at the wall directly behind where a whole row of fully prepared gourds was hanging. What would happen if the teacher caught sight of them?

Trembling inside, he awaited the worst, but at length the man exhausted his rhetoric and stamped angrily out of the house. Seibei heaved a sigh of relief.

Seibei's mother was sobbing softly. In a querulous whine she began to scold him, and in the midst of this, Seibei's father returned from his shop. As soon as he heard what had happened, he grabbed his son by the collar and gave him a sound beating. "You're no good!" he bawled at him. "You'll never get anywhere in the world the way you're carrying on. I've a good mind to throw you out into the street where you belong!" The gourds on the wall caught his attention. Without a word, he fetched his hammer and systematically smashed them to pieces one after another. Seibei turned pale but said nothing.

The next day the teacher gave Seibei's confiscated gourd to an old porter who worked in the school. "Here, take this," he said, as if handing over some unclean object. The porter took the gourd home with him and hung it on the wall of his small, sooty room.

About two months later the porter, finding himself even more hard pressed for money than usual, decided to take the gourd to a local curio shop to see if he could get a few coppers for it. The curio dealer examined the gourd carefully; then, assuming an uninterested tone, he handed it back to the porter saying: "I might give you five yen for it."

The porter was astounded, but being quite an astute old man, he replied coolly: "I certainly wouldn't part with it for that." The dealer immediately raised his offer to ten yen, but the porter was still adamant.

In the end the curio dealer had to pay fifty yen for the gourd. The porter left the shop, delighted at his luck. It wasn't often that the teachers gave one a free gift equivalent to a year's wages! He was so clever as not to mention the matter to anyone, and neither Seibei nor the teacher ever heard what had happened to the gourd. Yes, the porter was clever, but he was not clever enough: little did he imagine that this same gourd would be passed on by the curio dealer to a wealthy collector in the district for six hundred yen.

Seibei is now engrossed in his pictures. He no longer feels any bitterness either toward the teacher, or toward his father who smashed all his precious gourds to pieces.

Yet gradually his father has begun to scold him for painting pictures.

Questions

1. Is Seibei's father a villain? What does he want his son to be? Does Seibei feel ill-used? How is Naoya's story similar to "The Celestial Omnibus"?

2. Which has greater value a sen or a yen? Without using the dictionary, how do you know? Is there any reason you should remember which one has the greater value?

3. That Seibei is not a perfect child is a point the author must make. Why? How does he do it?

4. When Seibei has a son of his own, will Seibei behave as his father did?

5. Had Seibei's father or the teacher learned the porter's secret, would they see the beauty of the gourds?

6. How do we know a teacher had considerable status in Seibei's community? Americans usually think of the Japanese as extremely polite. Was the author concerned in any major way to disprove this stereotyped thought?

7. What would Robert Henri, who wrote "On Schools," page 102, have to say about Seibei's teacher? That Seibei is not crushed by his parents and teachers tells us what about the human spirit?

The Celestial Omnibus*

E. M. FORSTER

The boy who resided at Agathox Lodge, 28, Buckingham Park Road, Surbiton, had often been puzzled by the old sign-post that stood almost opposite. He asked his mother about it, and she replied that it was a joke, and not a very nice one, which had been made many years back by some naughty young men, and that the police ought to remove it. For there were two strange things about this sign-post: firstly, it pointed up a blank alley, and, secondly, it had painted on it, in faded characters, the words, "To Heaven."

"What kind of young men were they?" he asked.

"I think your father told me that one of them wrote verses, and was expelled from the University and came to grief in other ways. Still, it was a long time ago. You must ask your father about it. He will say the same as I do, that it was put up as a joke."

"So it doesn't mean anything at all?"

She sent him up-stairs to put on his best things, for the Bonses were coming to tea, and he was to hand the cake-stand.

It struck him, as he wrenched on his tightening trousers, that he might do worse than ask Mr. Bons about the sign-post. His father, though very kind, always laughed at him—shrieked with laughter whenever he or any other child asked a question or spoke. But Mr. Bons was serious as well as kind. He had a beautiful house and lent one books, he was a churchwarden, and a candidate for the County Council; he had donated to the Free Library enormously, he presided over the Literary Society, and had Members of Parliament to stop with him—in short, he was probably the wisest person alive.

Yet even Mr. Bons could only say that the sign-post was a joke—the joke of a person named Shelley.

"Of course!" cried the mother; "I told you so, dear. That was the name."

"Had you never heard of Shelley?" asked Mr. Bons.

"No," said the boy, and hung his head.

"But is there no Shelley in the house?"

"Why, yes!" exclaimed the lady, in much agitation. "Dear Mr. Bons, we aren't such Philistines as that. Two at the least. One a wedding present, and the other, smaller print, in one of the spare rooms."

"I believe we have seven Shelleys," said Mr. Bons, with a slow smile. Then he brushed the cake crumbs off his stomach, and, together with his daughter, rose to go.

°From *The Collected Tales of E. M. Forster.* Published 1947 by Alfred A. Knopf, Inc. Reprinted by permission.

The boy, obeying a wink from his mother, saw them all the way to the garden gate, and when they had gone he did not at once return to the house, but gazed for a little up and down Buckingham Park Road.

His parents lived at the right end of it. After No. 39 the quality of the houses dropped very suddenly, and 64 had not even a separate servants' entrance. But at the present moment the whole road looked rather pretty, for the sun had just set in splendour, and the inequalities of rent were drowned in a saffron afterglow. Small birds twittered, and the breadwinners' train shrieked musically down through the cutting—that wonderful cutting which has drawn to itself the whole beauty out of Surbiton, and clad itself, like any Alpine valley, with the glory of the fir and the silver birch and the primrose. It was this cutting that had first stirred desires within the boy— desires for something just a little different, he knew not what, desires that would return whenever things were sunlit, as they were this evening, running up and down inside him, up and down, up and down, till he would feel quite unusual all over, and as likely as not would want to cry. This evening he was even sillier, for he slipped across the road towards the sign-post and began to run up the blank alley.

The alley runs between high walls—the walls of the gardens of "Ivanhoe" and "Belle Vista" respectively. It smells a little all the way, and is scarcely twenty yards long, including the turn at the end. So not unnaturally the boy soon came to a standstill. "I'd like to kick that Shelley," he exclaimed, and glanced idly at a piece of paper which was pasted on the wall. Rather an odd piece of paper, and he read it carefully before he turned back. This is what he read:

S. AND C. R. C. C.

Alteration in Service.

Owing to lack of patronage the Company are regretfully compelled to suspend the hourly service, and to retain only the

Sunrise and Sunset Omnibuses,

which will run as usual. It is to be hoped that the public will patronize an arrangement which is intended for their convenience. As an extra inducement, the Company will, for the first time, now issue

Return Tickets!

(available one day only), which may be obtained of the driver. Passengers are again reminded that *no tickets are issued at the other end,* and that no complaints in this connection will receive consideration from the Company.

Nor will the company be responsible for any negligence or stupidity on the part of Passengers, nor for Hailstorms, Lightning, Loss of Tickets, nor for any Act of God.

For the Direction.

Now he had never seen this notice before, nor could he imagine where the omnibus went to. S. of course was for Surbiton, and R.C.C. meant Road Car Company. But what was the meaning of the other C.? Coombe and Malden, perhaps, or possibly "City." Yet it could not hope to compete with the South-Western. The whole thing, the boy reflected, was run on hopelessly unbusiness-like lines. Why no tickets from the other end? And what an hour to start! Then he realized that unless the notice was a hoax, an omnibus must have been starting just as he was wishing the Bonses goodbye. He peered at the ground through the gathering dusk, and there he saw what might or might not be the marks of wheels. Yet nothing had come out of the alley. And he had never seen an omnibus at any time in the Buckingham Park Road. No: it must be a hoax, like the sign-posts, like the fairy tales, like the dreams upon which he would wake suddenly in the night. And with a sigh he stepped from the alley—right into the arms of his father.

Oh, how his father laughed! "Poor, poor Popsey!" he cried. "Diddums! Diddums! Diddums think he'd walky-palky up to Evvink!" And his mother, also convulsed with laughter, appeared on the steps of Agathox Lodge. "Don't, Bob!" she gasped. "Don't be so naughty! Oh, you'll kill me! Oh, leave the boy alone!"

But all that evening the joke was kept up. The father implored to be taken too. Was it a very tiring walk? Need one wipe one's shoes on the doormat? And the boy went to bed feeling faint and sore, and thankful for only one thing—that he had not said a word about the omnibus. It was a hoax, yet through his dreams it grew more and more real, and the streets of Surbiton, through which he saw it driving, seemed instead to become hoaxes and shadows. And very early in the morning he woke with a cry, for he had had a glimpse of its destination.

He struck a match, and its light fell not only on his watch but also on his calendar, so that he knew it to be half-an-hour to sunrise. It was pitch dark, for the fog had come down from London in the night, and all Surbiton was wrapped in its embraces. Yet he sprang out and dressed himself, for he was determined to settle once for all which was real: the omnibus or the streets. "I shall be a fool one way or the other," he thought, "until I know." Soon he was shivering in the road under the gas lamp that guarded the entrance to the alley.

To enter the alley itself required some courage. Not only was it horribly dark, but he now realized that it was an impossible terminus for an omnibus. If it had not been for a policeman, whom he heard approaching through the fog, he would never have made the attempt. The next moment he had made the attempt and failed. Nothing. Nothing but a blank alley and a very silly boy gaping at its dirty floor. It *was* a hoax. "I'll tell papa and mamma," he decided. "I deserve it. I deserve that they should know. I am too silly to be alive." And he went back to the gate of Agathox Lodge.

There he remembered that his watch was fast. The sun was not risen; it would not rise for two minutes. "Give the bus every chance," he thought cynically, and returned into the alley.

But the omnibus was there.

It had two horses, whose sides were still smoking from their journey, and its two great lamps shone through the fog against the alley's walls, changing their cobwebs and moss into tissues of fairyland. The driver was huddled up in a cape. He faced the blank wall, and how he had managed to drive in so neatly and so silently was one of the many things that the boy never discovered. Nor could he imagine how ever he would drive out.

"Please," his voice quavered through the foul brown air. "Please, is that an omnibus?"

"Omnibus est," said the driver, without turning round. There was a moment's silence. The policeman passed, coughing, by the entrance of the alley. The boy crouched in the shadow, for he did not want to be found out. He was pretty sure, too, that it was a Pirate; nothing else, he reasoned, would go from such odd places and at such odd hours.

"About when do you start?" He tried to sound nonchalant.

"At sunrise."

"How far do you go?"

"The whole way."

"And can I have a return ticket which will bring me all the way back?"

"You can."

"Do you know, I half think I'll come." The driver made no answer. The sun must have risen, for he unhitched the brake. And scarcely had the boy jumped in before the omnibus was off.

How? Did it turn? There was no room. Did it go forward? There was a blank wall. Yet it was moving—moving at a stately pace through the fog, which had turned from brown to yellow. The thought of warm bed and warmer breakfast made the boy feel faint. He wished he had not come. His parents would not have approved. He would have gone back to them if the weather had not made it impossible. The solitude was terrible; he was the only passenger. And the omnibus, though well-built, was cold and somewhat musty. He drew his coat round him, and in so doing chanced to feel his pocket. It was empty. He had forgotten his purse.

"Stop!" he shouted. "Stop!" And then, being of a polite disposition, he glanced up at the painted notice-board so that he might call the driver by name. "Mr. Browne! stop; Oh, do please stop!"

Mr. Browne did not stop, but he opened a little window and looked in at the boy. His face was a surprise, so kind it was and modest.

"Mr. Browne, I've left my purse behind. I've not got a penny. I can't pay for the ticket. Will you take my watch, please? I am in the most awful hole."

"Tickets on this line," said the driver, "whether single or return, can be purchased by coinage from no terrene mint. And a chronometer, though it had solaced the vigils of Charlemagne, or measured the slumbers of Laura, can acquire by no mutation the double-cake that charms the fangless Cerberus of Heaven!" So saying, he handed in the necessary ticket, and, while the boy said "Thank you," continued: "Titular pretensions, I know it well, are vanity. Yet they merit no censure when uttered on a laughing lip, and in an homonymous world are in some sort useful, since they do serve to distinguish one Jack from his fellow. Remember me, therefore, as Sir Thomas Browne."

"Are you a Sir? Oh, sorry!" He had heard of these gentlemen drivers. "It *is* good of you about the ticket. But if you go on at this rate, however does your bus pay?"

"It does not pay. It was not intended to pay. Many are the faults of my equipage; it is compounded too curiously of foreign woods; its cushions tickle erudition rather than promote repose; and my horses are nourished not on the evergreen pastures of the moment, but on the dried bents and clovers of Latinity. But that it pays!—that error at all events was never intended and never attained."

"Sorry again," said the boy rather hopelessly. Sir Thomas looked sad, fearing that, even for a moment, he had been the cause of sadness. He invited the boy to come up and sit beside him on the box, and together they journeyed on through the fog, which was now changing from yellow to white. There were no houses by the road; so it must be either Putney Heath or Wimbledon Common.

"Have you been a driver always?"

"I was a physician once."

"But why did you stop? Weren't you good?"

"As a healer of bodies I had scant success, and several score of my patients preceded me. But as a healer of the spirit I have succeeded beyond my hopes and my deserts. For though my draughts were not better nor subtler than those of other men, yet, by reason of the cunning goblets wherein I offered them, the queasy soul was ofttimes tempted to sip and be refreshed."

"The queasy soul," he murmured; "if the sun sets with trees in front of it, and you suddenly come strange all over, is that a queasy soul?"

"Have you felt that?"

"Why yes."

After a pause he told the boy a little, a very little, about the journey's end. But they did not chatter much, for the boy, when he liked a person, would as soon sit silent in his company as speak, and this, he discovered, was also the mind of Sir Thomas Browne and of many others with whom he was to be acquainted. He heard, however, about the young man Shelley, who was now quite a famous person, with a carriage of his own, and about some of the other drivers who are in the service of the Company. Meanwhile the light grew stronger, though the fog did not disperse. It was now more like mist than fog, and at times would travel quickly across them, as if it was part of a cloud. They had been ascending, too, in a most puzzling way; for over two hours the horses had been pulling against the collar, and even if it were Richmond Hill they ought to have been at the top long ago. Perhaps it was Epsom, or even the North Downs; yet the air seemed keener than that which blows on either. And as to the name of their destination, Sir Thomas Browne was silent.

Crash!

"Thunder, by Jove!" said the boy, "and not so far off either. Listen to the echoes! It's more like mountains."

He thought, not very vividly, of his father and mother. He saw them sitting down to sausages and listening to the storm. He saw his own empty place. Then there would be questions, alarms, theories, jokes, consolations. They would expect him back at lunch. To lunch he would not come, nor to tea, but he would be in for dinner, and so his day's truancy would be over. If he had had his purse he would have bought them presents—not that he should have known what to get them.

Crash!

The peal and the lightning came together. The cloud quivered as if it were alive, and torn streamers of mist rushed past. "Are you afraid?" asked Sir Thomas Browne.

"What is there to be afraid of? Is it much farther?"

The horses of the omnibus stopped just as a ball of fire burst up and exploded with a ringing noise that was deafening but clear, like the noise of a blacksmith's forge. All the cloud was shattered.

"Oh, listen, Sir Thomas Browne! No, I mean look; we shall get a view at last. No, I mean listen; that sounds like a rainbow!"

The noise had died into the faintest murmur, beneath which another murmur grew, spreading stealthily, steadily, in a curve that widened but did not vary. And in widening curves a rainbow was spreading from the horses' feet into the dissolving mists.

"But how beautiful! What colours! Where will it stop? It is more like the rainbows you can tread on. More like dreams."

The colour and the sound grew together. The rainbow spanned an enormous gulf. Clouds rushed under it and were pierced by it, and still it grew, reaching forward, conquering the darkness, until it touched something that seemed more solid than a cloud.

The boy stood up. "What is that out there?" he called. "What does it rest on, out at that other end?"

In the morning sunshine a precipice shone forth beyond the gulf. A precipice—or was it a castle? The horses moved. They set their feet upon the rainbow.

"Oh, look!" the boy shouted. "Oh, listen! Those caves—or are they gateways? Oh, look between those cliffs at those ledges. I see people! I see trees!"

"Look also below," whispered Sir Thomas. "Neglect not the diviner Acheron."

The boy looked below, past the flames of the rainbow that licked against their wheels. The gulf also had cleared, and in its depths there flowed an everlasting river. One sunbeam entered and struck a green pool, and as they passed over he saw three maidens rise to the surface of the pool, singing, and playing with something that glistened like a ring.

"You down in the water—" he called.

They answered, "You up on the bridge—" There was a burst of music. "You up on the bridge, good luck to you. Truth in the depth, truth on the height."

"You down in the water, what are you doing?"

Sir Thomas Browne replied: "They sport in the mancipiary possession of their gold"; and the omnibus arrived.

The boy was in disgrace. He sat locked up in the nursery of Agathox Lodge, learning poetry for a punishment. His father had said, "My boy! I can pardon anything but untruthfulness," and had caned him, saying at each stroke, "There is *no* omnibus, *no* driver, *no* bridge, *no* mountain; you are a *truant,* a *gutter snipe,* a *liar.*" His father could be very stern at times. His mother had begged him to say he was sorry. But he could not say that. It was the greatest day of his life, in spite of the caning and the poetry at the end of it.

He had returned punctually at sunset—driven not by Sir Thomas Browne, but by a maiden lady who was full of quiet fun. They had talked of omnibuses and also of barouche landaus. How far away her gentle voice seemed now! Yet it was scarcely three hours since he had left her up the alley.

His mother called through the door. "Dear, you are to come down and to bring your poetry with you."

He came down and found that Mr. Bons was in the smoking-room with his father. It had been a dinner party.

"Here is the great traveller!" said his father grimly. "Here is the young gentleman who drives in an omnibus over rainbows, while young ladies sing to him." Pleased with his wit, he laughed.

"After all," said Mr. Bons, smiling, "there is something a little like it in Wagner. It is odd how, in quite illiterate minds, you will find glimmers of

Artistic Truth. The case interests me. Let me plead for the culprit. We have all romanced in our time, haven't we?"

"Hear how kind Mr. Bons is," said his mother, while his father said, "Very well. Let him say his Poem, and that will do. He is going away to my sister on Tuesday, and *she* will cure him of his alley-slopering." (Laughter.) "Say your Poem."

The boy began. "'Standing aloof in giant ignorance.'"

His father laughed again—roared. "One for you, my son! 'Standing aloof in giant ignorance!' I never knew these poets talked sense. Just describes you. Here, Bons, you go in for poetry. Put him through it, will you, while I fetch up the whisky?"

"Yes, give me the Keats," said Mr. Bons. "Let him say his Keats to me."

So for a few moments the wise man and the ignorant boy were left alone in the smoking-room.

"'Standing aloof in giant ignorance, of thee I dream and of the Cyclades, as one who sits ashore and longs perchance to visit—'"

"Quite right. To visit what?"

"'To visit dolphin coral in deep seas,'" said the boy, and burst into tears.

"Come, come! why do you cry?"

"Because—because all these words that only rhymed before, now that I've come back they're me."

Mr. Bons laid the Keats down. The case was more interesting than he had expected. *"You?"* he exclaimed. "This sonnet, *you?"*

"Yes—and look further on: 'Aye, on the shores of darkness there is light, and precipices show untrodden green.' It *is* so, sir. All these things are true."

"I never doubted it," said Mr. Bons, with closed eyes.

"You—then you believe me? You believe in the omnibus and the driver and the storm and that return ticket I got for nothing and—"

"Tut, tut! No more of your yarns, my boy. I meant that I never doubted the essential truth of Poetry. Some day, when you have read more, you will understand what I mean."

"But Mr. Bons, it *is* so. There *is* light upon the shores of darkness. I have seen it coming. Light and a wind."

"Nonsense," said Mr. Bons.

"If I had stopped! They tempted me. They told me to give up my ticket—for you cannot come back if you lose your ticket. They called from the river for it, and indeed I was tempted, for I have never been so happy as among those precipices. But I thought of my mother and father, and that I must fetch them. Yet they will not come, though the road starts opposite our house. It has all happened as the people up there warned me, and Mr. Bons has disbelieved me like every one else. I have been caned. I shall never see that mountain again."

"What's that about me?" said Mr. Bons, sitting up in his chair very suddenly.

"I told them about you, and how clever you were, and how many books you had, and they said, 'Mr. Bons will certainly disbelieve you.'"

"Stuff and nonsense, my young friend. You grow impertinent. I—well—I will settle the matter. Not a word to your father. I will cure you. To-morrow evening I will myself call here to take you for a walk, and at sunset we will go up this alley opposite and hunt for your omnibus, you silly little boy."

His face grew serious, for the boy was not disconcerted, but leapt about the room singing. "Joy! joy! I told them you would believe me. We will drive together over the rainbow. I told them that you would come." After all, could there be anything in the story? Wagner? Keats? Shelley? Sir Thomas Browne? Certainly the case was interesting.

And on the morrow evening, though it was pouring with rain, Mr. Bons did not omit to call at Agathox Lodge.

The boy was ready, bubbling with excitement, and skipping about in a way that rather vexed the President of the Literary Society. They took a turn down Buckingham Park Road, and then—having seen that no one was watching them—slipped up the alley. Naturally enough (for the sun was setting) they ran straight against the omnibus.

"Good heavens!" exclaimed Mr. Bons. "Good gracious heavens!"

It was not the omnibus in which the boy had driven first, nor yet that in which he had returned. There were three horses—black, gray, and white, the gray being the finest. The driver, who turned round at the mention of goodness and of heaven, was a sallow man with terrifying jaws and sunken eyes. Mr. Bons, on seeing him, gave a cry as if of recognition, and began to tremble violently.

The boy jumped in.

"Is it possible?" cried Mr. Bons. "Is the impossible possible?"

"Sir; come in, sir. It is such a fine omnibus. Oh, here is his name—Dan some one."

Mr. Bons sprang in too. A blast of wind immediately slammed the omnibus door, and the shock jerked down all the omnibus blinds, which were very weak on their springs.

"Dan . . . Show me. Good gracious heavens! we're moving."

"Hooray!" said the boy.

Mr. Bons became flustered. He had not intended to be kidnapped. He could not find the door-handle, nor push up the blinds. The omnibus was quite dark, and by the time he had struck a match, night had come on outside also. They were moving rapidly.

"A strange, a memorable adventure," he said, surveying the interior of the omnibus, which was large, roomy, and constructed with extreme regularity, every part exactly answering to every other part. Over the door (the handle of which was outside) was written, "Lasciate ogni baldanza voi che entrate"—at least, that was what was written, but Mr. Bons said that it was

Lashy arty something, and that baldanza was a mistake for speranza. His voice sounded as if he was in church. Meanwhile, the boy called to the cadaverous driver for two return tickets. They were handed in without a word. Mr. Bons covered his face with his hand and again trembled. "Do you know who that is!" he whispered, when the little window had shut upon them. "It is the impossible."

"Well, I don't like him as much as Sir Thomas Browne, though I shouldn't be surprised if he had even more in him."

"More in him?" He stamped irritably. "By accident you have made the greatest discovery of the century, and all you can say is that there is more in this man. Do you remember those vellum books in my library, stamped with red lilies? This—sit still, I bring you stupendous news!—*this is the man who wrote them.*"

The boy sat quite still. "I wonder if we shall see Mrs. Gamp?" he asked, after a civil pause.

"Mrs.—?"

"Mrs. Gamp and Mrs. Harris. I like Mrs. Harris. I came upon them quite suddenly. Mrs. Gamp's bandboxes have moved over the rainbow so badly. All the bottoms have fallen out, and two of the pippins off her bedstead tumbled into the stream."

"Out there sits the man who wrote my vellum books!" thundered Mr. Bons, "and you talk to me of Dickens and of Mrs. Gamp?"

"I know Mrs. Gamp so well," he apologized. "I could not help being glad to see her. I recognized her voice. She was telling Mrs. Harris about Mrs. Prig."

"Did you spend the whole day in her elevating company?"

"Oh, no. I raced. I met a man who took me out beyond to a race-course. You run, and there are dolphins out at sea."

"Indeed. Do you remember the man's name?"

"Achilles. No; he was later. Tom Jones."

Mr. Bons sighed heavily. "Well, my lad, you have made a miserable mess of it. Think of a cultured person with your opportunities! A cultured person would have known all these characters and known what to have said to each. He would not have wasted his time with a Mrs. Gamp or a Tom Jones. The creations of Homer, of Shakespeare, and of Him who drives us now, would alone have contented him. He would not have raced. He would have asked intelligent questions."

"But Mr. Bons," said the boy humbly, "you will be a cultured person. I told them so."

"True, true, and I beg of you not to disgrace me when we arrive. No gossiping. No running. Keep close to my side, and never speak to these Immortals unless they speak to you. Yes, and give me the return tickets. You will be losing them."

The boy surrendered the tickets, but felt a little sore. After all, he had found the way to this place. It was hard first to be disbelieved and then to be lectured. Meanwhile, the rain had stopped, and moonlight crept into the omnibus through the cracks in the blinds.

"But how is there to be a rainbow?" cried the boy.

"You distract me," snapped Mr. Bons. "I wish to meditate on beauty. I wish to goodness I was with a reverent and sympathetic person."

The lad bit his lip. He made a hundred good resolutions. He would imitate Mr. Bons all the visit. He would not laugh, or run, or sing, or do any of the vulgar things that must have disgusted his new friends last time. He would be very careful to pronounce their names properly, and to remember who knew whom. Achilles did not know Tom Jones—at least, so Mr. Bons said. The Duchess of Malfi was older than Mrs. Gamp—at least, so Mr. Bons said. He would be self-conscious, reticent, and prim. He would never say he liked any one. Yet, when the blind flew up at a chance touch of his head, all these good resolutions went to the winds, for the omnibus had reached the summit of a moonlit hill, and there was the chasm, and there, across it, stood the old precipices, dreaming, with their feet in the everlasting river. He exclaimed, "The mountain! Listen to the new tune in the water! Look at the camp fires in the ravines," and Mr. Bons, after a hasty glance, retorted, "Water? Camp fires? Ridiculous rubbish. Hold your tongue. There is nothing at all."

Yet, under his eyes, a rainbow formed, compounded not of sunlight and storm, but of moonlight and the spray of the river. The three horses put their feet upon it. He thought it the finest rainbow he had seen, but he did not dare to say so, since Mr. Bons said that nothing was there. He leant out—the window had opened—and sang the tune that rose from the sleeping waters.

"The prelude to Rhinegold?" said Mr. Bons suddenly. "Who taught you these *leit motifs?*" He, too, looked out of the window. Then he behaved very oddly. He gave a choking cry, and fell back on to the omnibus floor. He writhed and kicked. His face was green.

"Does the bridge make you dizzy?" the boy asked.

"Dizzy!" gasped Mr. Bons. "I want to go back. Tell the driver."

But the driver shook his head.

"We are nearly there," said the boy. "They are asleep. Shall I call? They will be so pleased to see you, for I have prepared them."

Mr. Bons moaned. They moved over the lunar rainbow, which ever and ever broke away behind their wheels. How still the night was! Who would be sentry at the Gate?

"I am coming," he shouted, again forgetting the hundred resolutions. "I am returning—I, the boy."

"The boy is returning," cried a voice to other voices, who repeated, "The boy is returning."

"I am bringing Mr. Bons with me."

Silence.

"I should have said Mr. Bons is bringing me with him."

Profound silence.

"Who stands sentry?"

"Achilles."

And on the rocky causeway, close to the springing of the rainbow bridge, he saw a young man who carried a wonderful shield.

"Mr. Bons, it is Achilles, armed."

"I want to go back," said Mr. Bons.

The last fragment of the rainbow melted, the wheels sang upon the living rock, the door of the omnibus burst open. Out leapt the boy—he could not resist—and sprang to meet the warrior, who, stooping suddenly, caught him on his shield.

"Achilles!" he cried, "let me get down, for I am ignorant and vulgar, and I must wait for that Mr. Bons of whom I told you yesterday."

But Achilles raised him aloft. He crouched on the wonderful shield, on heroes and burning cities, on vineyards graven in gold, on every dear passion, every joy, on the entire image of the Mountain that he had discovered, encircled, like it, with an everlasting stream. "No, no," he protested, "I am not worthy. It is Mr. Bons who must be up here."

But Mr. Bons was whimpering, and Achilles trumpeted and cried, "Stand upright upon my shield!"

"Sir, I did not mean to stand! something made me stand. Sir, why do you delay? Here is only the great Achilles, whom you knew."

Mr. Bons screamed, "I see no one. I see nothing. I want to go back." Then he cried to the driver, "Save me! Let me stop in your chariot. I have honoured you. I have quoted you. I have bound you in vellum. Take me back to my world."

The driver replied, "I am the means and not the end. I am the food and not the life. Stand by yourself, as that boy has stood. I cannot save you. For poetry is a spirit; and they that would worship it must worship in spirit and in truth."

Mr. Bons—he could not resist—crawled out of the beautiful omnibus. His face appeared, gaping horribly. His hands followed, one gripping the step, the other beating the air. Now his shoulders emerged, his chest, his stomach. With a shriek of "I see London," he fell—fell against the hard, moonlit rock, fell into it as if it were water, fell through it, vanished, and was seen by the boy no more.

"Where have you fallen to, Mr. Bons? Here is a procession arriving to honour you with music and torches. Here come the men and women whose names you know. The mountain is awake, the river is awake, over the racecourse the sea is awaking those dolphins, and it is all for you. They want you——"

There was the touch of fresh leaves on his forehead. Some one had crowned him.

T   E   Λ   O   Σ[1]

From the *Kingston Gazette, Surbiton Times,* and
Raynes Park Observer.

The body of Mr. Septimus Bons has been found in a shockingly mutilated condition in the vicinity of the Bermondsey gas-works. The deceased's pockets contained a sovereign-purse, a silver cigar-case, a bijou pronouncing dictionary, and a couple of omnibus tickets. The unfortunate gentleman had apparently been hurled from a considerable height. Foul play is suspected, and a thorough investigation is pending by the authorities.

Questions

1. "Celestial" has to do with heaven. What transportation (omnibus) do you anticipate the author will provide his fictional characters?

2. A poet named Shelley had tacked up the notice the boy saw. Why didn't the author of the story have the notice put up by a politician, a religious leader, a scientist, a teacher, or an entertainer?

3. How many copies of Shelley's poems did Mr. Bons have at his house? What does the author accomplish with this detail?

4. As a punishment for lying about the trip, what was the boy made to do? What influence would such punishment tend to have on a youngster?

5. The first coach or omnibus was decorated in a very fanciful way. The second coach was severely plain. Although perhaps you have not read the writings of Sir Thomas Browne or Dante, what can you predict about their writings because of the coach each drove?

6. If the boy had made a third journey, why should Emily Dickinson be his coachman? See her poems on pages 96 and 224.

7. Mr. Bons used art for what purpose? He says, just before his fall, "I bound you in vellum (leather)." Should art be "used"? Should it be bound in leather?

---

[1] A Greek word meaning "The End."

Conditioning the Children*

ALDOUS HUXLEY

The D.H.C. and his students stepped into the nearest lift and were carried up to the fifth floor.

INFANT NURSERIES. NEO-PAVLOVIAN CONDITIONING ROOMS, announced the notice board.

The Director opened a door. They were in a large bare room, very bright and sunny; for the whole of the southern wall was a single window. Half a dozen nurses, trousered and jacketed in the regulation white viscose-linen uniform, their hair aseptically hidden under white caps, were engaged in setting out bowls of roses in a long row across the floor. Big bowls, packed tight with blossom. Thousands of petals, ripeblown and silkily smooth, like the cheeks of innumerable little cherubs, but of cherubs, in that bright light, not exclusively pink and Aryan, but also luminously Chinese, also Mexican, also apoplectic with too much blowing of celestial trumpets, also pale as death, pale with the posthumous whiteness of marble.

The nurses stiffened to attention as the D.H.C. came in.

"Set out the books," he said curtly.

In silence the nurses obeyed his command. Between the rose bowls the books were duly set out—a row of nursery quartos opened invitingly each at some gaily coloured image of beast or fish or bird.

"Now bring in the children."

They hurried out of the room and returned in a minute or two, each pushing a kind of tall dumb-waiter laden, on all its four wire-netted shelves, with eight-month-old babies, all exactly alike (a Bokanovsky Group, it was evident) and all (since their caste was Delta) dressed in khaki.

"Put them down on the floor."

The infants were unloaded.

"Now turn them so that they can see the flowers and books."

Turned, the babies at once fell silent, then began to crawl towards those clusters of sleek colours, those shapes so gay and brilliant on the white pages. As they approached, the sun came out of a momentary eclipse behind a cloud. The roses flamed up as though with a sudden passion from within; a new and profound significance seemed to suffuse the shining pages of the books. From the ranks of the crawling babies came little squeals of excitement, gurgles and twitterings of pleasure.

The Director rubbed his hands. "Excellent!" he said. "It might almost have been done on purpose."

The swiftest crawlers were already at their goal. Small hands reached out uncertainly, touched, grasped, unpetaling the transfigured roses, crumpling the illuminated pages of the books. The Director waited until all were happily busy. Then, "Watch carefully," he said. And, lifting his hand, he gave the signal.

The Head Nurse, who was standing by a switchboard at the other end of the room, pressed down a little lever.

There was a violent explosion. Shriller and ever shriller, a siren shrieked. Alarm bells maddeningly sounded.

The children started, screamed; their faces were distorted with terror.

"And now," the Director shouted (for the noise was deafening), "now we proceed to rub in the lesson with a mild electric shock."

He waved his hand again, and the Head Nurse pressed a second lever. The screaming of the babies suddenly changed its tone. There was something desperate, almost insane, about the sharp spasmodic yelps to which they now gave utterance. Their little bodies twitched and stiffened; their limbs moved jerkily as if to the tug of unseen wires.

"We can electrify that whole strip of floor," bawled the Director in explanation. "But that's enough," he signalled to the nurse.

The explosions ceased, the bells stopped ringing, the shriek of the siren died down from tone to tone into silence. The stiffly twitching bodies relaxed, and what had become the sob and yelp of infant maniacs broadened out once more into a normal howl of ordinary terror.

"Offer them the flowers and the books again."

The nurses obeyed; but at the approach of the roses, at the mere sight of those gaily-coloured images of pussy and cock-a-doodle-doo and baa-baa black sheep, the infants shrank away in horror; the volume of their howling suddenly increased.

"Observe," said the Director triumphantly, "observe."

Books and loud noises, flowers and electric shocks—already in the infant mind these couples were compromisingly linked; and after two hundred repetitions of the same or a similar lesson would be wedded indissolubly. What man has joined, nature is powerless to put asunder.

"They'll grow up with what the psychologists used to call an 'instinctive' hatred of books and flowers. Reflexes unalterably conditioned. They'll be safe from books and botany all their lives." The Director turned to his nurses. "Take them away again."

Still yelling, the khaki babies were loaded on to their dumb-waiters and wheeled out, leaving behind them the smell of sour milk and a most welcome silence.

Questions

1. We often say a person's job conditions him. Give examples. How does a housepainter's work condition him? A teacher's?

2. What will the babies in the world of the future described in this excerpt be conditioned to? How will they be conditioned?

3. Might *Some Conditioners of Man* be the title of this book? Do the words "shapers" and "conditioners" mean the same to you?

4. Might the "I" in "mr. youse needn't be so spry" (p. 223) have been conditioned as were the babies here?

5. In your estimation is Huxley concerned only with the world of the future? If beauty, color, books, shapes, and pictures are of secondary or of less importance in your life, how were you so conditioned?

6. Does the artist stack the deck in favor of the madmen (the artists)?

If Thou of Fortune Be Bereft*

James Terry White

If thou of fortune be bereft
And in thy store there be but left
Two loaves,
Sell one,
And with the dole
Buy hyacinths to feed thy soul.

Questions

1. If you have no money (bereft of fortune) and have but two loaves of bread, what does the poet advise you to do?

2. What are you to do with the loaf you do not sell?

3. When the babies described in the Huxley selection have grown, what hyacinths will feed their souls?

4. The poet says "hyacinths," not dandelions and thistles or juniper berries and poppies. How do the three groups of plants differ?

Introduction to Songs of Innocence

William Blake (1757–1827)

Piping down the valleys wild,
    Piping songs of pleasant glee,
On a cloud I saw a child,
    And he laughing said to me:

---

* Reprinted by permission of James T. White & Company, Publishers.

"Pipe a song about a Lamb!"
    So I piped with merry cheer.
"Piper, pipe that song again";
    So I piped; he wept to hear.

"Drop thy pipe, thy happy pipe;
    Sing thy songs of happy cheer!"
So I sang the same again,
    While he wept with joy to hear.

"Piper, sit thee down and write
    In a book, that all may read."
So he vanished from my sight;
    And I plucked a hollow reed,

And I made a rural pen,
    And I stained the water clear,
And I wrote my happy songs
    Every child may joy to hear.

Questions

1. After asking the piper to play music and to sing, what does the child ask him to do?

2. Are the piper and the child in the country or in the city?

3. Is the piper giving the children the equivalent of what the writer for "the slicks" (p. 134) gives the adults? Is there "good" art and "bad" art for children in the same way there is good and bad art for adults?

4. React to this statement: "The difference between a bad and good artist is simply the difference between the cook and the chef. The one follows a recipe, the other creates."

5. What does bad art do to adults? To children?

Madman's Song*

ELINOR WYLIE

Better to see your cheek grown hollow,
Better to see your temple worn,
Than to forget to follow, follow,
After the sound of a silver horn.

Better to bind your brow with willow
And follow, follow until you die,
Than to sleep with your head on a golden pillow,
Nor lift it up when the hunt goes by.

Better to see your cheek grown sallow
And your hair grown gray, so soon, so soon,
Than to forget to hallo, hallo,
After the milk-white hounds of the moon.

Questions

1. It is better to see you grow sick, to see you grow old, or even to see you die than for what to happen?

2. What are the "silver horn," the "hunt," and the "milk-white hounds of the moon" symbols of?

3. Does the poet mean you will not get sick, grow old, and die if you do what she tells you?

4. Why does she call the poem "Madman's Song"? (Remember the story "Black Is My Favorite Color" from a collection of stories called *Idiots First*.)

5. How does Seibei's father (see "Seibei's Gourds") regard him?

6. In American folklore what role is assigned to the artist, to the Negro, to the gambler, to the prostitute, to the teacher, to mother, to father, to puppies, to sex, and to money?

Lantern in the Snow*

ROBERT P. TRISTRAM COFFIN

This thing is beautiful, I know,
A lantern burning in the snow,
Which diggers left so men might see
Their hole beneath my lilac tree.

The lantern makes a spot of gold,
Alien to the dark and cold,
Burning steady as it can,
As if a warm, good part of man
Were left outside there in the night
To go on working, giving light.

*Reprinted with permission of The Macmillan Company from *Collected Poems* by Robert P. Tristram Coffin. Copyright 1939 by The Macmillan Company.

The glow strikes down and shows the ground
A single solitary mound
Of whiteness set in vacant space.

The light strikes up and shows the grace
Of the lilac's limbs and bark,
An open fan against the dark.
The snow falls round the common thing
And makes a dim, mysterious ring
Of flaky flame that wheels and turns
As the lonely lantern burns.

There are only four or five
Such sights for any man alive
In all the years he has to go
Like this lantern in the snow.

Questions

1. Why did the workers leave the lantern in the snow?

2. Obviously, what is the time?

3. How many times in our lives do we see such sights, according to the poet? Do you agree with him? Explain.

4. Norman in "Chaos, Disorder and the Late Show" would approve of the men setting out the lantern. Would he see what the poet sees? Explain.

5. If the artist is our eyes and ears because we are so busy, why might an impostor be tempted to pretend to be an artist?

6. Do you imagine the workers in the poem "Lantern in the Snow" have read Gibran's poem "On Work"?

Composed upon Westminster Bridge

WILLIAM WORDSWORTH (1770–1850)

Earth has not anything to show more fair:
Dull would he be of soul who could pass by
A sight so touching in its majesty:
This city now doth, like a garment, wear
The beauty of the morning; silent, bare,
Ships, towers, domes, theatres, and temples lie
Open unto the fields, and to the sky;
All bright and glittering in the smokeless air.

Never did sun more beautifully steep
In his first splendour, valley, rock, or hill;
Ne'er saw I, never felt, a calm so deep!
The river glideth at his own sweet will;
Dear God! the very houses seem asleep;
And all that mighty heart is lying still!

Questions

1. Earth has not anything more fair to show than what?

2. A South Sea island is supposed to be the spot that has the qualities Wordsworth describes. Is Wordsworth joking?

3. "Mighty heart" in the last line is used to make us feel positive or negative? Does Wordsworth seem to say, "The people—yes!" or "The people—no!"?

mr. youse needn't be so spry*

E. E. CUMMINGS

mr. youse needn't be so spry
concernin questions arty

each has his tastes but as for i
i likes a certain party

gimme the he-man's solid bliss
for youse ideas i'll match youse

a pretty girl who naked is
is worth a million statues

Questions

1. Cummings wants to give a sound to the "I." What is the sound, and how does Cummings achieve the sound?

2. Who is the "mr." Cummings refers to?

3. What does the "I" want to match with "the he-man's solid bliss"?

4. What is worth a million statues?

---

5. Is or isn't Cummings cutting his own throat with this poem? What is worth a million poems?

6. The pretty, naked girl; the lantern in the snow; London from Westminster Bridge; the "Fiddler of Dooney" are the hyacinths we fail to see—do you agree?

7. In the "mr." is Cummings setting up a straw man to knock down? What do Cummings and Saroyan have in common?

8. Reply to the person who says, "There's not much difference between the "I" in the poem, and the animal who operates at the level of instinct—food, sex, shelter, and elimination of wastes. There are apparently no other necessities."

To Make a Prairie*

EMILY DICKINSON

To make a prairie it takes a clover and one bee,
One clover, and a bee,
And revery.
The revery alone will do,
If bees are few.

Questions

1. The boy in "The Celestial Omnibus" wondered what was the real world—the one he visited or the one he lived in. What answer would Emily Dickinson give him?

2. The fine arts transported the boy in "The Celestial Omnibus." Norman's mother in "Chaos, Disorder and the Late Show" was transported by the popular arts. As Dickinson uses it, what does "revery" mean? When will the world be such that being "transported" will not be necessary?

---

*From *The Complete Poems of Emily Dickinson* published by Little, Brown and Company.

The Artist*

ROBERT HENRI

I have no sympathy with the belief that art is the restricted province of those who paint, sculpt, make music and verse. I hope we will come to an understanding that the material used is only incidental, that there is artist in every man; and that to him the possibility of development and of expression and the happiness of creation is as much a right and as much a duty to himself, as to any of those who work in the especially ticketed ways.

There is much talk of the "growth of art" in America, but the proof offered deals too often with the increase in purchases. I'm sure it often happens that the purchaser believes he has done his art bit for himself and for the public, when he has bought. Being a struggling artist myself, far be it from me to say he should not buy! But buying is not enough. We may build many imitation Greek temples and we may buy them full of pictures, but there is something more—in fact the one thing more which really counts before we can be an art nation—we must get rid of this outside feeling of looking in on art. We must get on the inside and press out.

Art is simply a result of expression during right feeling. It's a result of a grip on the fundamentals of nature, the spirit of life, the constructive force, the secret of growth, a real understanding of the relative importance of things, order, balance. Any material will do. After all, the object is not to *make art,* but to be in the wonderful state which makes art inevitable.

In every human being there is the artist, and whatever his activity, he has an equal chance with any to express the result of his growth and his contact with life. I don't believe any real artist cares whether what he does is "art" or not. Who, after all, knows what is art? Were not our very intelligent fathers admirers of Bouguereau, and was not Bouguereau covered with all the honors by which we make our firsts, and were they not ready to commit Cézanne to a madhouse? Now look at them!

I think the real artists are too busy with just being and growing and acting (on canvas or however) like themselves to worry about the end. The end will be what it will be. The object is intense living, fulfillment; the great happiness in creation. People sometimes phrase about the joy of work. It is only in creative work that joy may be found.

Art when really understood is the province of every human being.

It is simply a question of doing things, anything, well. It is not an outside, extra thing.

When the artist is alive in any person, whatever his kind of work may be, he becomes an inventive, searching, daring, self-expressing creature. He becomes interesting to other people. He disturbs, upsets, enlightens, and he opens ways for a better understanding. Where those who are not artists are trying to close the book, he opens it, shows there are still more pages possible.

The world would stagnate without him, and the world would be beautiful with him; for he is interesting to himself and he is interesting to others. He does not have to be a painter or sculptor to be an artist. He can work in any medium. He simply has to find the gain in the work itself, not outside it.

Museums of art will not make a country an art country. But where there is the art spirit there will be precious works to fill museums. Better still, there will be the happiness that is in the making. Art tends towards balance, order, judgment of relative values, the laws of growth, the economy of living —very good things for anyone to be interested in.

The work of the art student is no light matter. Few have the courage and stamina to see it through. You have to make up your mind to be alone in many ways. We like sympathy and we like to be in company. It is easier than going it alone. But alone one gets acquainted with himself, grows up and on, not stopping with the crowd. It costs to do this. If you succeed somewhat you may have to pay for it as well as enjoy it all your life.

Questions

1. If art is the province of every human being, why aren't all human beings artists?

2. Henri says "Where those who are not artists are trying to close the book, he (the artist) opens it, shows there are still more pages possible." What does "to open the book" mean?

3. "The object is not to make art, but to be in the wonderful state that makes art inevitable." Explain.

4. How would Henri probably react to the sectioning of this text?

The Cock and the Jewel*

ÆSOP

A brisk young Cock, in company with two or three Pullets, was scratching around on a dunghill for something to entertain them with when he happened to hit upon a jewel. He knew that it was good enough, for it sparkled with an excellent luster, but not knowing what to do with it he endeavored to cover his ignorance under a gay contempt. So, shrugging his wings and shaking his head, he put on a grimace and expressed himself thus: "Indeed you are a very fine thing, but I know not what business you have here. I do not hesitate to declare that my taste lies quite another way, and I had rather have one grain of dear, delicious barley than all the jewels under the sun."

Questions

1. How might the Cock have reacted to the jewel? How did he react?

2. No matter how the Cock reacted to the jewel, what are you willing to predict about the Pullets' behavior? Do the Pullets and the people in "The History of Susanna" fall in the same category?

3. In the context of this section of the text, what is the jewel?

4. Seibei's father and his teacher behaved in what way toward Seibei and his gourds? Were the two men "sensible" or "silly," as the terms are used in this fable. Are most men like the father and teacher or like the Cock?

The Dog and the Wolf*

ÆSOP

A lean, hungry, half-starved Wolf happened, one moon-shiny night, to meet with a jolly, plump, well-fed Dog. After the first compliments were passed the Wolf said, "You look extremely well; I protest, I think I never saw a more graceful, comely person. How comes it, I beseech you, that you should live so much better than I? I may say without vanity, that I venture fifty times more than you do and yet I am almost ready to perish with hunger." The Dog answered very bluntly, "Why, you may live as well if you will do the same as I do." "Indeed! What is that?" said he. "Why," said the Dog, "only to guard the house anights and keep it from thieves." "With all my heart," replied the Wolf, "for at present I have but a sorry time of it, and to change my hard lodging in the woods where I endure rain, frost, and snow, for a warm roof over my head and a bellyful of good victuals, will be no bad bargain." "True," said the Dog, "therefore you have nothing more to do but to follow me." Now as they were jogging on together the Wolf spied a crease in the Dog's neck and having a strange curiosity could not forbear asking him what it meant. "Pugh! nothing," said the Dog. "Nay, but pray," said the Wolf. "Why?" said the Dog. "If you must know, I am tied up in the daytime because I am a little fierce and may bite people, and am only let loose anights. But this is done with design to make me sleep adays more than anything else, and as soon as the twilight appears, out I am turned and may go where I please. Then my master brings me plates of bones from the table with his own hands; and whatever scraps are left by any of the family, all fall to my share, for you must know I am a favorite with everybody. So you see how you are to live. Come, come along. What is the matter with you?" "No," replied the Wolf, "I beg your pardon, keep your happiness to yourself. Liberty is the word with me and I would not be a king upon the terms you mention."

Questions

1. The dog had security and the wolf did not. What price did the dog pay?

2. What is the greater desire of most men, security or freedom? How is the desire acquired?

3. The fine artist and the popular artist meet and converse on the street. Describe the two and reproduce their conversation.

or

4. A fine artist, short of money, food, art supplies, and popularity bemoans his condition and casts aspersions at a popular artist who is long on money, food, art supplies, and popularity. A wise old man speaks to the fine artist, saying, "_____." Complete the fable.

High Yaller

(*painting—see p. 194*)

REGINALD MARSH

Connoisseurs of Prints

(*etching—see p. 195*)

JOHN SLOAN

Questions

1. With what are the men and women in the Sloan picture vitally concerned? Does Sloan want you to like the men and women? Does the picture perpetuate a stereotype about art?

2. How does Marsh want the viewer to feel about the girl in his picture? What is her concern?

3. To live one's life as a work of art, how would one have to live? Who comes closer in your estimation to living his life as a work of art, the figures in the Sloan picture or the girl in Marsh's?

4. The Marsh picture is dated 1934. Do you imagine Marsh would use the same title today? How might members of various groups (racial, socioeconomic, religious, or political) respond to the painting?

5. The quotation "Fine art is the only teacher except torture" is given on page 196. If fine art is an effective and painless method of shaping man—to a greater awareness? to a greater humanity?—how do you account for Sloan's and Daumier's (see title pages) pictures? [The pictures show people who are immersed in art and they appear so mean-spirited, so aloof, so inhumane.]

Questions on "Buffalo Dusk," (see page 230)

1. What directions would you give to a group of people who were going to read "Buffalo Dusk" aloud?

2. How do you feel at the close of the poem? Is what you feel entirely Sandburg's doing? Explain.

3. If someone says, "But the buffalo are not gone. There are buffalo at the zoo," what would you reply?

4. "Buffalo Dusk" could have appeared earlier in the text—in the section on school or simply earlier in this section. Is the anthologist attempting to shape you?

Moonrise, Hernandez, New Mexico

(photograph—see p. 230)

ANSEL ADAMS

Questions

1. One of the purposes of the artist is to communicate and perhaps to shape you to his way of thinking, feeling, seeing, hearing, and moving. In your estimation, what does Ansel Adams attempt to shape you to here?

2. "Buffalo Dusk" and "Moonrise, Hernandez, New Mexico" come at the text's close. Are the poem and photograph radically different?

3. How, in your estimation, is the anthologist who put together the text and the very question you are reading attempting to shape you?

4. Because no man is an island and consequently you cannot avoid shaping and being shaped, what is (are) the most effective way(s) of shaping man?

Buffalo Dusk*

CARL SANDBURG

The buffaloes are gone.
And those who saw the buffaloes are gone.
Those who saw the buffaloes by thousands and
how they pawed the prairie sod into dust
with their hoofs, their great heads down
pawing on in a great pageant of dusk,
Those who saw the buffaloes are gone.
And the buffaloes are gone.

Moonrise, Hernandez, New Mexico
Photograph by Ansel Adams

* From *Smoke and Steel* by Carl Sandburg, copyright, 1920, by Harcourt, Brace & World, Inc.; renewed, 1948, by Carl Sandburg. Reprinted by permission of the publisher.

INDEX OF ARTISTS AND TITLES

Index of Artists and Titles*

* Titles of selections are italicized.